GROUP WORK

FOUNDATIONS AND FRONTIERS

GROUP WORK

New York

1955

Foundations & Frontiers

Edited by

HARLEIGH B. TRECKER

WHITESIDE, INC.
and

WILLIAM MORROW AND COMPANY

CONTENTS

PART TWO

THE FRONTIERS OF GROUP WORK

x | *Contents*

INDEX OF CONTRIBUTORS

ARMSTRONG, Robert N.—Program Director, Erie Neighborhood House, Chicago, Illinois.

AULT, Laura—Associate Metropolitan Executive Director, YWCA of Detroit, Michigan

BRAGER, George—Executive Director, Mount Vernon YM-YWHA, Mount Vernon, New York

BRIGHT, Sallie E.—Associate Director, Department of Public Interest, Community Service Society, New York, New York

CARNER, Lucy—Executive Secretary of the Division on Education and Recreation of the Welfare Council of Metropolitan Chicago, Chicago, Illinois

COYLE, Grace L.—Professor of Social Group Work, School of Applied Sciences, Western Reserve University, Cleveland, Ohio

CRAWFORD, Mary E.—Consultant: Group Worker, Cleveland Rehabilitation Center, Cleveland, Ohio

DEMARCHE, David F.—Director of Program and Research, United Service Organizations Incorporated, New York, New York

FISHER, Raymond—Associate Professor of Social Group Work, School of Applied Social Sciences, Western Reserve University, Cleveland, Ohio

FRANKEL, Godfrey—Director, Heights Branch Jewish Community Centers of Cleveland, Cleveland Heights, Ohio

GREEN, Marvin—Formerly Group Work Consultant, Division of Community Education, New York City Board of Education, New York, New York

ISKANDER, G. Michael—Student Work Secretary, Cairo YMCA, Cairo, Egypt

KINDELSPERGER, Kenneth W.—Associate Professor of Social Work, Syracuse University—University of Buffalo, Graduate Program in Social Work, Syracuse, New York

KLEIN, Alan F.—Associate Professor, University of Toronto School of Social Work, Toronto, Canada

KOLODNY, Ralph L.—Assistant Director, Department of Neighborhood Clubs, Children's Aid Association of Boston, Massachusetts

KONOPKA, Gisela—Associate Professor of Social Work, University of Minnesota, Minneapolis, Minnesota

LINDEMAN, Eduard C. (deceased)—Professor of Philosophy, New York School of Social Work. Consultant to New York City Adult Education Council, New York. Chairman of National Child Labor Committee

MAXWELL, Jean M.—Associate Professor of Social Work, School of Public Administration and Social Service, New York University, New York, New York

NORTHEN, Helen E.—Associate Professor of Social Work, School of Social Work, University of Southern California, Los Angeles, California

OWEN, Monica Burrell—National Field Worker, Play Schools Association, New York, New York

PENNOCK, Mary E.—Group Worker, Wilder Child Guidance Clinic, Minneapolis, Minnesota

PHILLIPS, Helen U.—Chairman Social Group Work Department, School of Social Work, University of Pennsylvania, Philadelphia, Pennsylvania

POLANSKY, Norman A.—Social Psychologist, Austen Riggs Center, Stockbridge, Massachusetts

PYLES, Joseph B.—Group Worker West Side Community House, Cleveland, Ohio

SCHEIDLINGER, Saul—Consultant in Group Therapy, Division of Family Services, Community Service Society of New York, New York

SHAPIRO, Sidney—Young Adult and Adult Division Head, Springfield Jewish Community Center, Springfield, Massachusetts

SLAVSON, S. R.—Group Therapy Consultant, Jewish Board of Guardians, New York City, New York

SLOAN, Marion B.—Supervisor Social Group Work Research Project #55 Cleveland Receiving Hospital, Cleveland, Ohio

TROPP, Emanuel—Assistant Director Greater Miami Jewish Community Center, Miami, Florida

WEYKER, Grace—Chief Social Worker, Wilder Child Guidance Clinic, Minneapolis, Minnesota

GROUP WORK

FOUNDATIONS AND FRONTIERS

Introduction

THIS is a book which thousands of group workers have helped to write. Within these pages we have assembled the best of professional thinking and practice from the past decade and a half. Here we have foundation and frontier material basic to the future development of group work.

The American Association of Group Workers was established in 1946. It is a professional association of approximately 2500 group workers whose purpose is "To promote association among education, recreation and group workers; to raise the standards of competence among practitioners; to encourage continued study of the basic body of knowledge and skills essential to professional practice; to improve personnel practices, including professional education; to encourage research; to provide individual and corporate action on matters affecting the field of practice."

Actually the American Association of Group Workers began in 1936. The association was then known as the National Association for the Study of Group Work. Its original purpose was "To encourage the study of group work. Through the coordination of discussion and inquiry, through publications, and through an annual conference, the Association aims to help clarify and refine both the philosophy and the practice of group work." In 1939 the Association changed its name to the American Association for the Study of Group Work. It retained its original membership requirement, namely, "membership in the association requires only that one manifest a genuine interest in group work as an emerging profession and be willing to share critically and creatively across agency lines in cooperative inquiry." After ten years as an association general in membership and devoted to the study of group work, the members decided to become a professional association in 1946 and have operated in this fashion for the past nine years. Obviously this development into a professional association modified the membership requirements and, from 1946 forward, membership was limited to those persons who had professional training for group work. In 1949, after several years of study, an A.A.G.W. committee under the chairmanship of Dr. Grace L. Coyle produced a report entitled "Definition of the Function of the Group Worker." This statement was adopted by the association and has become the official description of the function of the professional group worker. It reads as follows:

The Group Worker enables various types of groups to function in such a way that both group interaction and program activities contribute to the growth of the individual, and the achievement of desirable social goals.

The objectives of the group worker include provision for personal growth according to individual capacity and need, the adjustment of the individual to other persons, to groups and to society, and the motivation of the individual toward the improvement of society; the recognition by the individual of his own rights, abilities, and differences of others.

Through his participation the group worker aims to effect the group process so that decisions come about as a result of knowledge and a sharing and integration of ideas, experiences and knowledge, rather than as a result of domination from within or without the group.

Through experience he aims to produce those relations with other groups and the wider community which contribute to responsible citizenship, mutual understanding between cultural, religious, economic or special groupings in the community, and a participation in the constant improvement of our society toward democratic goals.

The guiding purpose behind such leadership rests upon the common assumptions of a democratic society; namely, the opportunity for each individual to fulfill his capacities in freedom, to respect and appreciate others and to assume his social responsibility in maintaining and constantly improving our democratic society.

Underlying the practice of group work is a knowledge of individual and group behavior and of social conditions and community relations which is based on the modern social sciences.

On the basis of this knowledge the group worker contributes to the group with which he works a skill in leadership which enables the members to use their capacities to the full and to create socially constructive group activities.

He is aware of both program activities and of the interplay of personalities within the group and between the group and its surrounding community.

According to the interests and needs of each, he assists them to get from the group experience the satisfactions provided by the program activities, the enjoyment and personal growth available through the social relations, and the opportunity to participate as a responsible citizen.

The group worker makes conscious use of his relation to the group, his knowledge of program as a tool, and his understanding of the individual and of the group process, and recognized his responsibility both to individuals and groups with whom he works and the larger social values he represents.

The idea for this volume arose when as President of the American Association of Group Workers, I began to review the history and accomplishments of the Association. At the December, 1953, meeting of the Board, I said that in my judgment the period of 1939-54 was rich with significance in the development of group work. During these years through our professional publications, particularly our quarterly journal *The Group*, the theoretical foundations of group work had been discussed by numerous practitioners. Their experiences, ideas and thoughtful formulations had been shared with their colleagues through the medium of professional publications. I said I thought we should make this material available in an organized permanent form easily accessible to the public. Hence the decision was made to select the outstanding articles from *The Group* and to present them in this form.

There was another compelling reason for this decision. For several years the several professional associations in social work had been moving toward the merger of their separate associations into one integrated professional body. Present plans call for the creation of the National Social Workers Association in 1955, with group work becoming a section within it. Therefore it seemed doubly important that we preserve the best thinking available as the basis for future developments in group work.

It was at this point that we decided to take another step, namely, to turn prophetic. We decided that we might speculate about our future responsibilities as group workers. We decided it would be interesting to attempt to forecast the major developments that would emerge during the period ahead. As a result of this thinking a letter was developed and sent to a selected list of group workers located in various cities throughout the country. They were asked to write a letter in which they would present their thinking as to the major tasks ahead of group work in the next decade. Specifically they were asked to react to the following questions:

(1). What are the most important tasks for group workers to work on in the next decade:

    (a) on the national level through the new single association?

    (b) on the local level through chapters?

(2). What current developments and trends in group work impress you as being worthy of continued or further study and emphasis in the period ahead?

(3.) What do you see as being the most significant social, economic, political trends today which group workers need to study and understand because of their likely influence in the future?

(4.) What areas of research should group workers concentrate upon in the next decade?

So we present to the reader this book, "Group Work Foundations and Frontiers." In Part I, "The Foundations of Group Work," we offer 30 articles that have appeared in *The Group* during the 1939-54 period. In some cases, the articles appeared in our annual report. It was a difficult job for me to select the articles. I am certain that my choices would not agree in every case with choices that other people might make. I am sure, too, that many excellent articles have been omitted simply because we could not reproduce all of them. In rereading each issue of *The Group* for this period and in making my selections, I tried to follow these criteria: The articles should be well-written and should possess lasting value as reference material. The articles should be illustrative of trends in group work and should be stimulating and thought-provoking. Naturally the articles should represent a variety of points of view and should be representative of long-term development. I am solely responsible for the articles chosen. I believe that each one of them has served and will continue to serve a real purpose in group work.

Actually in Part I of the book we have writings from 32 different people, some of these persons are professional educators in group work and others are group work practitioners. I deliberately weighed the choice toward the latter because in my judgment the practitioners are the ones who have made the richest contribution in recent years. It has long been known that professional organization members must communicate the results of their practice with their fellow members. Certainly some of our major learnings in the period just concluded have come from the group workers themselves.

In deciding upon an arrangement of the articles, an attempt was made to combine the historical and developmental approaches. Material which would tend to accent the democratic values and democratic philosophy upon which group work is based was presented first. Next there is a consideration of the objectives of group work, and group work and case work, and group work and recreation. We next moved to a consideration of understanding individual and group behavior, and then selected pieces dealing with group work with different age groups. Because group work has become so useful in specialized settings such as hospitals, we presented material on this subject. Next we included pieces on group work and social action and group work services in the community. We included a section on group work supervision and a section on refining the group work process. In addition, we selected material on professional developments in group work. It is to be hoped that readers will be able to capture some feeling of the continuous forward movement of group work during our recent past.

In Part II of this book which we have called the "Frontiers of Group Work," we have an experiment in writing. Key group workers from all over the country have contributed their ideas to this section of the book. In a sense it might be described as "A Conference by Correspondence." Forty-two people from 15 different states replied to the letter. Over one hundred pages of single-spaced typewritten copy were received. Often the reply represented the results of a discussion conducted by group workers in the local chapter. The material which came in was thoughtful, provocative and stimulating. Certainly many thanks are due to this group of people. Their names are listed at the beginning of Part II of the book. I have summarized their replies and have attempted to prepare an agenda for the future development of group work. I have tried to capture the essence of their thinking. I have not labeled ideas as belonging to particular individuals but have selected those ideas which are representative of the thinking of many. In many cases I have quoted material because the quotation seemed to say in direct and interesting fashion the thinking of many people. Actually the frontiers of group work are endless; there are exciting prospects for the future. This is a systematic attempt to spell out what we ought to be working on. To be sure, the summary is only a beginning and it may cause discussion and debate. The fact remains that there is much ahead of us and great opportunities before us.

In completing this introduction I wish to express my thanks to Mrs. Janet Korpela, Executive Secretary of the Association, Mrs. Janie McGuffin, Administrative Secretary, and Mrs. Irene Nass of the staff. All of these folks have worked hard to put our copy in shape for the publisher. In addition I wish to express my appreciation to Mrs. Grace Darling, Editor of Whiteside for her interest and for her help in bringing this material into print. Furthermore Mr. Murray Schneier, a graduate student in group work at the University of Connecticut School of Social Work, did his master's degree research project on "A History of the American Association of Group Workers 1936-53." His contribution has been of great value to me in planning the design for this book. Most of all I wish to thank the people who shared so willingly their ideas and their thoughts. Without their conscientious attention to the questions which I raised, we would not have been able to develop our theme.

With all of this said the reader is invited now to venture forth on what I hope will be a rewarding journey into our recent past and an exciting projection into our inviting future.

HARLEIGH B. TRECKER
President,
American Association of Group Workers

September 15, 1954

Part One

THE FOUNDATIONS OF GROUP WORK

Selected Articles from
The Group, 1939–1954

1

Group Work and Democratic Values

THE ROOTS OF DEMOCRATIC CULTURE
By Eduard C. Lindeman

I HAVE the feeling that American citizens are becoming somewhat wearied over the sound of the word "democracy," and to me the word is so precious that I hesitate for fear that I may contribute to its debasement. But this very hesitancy is a part of my desire to discuss democracy with you since it is my feeling that most of the current dissertations on democracy are lacking in realistic content. The word still exercises a "pull" on our emotions, but so far as I can determine we have done very little to provide it with genuine meanings, that is, meanings suitable to our time. But I know that the task which I have set for myself is one which requires the collaboration of many minds and that what I have to say has not been sufficiently refined by criticism. So far as I know what I mean to say, it is this: *If democracy is to be considered as a mode of life, we should be able to describe its basic requirements and hence furnish clearly-definable tests for our performances.* In other words, I am striving to furnish some realistic content for the term "democracy" in order to endow it with logical as well as behavioristic and emotional meaning.

A *culture* may be said to be a pattern or design of life founded upon certain basic assumptions regarding the nature of man, the function of organized society, the relation between the individual and the group, and the meanings to be ascribed to truth, justice, goodness, and beauty. The traditional proponents of democracy, for example, have assumed that freedom is a requirement of individual growth; they have assumed that the individual is an end in himself and that it is never justifiable to use him as means to achieve other or extrinsic ends. These are fundamental concepts of life and when they permeate a given collection of people they constitute a background for culture. It is not my intention, however, to carry this theme further because what I am proposing tonight is not a theoretical interpretation of culture nor of democracy. I should like to avoid both the false clarity of the ideologists and the pretentious profundity of the academicans in my attempt to explain what experience would be like in a democratic culture.

Democracy is not a necessary or inevitable pattern of culture. It is not "written in the stars" that the democratic way of life shall succeed. Democracy is simply a program for meeting human needs, and like every other program it consists of two parts, namely, goals and methods. Also, like every other program it must be tested by its concrete consequences and not by emotional or mystical devotions. Democracy is, probably, the most difficult form of human society ever conceived and its difficulties tend to increase as life becomes more complicated. In the first place, the democratic concept of experience runs counter to what may be called the "law of human inertia"; we are all lazy and would be content if the necessary functions of society were looked after by someone other than ourselves.

But, democracy requires participation on a cumulative scale. Also, democracy appears to be in opposition to the prevailing patterns of family life; families tend to create for children increased dependence, whereas democracy asks for increased self-reliance. Democracy seems to work with a fair degree of efficiency when the social units are comparatively small, but most of our social units tend to increase in size, so much so as to make the famous phrase of Justice Louis Brandeis "The Curse of Bigness" carry an almost sinister meaning. Our societies tend to become more and more technological in character, which means that we require an ever-increasing compliment of specialists; but the specialists we have thus far trained have done a great deal to make democracy unworkable. Finally, expanding literacy is in itself a democratic liability since it appears to make the masses more susceptible to demagoguery. These are all difficulties which the adherents of democracy cannot afford to neglect. If, having recognized the difficulties, they still believe that the democratic way of life is preferable to any other, they must be prepared to take the next step which I conceive to be the formulation of tests which may be applied to both personal and collective behavior in order to determine what is required of those who wish to live a democratic life.

Democracy does not possess *a priori* validity. Its roots do not lie in history nor in ideological assumptions. Its roots are to be found in the practice of living, in day-by-day human experience. A democratic culture is, of course, an ideal and like all other cultural entities, it represents a conscious striving toward the ideal accompanied by an awareness that the ideal will never be completely realized. But, I assume that there is no satisfactory practice of life which does not include ideal elements, and to me the term "ideal" does not mean unreal but rather the presence of an enlarging and expanding goal. Experience loses its compulsive meaning when there is an absence of conscious or ideal striving. Those who attempt to laugh democracy out of court by deriding its idealism are at the same time positing new ideals for anti-democratic culture. Enthusiasm is always born of idealism. Creativeness springs only from ideals, and "if we are to preserve culture, we must continue to create it."

The tests for democratic culture which follow are derived from my understanding of the contributions which have come primarily from social, humanistic, and philosophic studies, but throughout I have striven also to subject my ideas to the criteria of science in general. The errors which occur must, therefore, be attributed to my faulty understanding of those interpretations of man and his world which have thus far emanated from research.

(1) I assume in the first place that a democratic culture rests upon an economic base and that it can flourish only when economic income is being distributed in such manner as to make a rising standard of living possible for all people. There can be no realistic democratic culture in a society in which wealth tends to concentrate while insecurity and dependence characterize the experience of any appreciable proportion of the total population. On the basis of this contention we can thus test our behavior by asking if we are consciously striving to bring about a greater equalization of wealth and income. If such striving is not a part of our daily living, we may then conclude that to this extent we are not participating in democratic culture.

(2) The structural strength of non-democratic societies is derived from a sense of unity and is fortified by conditions of uniformity and regimentation. The structural strength of democracy is a dynamic equilibrium which is a derivative of conflict. The strength of democracy is comparable to that of the arch in architecture: the arch is capable of sustaining great weight because its two major elements are juxtaposed, in con-

flict. Similar analogies may be found in engineering, as, for example, in the opposing stresses which give strength to a bridge. Or, one may seek comparisons in the organic sphere: walking is a kind of continual falling; the reason we do not fall is the fact that our muscular system exists in pairs, each unit of a pair pulling in an opposite direction. Dancing is, perhaps, an even better illustration since in this form of walking rhythm is added to structural strength. The rhythm of democracy is a product of conflict and only those can enjoy life in a democratic culture who are prepared to confront unending conflicts, to live in a perpetual atmosphere of dynamic instability.

(3) Conflict is not in and of itself creative, but only through conflicts are situations demanding change precipitated. Sameness produces sameness and difference produces difference. In a democratic culture difference itself is valued because of its disturbing tendency to challenge the *status quo*. A democratic culture can hence tolerate (rather invite) a wide variety of personality types, numerous religions, divergent races, mixed authorities, and regional inconsistences. Democracy is thus latent with innovation, filled with surprises. Its logic is pluralistic, open to many and diverse consequences. Those who are not conditioned to enjoy the exciting experiences which differences elicit cannot be happy in a democratic culture. Those who strive to eliminate difference and to annihilate those with whom they differ are obviously enemies of democracy. Practical tests derived from this principle appear in our daily living with such profuseness that further illustration is unnecessary.

(4) In a democratic culture each individual participant must feel that the attainment of personal dignity is a possibility for him as well as for all his fellows. Hence, in democratic societies there will be found a constant tendency to provide an environment in which individuals may discover and experience the sources of dignity. The slave loses his dignity and likewise his master. The individual who is manipulated by others, who be-

comes a means for another's ends, cannot achieve dignity. Anger and hatred are enemies of self-possession, and he who is not self-possessed is undignified. On the other hand, whoever experiences affection and fellowship is thereby dignified. From this discussion it will appear that dignity is conceived to be a quality of worthiness which the individual cannot acquire by and for himself but only by reason of his social relationships. This I believe to be true, but the sources of dignity are not single but rather diverse. A person has already acquired considerable dignity when he is permitted to perform useful work. He becomes self-sustained through his labor, and he is dignified by its social value. Parenthetically, it is for this reason that work programs for persons involuntarily unemployed belong within a democratic concept of culture. Exploiters, parasites and wasters sink to lower and lower levels of esteem and are ultimately discounted. The proper distinction between leisure and idleness is that the former is earned whereas the latter is merely taken. A shabby tramp lolling in the shade of a box-car and seeking his living from the labor of others is no more undignified than the well-fed inheritor of wealth idling away his time on the deck of his private yacht. Leisure is a source of dignity only when it has been earned through useful labor. An unemployed person, for example, soon loses the capacity to enjoy his leisure and in a strict sense he has no leisure. Without labor and without true leisure he soon loses his dignity, his sense of worth. But, it is equally true that the unemployed person who is set to work at tasks which have no economic value or social importance also loses his dignity and becomes the butt of common jokes.

I am never quite sure what people mean when they speak of and give high praise to a "sense of humor." Often they seem to mean that a person has a sense of humor if he laughs easily and frequently. But laughter is certainly not the essence of humor. Many persons laugh in order to conceal embarrassment, and a great deal of laughter, likewise, causes embarrassment in others. Nervous laughter, tittering and giggling are not the result of having seen the world in a delightful aspect, but are rather the consequences of lost perspective. True humor rests upon "a reasoned and confident attitude toward life" and is thus the source of genuine dignity. I have frequently noted in the photographs of the various European dictators and their cohorts that there appears to be a conscious striving on their part to appear dignified. The result is stuffiness and pomposity. Badges and uniforms were invented, I presume, in order to invest individuals with dignity, but authentic dignity is natural, not decorative. The sense of humor which lends dignity to persons is, I presume, associated with a capacity for viewing life and experience as drama, sometimes tragic and sometimes comical, but always unpredictable, fraught with surprise. Unaffected humor is also a social attribute. To be able to laugh *with* others is to break down some of those barriers which block social experience. Humor is hence a socializing influence. To laugh *at* others is likewise a method for closing the channels of fellowship.

The reason I have laid so much stress upon humor as a source of dignity is two-fold: in the first place, serious-minded philosophers have, I believe, too long neglected its hygienic function, and in the second place, this happens to be a grim era of history, a period in which earnest persons may readily lose their perspective; to be able to see what is humorous in the present is a sign that we are not wholly "caught" by immediacy, that we can endure the present because we see it in relation to a long past and a long future.

We can be assured that our lives are democratically oriented, if, then, we achieve personal dignity through affectionate relations with others, through socially-useful labor, through earned leisure which allows play to become, not an escape from, but a complement for work, and through that variety of humor which denotes absence of fear, a reasoned perspective.

(5) In a democratic society the ultimate judgments with respect to values and goals must rest with the people, for in a democracy "nothing can be done for the people except what the people do for themselves." But, this means that the people must be so educated as to make the judging process one in which emotions and feelings are tempered by reason and fact. A culture may be said to be democratic when the relevant and pertinent facts affecting the lives of the people are being made readily accessible. In a democratic society, the instruments of research and of communication cannot be monopolized by a group or a class. Those who possess enough wealth to control, let us say the press, are not to be trusted with the responsibility of furnishing the appropriate facts. Their personal and class interests will automatically create "blind-spots" and discolorations.

We live in a propaganda age. One ruthless Minister of Propaganda, Herr Goebbels, insists that "propaganda knows neither truth nor falsehood, but only what it wants." The modern propaganda method is one which attempts to influence the conduct of people by means of an appeal, primarily in terms of emotions, made on behalf of a preconceived end. But, it is precisely the ends of life which constitute the proper domain of the people. The people cannot arrive at a valid conception of ends unless they are in possession of the relevant facts. If they are not to be "tricked" by demagogues and propagandists, they must be trained to understand the devious methods employed by these end-gainers and power-seekers. The distinction between education and propaganda is simple: in the former there is visible a constant aim to formulate ends and then to invent means which are consonant with those ends; in the latter there is a constant tendency to utilize whatever means are available to achieve ends already determined. Upon the basis of its discrimination a democratic form of education becomes possible.

We may then conclude that our behavior has a democratic tendency when we are consciously striving to make facts more accessible, and when we are exercising vigilance with respect to propaganda and its methods.

(6) Lay moralists and even trained philosophers frequently treat the problem of values as though we were in possession of infallible criteria for detecting the difference between truth and falsehood, right and wrong, ugliness and beauty, righteousness and evil, equity and injustice, et cetera. Moral training thereupon becomes a matter of indoctrination rather than inquiry, and progressive experience which so often contradicts the established doctrine, is frustrated and denied. Under the aegis of this type of morality old evils may persist if for no other reason than their prior establishment.

Another error, so it seems to me, is to regard values as separate entities, operating in compartments of experience. Thus, a man may be privately "good" if he obeys the current *mores*, even though he makes no contribution to the public good. He may be considered a "good" man if he adheres to the moral code but at the same time neglects or even prevents expressions of beauty.

A more reasonable and certainly a more fruitful attitude toward the problem of values, so it seems to me, is one which regards the whole of experience as shot through and through with values, and then to assume that all values are interrelated. A value found in one context immediately serves the function of nourishing and sharpening the sense of values in all other contexts, given the absence of conscious exclusions.

The above theory of values furnishes a basis for fresh reflections concerning the complex questions of truth, goodness, justice, and beauty, and leads to the consideration of additional democratic tests. In an aristocratic society, for example, the arts serve a small class whose members finally become its patrons. In a democratic culture, all the people are expected to be participants in the arts. "For art," writes one of our sensitive critics, "is not a separate chamber of life or the exclusive property of cultivated people. It goes down through the whole structure of life. It is the words we speak and the clothes we wear and the friendships we cultivate in passing and the stamp of individuality we give to our homes. . . . The raw materials of art are the commonest property we have at our disposal—mind and heart, eyes and hands. . . . There is nothing occult about art." (Brooks Atkinson in *Art for Our Sake.*)

To select, then, one of the units in the cluster of interrelated values, it may be stated that behavior tends to become oriented in the direction of democratic culture to the extent that we as individuals participate in esthetic expression, and aid in making such participation possible for the masses.

(7) Professionalism is the natural consequence of either science or specialization. A professional person is one who has acquired certain bodies of knowledge and skills which he is able to utilize in services for which he is remunerated. As science throws more and more light upon the realities involved in these services there occurs another natural tendency, namely, specialization. In a scientific civilization everybody will tend to become a specialist about something. A quality of prestige and dignity attaches to the successful specialist. If he performs an essential function, he thereby gains security. But, he may also cultivate a certain pride, a conceit which serves to insulate him from the laymen, and frequently from other specialists. His specialization may then become the means of establishing barriers between him and his fellows. He may consciously strive to use language which few can understand; he may consider his specialty as superior to all others; he may, in short, become a professional snob.

A thorough-going treatment of the above problem would carry me too far afield, that is, to a consideration of the relationship between science and democracy in general, a theme which must be reserved for another occasion, and hence I shall content myself with saying that we may test out behavior and its consonance with democratic culture by the degree of respect which we exercise towards the amateur.

(8) We have heard a great deal in recent years about the subject of indoctrination in education, and from my viewpoint most of this discussion has been beside the point. If absence of indoctrination implies education without a goal of any sort, then the current debate loses all meaning. If, on the other hand, indoctrination is taken to mean an attempt on the part of an individual teacher to "convert" his pupils so that they will accept, on penalty of possible classroom failure, his political, economic, social or religious doctrines, then it may be safely stated that no such right exists in a democratic system of public education. The chief function of education in a democracy is to enable the learner to expand the range of his individual capacities and his social relationships. Education is the natural ally of freedom. This implies that the teacher is also to be free, free, first of all, to explore facts regardless of the conclusions to which they may lead, and, in the second place, free to be a whole person, a citizen as well as a teacher. The teacher who has no convictions becomes a half-animate, routinized, mechanized, uninspired automaton. The teacher who has convictions which he conceals or disguises because of fear or compulsion becomes an intellectual coward. His pupils will soon find him out, for while they are still young they remain unafraid of both facts and opinions.

Should teachers, then, in a democratic state teach democracy? The answer is obviously affirmative, providing, first, that democratic striving is a national trait, and second, that they themselves actually believe in the democratic way of life. But, they should do much more than teach *about* democracy: they should allow their pupils and their associates to experience democracy in practice. It would be absurd to expect American youth, for example, to be staunch supporters of democratic culture if their educational experiences had provided them with no opportunities for its practical utilization. It is, happily or unhappily, a law of human behavior that we can be genuinely loyal only to that which we have experienced. Sound teaching proceeds by the rule of contrasts and progressive discriminations, and hence pupils should also be allowed to acquaint themselves with anti-democratic conceptions and practices. Millions of people in the contemporary world no longer believe in democracy. This is a portentous fact and should not be concealed from learners. There are many and various interpretations of democracy. Some believe, for example, that democracy means individualism, the freedom to do as one likes regardless of the consequences to others; some believe that democracy means a minimum of governmental intervention in the sphere of economics while others believe that democracy can only be preserved if government assumes a greater control over economic processes; some believe that political democracy may remain a reality without a corresponding social and economic democracy, and others believe the exact opposite. These are all suitable problems for education.

I may conclude by stating that our behavior may be tested, in relation to education, by the degree of truthfulness with which we confront the problems arising from democratic striving. This statement prompts me to repeat that the roots of democratic culture do not lie in theories and conceptions, but rather in conduct, in experience and its satisfactions. If these roots do not strike deep into the "soil" of human personality, they will be easily destroyed by their external enemies, or they will wither away and die for want of nutriment and exercise. Whenever in history the people have thought and felt and lived democracy there has been cast upon human experience a sharp luminosity. Fears were dispelled and hopes renewed. And, whenever in history tyranny and despotism have succeeded to power, human experience has been shadowed by suspicion, anger and bitterness.

Thus far I have spoken more specifically about those tests which may be applied to our personal behavior, but the time has now come, I believe, when all sincere believers in democracy must also apply these or similar tests to our nation itself. To what extent have we as a people deviated from the democratic pathway? To what degree have we already "slipped" from our democratic base? Has democracy already become a hallowed symbol from which much of reality has been abstracted? I do not know the precise answers to these questions, but I do know that a dark shadow lies athwart our future and that in these days to come men are to be tested once again; their hearts are to be searched and their minds challenged, for the cherished ideal of democracy is once more in peril.

LEADERSHIP AND DEMOCRACY ARE COMPATIBLE *By S. R. Slavson*

In the past few years, many changes have been made in the concepts concerning effective leadership of groups. Thinking has come slowly but surely away from the concept of a leader as a person with authority over the group (autocratic), has swung to the other extreme of thinking of the leader as a person outside the group (laissez-faire), *and has come to rest at the point where the leader is thought of as an integral part of the group in a democratic relationship. In this change, however, confusion has arisen because a false rigidity has been given to the concept of democratic leadership. The problems that arise as a result of this confusion were discussed thoroughly at a panel luncheon held on Friday, June 6, 1941, at Atlantic City, under the leadership of Mr. LeRoy E. Bowman. Mr. S. R.*

Slavson, one of the panel members, summarizes the major points brought out in this discussion.

Note should be made also of the interesting method Mr. Bowman, an expert in discussion methods, used to stimulate discussion. Instead of the panel members sitting isolated on a platform in front of the group, they were seated among the audience and made their comments from the floor. In this way, other members of the audience were encouraged to enter into the discussion.—Editor.

The two major aims of group work are: (1) to develop personality to its greatest capacity in terms of interest, expression and the creative life; and (2) to experience group living with the view of evolving attitudes and interests for participation in a democratic society. It is essential for group workers to develop those practices that will make development of personality and social attitudes compatible with guidance and leadership. The question that often puzzles one is: How can leadership and real democracy co-exist? Does not the leader check free expression and group autonomy? The Iowa experiments in "social climates," directed by Dr. Kurt Lewin and his associates, focused attention in recent months on this problem. These experiments tested under controlled conditions the effect upon small groups of boys of autocratic, democratic and *laissez-faire* leadership. The results show that democratic leadership—as against the other two types—vitalizes the group as a whole, releases the creative impulse in individuals, and reduces to a significant extent aggressive and antisocial acts among the members of the group. Despite these findings, democratic leadership often fails either because of the unreadiness of the group or because the leader is unable to apply the democratic method constructively.

A group of boys of first-generation Americans, whose parents have come from a part of the world where parental, church and governmental authority are particularly repressive, is an example of this point. This club consisted of about twelve boys, whose ages ranged from ten to fifteen years. The leader had a good intellectual appreciation of democratic leadership and proceeded to apply his theoretical knowledge to this club. After a difficult struggle to develop a program, the boys walked out in a huff, demanding another leader. They wanted a leader that would "make us be good." It seems that this group was not ready for the type of work the leader had in mind, because self-direction and group action were alien to their experience. Group action and participation had to be introduced slowly here. The group needed a preparatory period. This the leader could not understand.

Another leader, who had attempted the same type of program too early in his group's development and failed, formulated the cause of his failure in the ready statement: "I made the mistake of being too democratic."

The basic error in both situations would seem to lie in the fact that the leaders conceived democracy as a process of organization, and administrative procedure, and a discussion method. Actually, democracy is an attitude of mind toward oneself and toward the group. Democracy reveals itself most through attitudes and values, rather than through a pattern and procedure. These leaders, therefore, set out to apply a method without the buttressing attitudes that are essential to a true democracy. If attitudes and intents are truly democratic, democratic forms emerge from the situation itself.

When Democracy becomes Tyranny

To impose a form, even if it is a democratic one, is an autocratic act, and may result in tyranny and even dishonesty. On the other hand, if the attitudes of the leader are genuinely democratic and he has, at the same time, educational insight, he will help develop procedures that are best suited to the educational needs of the group at any given time.

A leader of a club of boys, twelve years old, urged the boys to adopt the democratic method. The group rejected the idea. The leader, however, insisted that it was the proper method to use. In spite of the boys' feelings in the matter, he set up a "democratic form of government." Having sensed the authority of the worker, the club accepted the situation and proceeded with its business. One of the matters that came before the group was a suggestion to arrange for a raffle. The leader thought this was a good opportunity to hold a "democratic discussion." He told them to come to the next meeting prepared to discuss the question. The leader was the only one who spoke against the raffle—and for a good reason, as we shall soon see. The vote of the members, however, was in favor of the raffle, the leader being the only one who voted against it. After the vote was taken, the leader told the group that there was a rule in the House against gambling, so that no raffle could be held. When questioned why he permitted the group to go through with this lengthy discussion only to be frustrated by an arbitrary rule of the House, he said that he wanted to give the boys "an experience in the democratic process." The misconception of democracy here is quite evident. Here the process has been divorced from the intent and led to a highly autocratic, tyrannical result. In addition, it frustrated the members and undoubtedly made them resentful.

Fit the Method to the Situation

The ability to recognize different situations that require corresponding types of handling is an important part of the equipment of a group leader. To insist upon one type of leadership despite the reality of the situation and the readiness of the group is a form of fanaticism alien to a good education. If education is a *leading-out* process, it must utilize the state in which pupils or group members are. It is, therefore, frequently necessary to apply different types of leadership to suit the situation at hand. Thus, in democratic group work we need to apply authoritarian, democratic and *laissez-faire* leadership, just as a good parent uses these three methods, or a combination of them.

Freedom has its Limitations

Group work does not occur in *vacuo* as though no external limitations, sanctions or restraints exist. It would have been by no means contrary to democratic education if the leader had told the boys, even before they began to discuss a raffle, that they could not hold one. There are always present cultural limitations on the individual. If the cultural sanctions are designed to strip the individual of personal autonomy, they become autocratic and destructive. But if personal autonomy is guaranteed within the defined limitations set up by the larger culture—the family, classroom, center, municipality or nation— the fundamentals of freedom and democracy are not violated. It would have been quite proper for the leader of the group that planned a raffle to state the conditions under which the group could operate as part of the larger recreational set-up. The leader must be clear, however, as to his own attitude in this connection. Everyone has a desire to be in authority. This desire is rooted deeply in us and has to be consciously checked. If there is a genuine and honest desire on the part of the leader to help children and young people become free from their own selfish impulses, he must face them with the inevitable limitations that life imposes on them.

The Leader Must Counteract Dependence

One of the important services of formal and informal education is to free the individual from his emotional and intellectual dependence upon others. This dependence originates in infancy as a result of the child's physical helplessness, intellectual confusion and the emotional ties that inevitably arise in the family. Since democracy can function adequately only when its citizens are emotionally and intellectually mature, it is necessary that we gradually wean our group members from their early dependencies. This must be accomplished through gradual diminution of adult participation, not by complete and sudden withdrawal. Withdrawal of help and authority may mean to the child that he is being rejected. An example of this is the leader in a summer play school who set up art materials and other arts and crafts supplies in a room, but gave the children no guidance, help or suggestions as to how to use them. The children, who had no previous experience with these materials, were bewildered and unable to utilize constructively the opportunities offered them. Another instance is the leader of a club who, when he was asked how the democratic process was going, said, "Well, if it doesn't work, I can always smack 'em down."

The sudden or over-speedy application of freedom can be almost as disturbing to a group as the application of too strict authority and domination. This is particularly serious to very young children who have not as yet learned to restrain their aggressive and impulsive acts. Aggressiveness in young children, if unchecked, feeds upon itself and mounts to ever higher intensity. It is necessary for the adult to divert or control it, for in some stages of development the group needs and wants the protection against its own "bad" impulses.

The factor of age must be considered in any discussion of leadership. Leadership can become more relaxed as children grow older, acquire inner direction to their behavior from experience with other people and groups, and have more definite interests that keep them occupied.

Authority Has Its Place and Its Limits

It is to be expected that sometimes the wishes of the group may not conform with the rules of the staff or the boards of directors in a group work agency. Although it is essential that members of a group participate in formulating these rules and be free to criticize them, the basic aims of democracy are not defeated if we insist upon conformity to the rules once they are promulgated. A large institution cannot possibly please every individual. There must be some basic rules and routines that are essential to its orderly functioning. These may not be acceptable to each and every one. Those who find themselves in disagreement must be free to criticize and try to alter them. But while doing so, they must conform. Conformity to group rules is part of training for democracy. Democracy guarantees freedom, but it also imposes responsibilities. One of these responsibilities is not to undermine the foundations upon which the group's freedom is built. Rules in a democracy are made so that the greatest good may accrue to the greatest number. An individual who transgresses them is not activated by the democratic spirit. He is rather prompted by his individualistic impulses.

The ability to deal with discontent is an important part of the equipment of leadership. The leader with an educational point of view must accept resentment from group members. He must allay it through his own accepting attitudes, and sometimes through discussion or explanation. He must always remember that, when he is accepted by the group because of his kindness, the group and the individuals in it will not be hostile and will at least listen to reason. By permitting them to express disagreement, the leader develops in his members attitudes of critical evaluation and independence. In formal education, all must participate equally in the improvement of the conditions that help everyone to a better life.

Only the Secure and Strong Can Give Freedom to Others

To give people freedom of expression and action requires a basic security within the leader himself. Only those people who are certain, without reservation, of their ability to control a group if they should so desire can give freedom to that group. This must be considered a basic psychologic law of democracy. Rules, regulations, programs, authority and repression are the tools of those who fear the situation. A person who feels secure feels no need to resort to external props of this nature. He faces each situation as it occurs in a free interaction between himself and the group. Persons so secure are not afraid to use authority if it is in the best interests of the group and the individuals in it. Restraint by an adult is not entirely outside the purview of democratic function. At all times, however, it must be remembered that the leader is not one who is in control of the situation, but is rather one who gives freedom to a degree that the group can make constructive use of it. It must also be remembered that the leader gets considerable security from the fact that he knows what to do next in terms of programs and activities. Knowledge is power here as in other relations.

Patience is a Virtue Even for Leaders

In manual activity and learning, children pass through five stages in development: (1) acclimatization; (2) manipulation; (3) experimentation; (4) reflection; and (5) socialization. Leaders in education must be aware of this and be patient with the slow growth of pupils and club members. An example of this comes from a center in a Southern city. This center is maintained for members of one religious sect and was avoided by all others in the neighborhood. The head worker felt the need for implanting a feeling of unity in the community. He invited a group of boys of another religious persuasion to come into the center "just to look around." They came and seemed to like the place. They came again and soon began to play with the regular members of the center. The newcomers participated more and more in activities and soon brought others from their group into the building. Although it took a considerable period, there has developed a community spirit irrespective of religion.

At first the newcomers walked around the building and observed the members of the center at play and at work. This was the period of acclimatization. When they began to play from time to time and work with the others, they were manipulating the situation to see how it would affect them. They experimented with the new opportunities when they brought in their friends to see what their reactions would be. Later, discussions were held concerning their attitude toward the center and the center's attitude toward them. This was the reflective period. When they became completely absorbed and participated fully in the play and work of the center, the period of socialization had been reached.

These stages take place in the use of freedom as well as in the application of democracy. We cannot rush any of these, and the leader must bide his time. Group work is education *for* democracy *through* democracy in slow and gradual stages.

In Summary

In summary, we may say the following concerning leadership of groups:

1. No type of leadership can be applied rigidly. Different situations require different leadership.

2. Democratic leadership lies in an attitude as well as in a method.

3. Democracy is an outcome of the interaction of the leader and the group, and the leader participates in it to a degree that helps members become independent and self-reliant.

4. One of the chief functions of leadership is training for democratic participation.

5. Another function of leadership is to decrease the dependence of the members upon adult authority.

6. Democracy includes limitations and sanctions evolved by the larger culture or group to which the individual must conform, even though he may work to effect changes in it.

7. The security of the group is based upon the security of the leader. Only people who feel secure can give freedom to others.

8. It is necessary to evaluate the term "leader." It is quite possible that it suggests domination. A term such as "counselor" or "advisor" may be more desirable.

9. Democratic leadership expresses itself through: (a) releasing free expression of group members; (b) graduated authority; (c) integration among groups; (d) manipulation; (e) persuasion; and many other forms. There is no particular method in which leadership expresses itself. Rather, basically, it is a matter of intent and attitude toward a group and the situations as they arise.

PANEL MEMBERS

LeRoy E. Bowman, *Leader*

Patricia Alsop
M. W. Beckleman
Homer Bishop
Nathan Cohen
Jean Schick Grossman
Helen Hall
Charles E. Hendry

Paul M. Limbert
Mary Longley
Walter Ludwig
A. H. Murray
Ann Elizabeth Neely
S. R. Slavson
Hilda Smith
Arthur L. Swift, Jr.

2

Objectives of Group Work

LETTING THE PUBLIC IN ON GROUP WORK OBJECTIVES *By Sallie E. Bright*

PERHAPS the greatest service I can render is made possible because I am *not* a group worker. Maybe that will give me a kind of objectivity, which is the thing needed most of all when we are tackling the problem of interpretation.

I should like to approach the question of interpretation from two angles, if I may. First, I should like to talk about what the public knows about group work *now;* and, second, I should like to see if we can sort out together some of the interpretation problems and possibilities in group work.

This isn't going to be a talk on how to do publicity. There isn't time to go into mechanics, and anyway I don't think the mechanics of publicity are our real problem at all. I realize that not many group work agencies have writers and public relations people on the staff; I realize, too, that training in interpretation in schools of social work is inadequate. But I am relying on the fact that group workers, believing as they do in the learning process, will learn to do the mechanics or will get

35

the money to engage specialists. All this is not nearly so important at this point as the fact that we must settle some basic questions about the *message* of group work. We certainly have to decide what we are going to say before we go into the problem of how we shall say it.

On the first question—what the public knows about group work now—I haven't made a public opinion poll, but I am in something of a strategic position because group work materials, written for the public, pour into the office of the National Publicity Council every day; and, using myself as a guinea pig, I can make a stab at deducing what the public must be learning from these materials—booklets, folders, annual reports, posters, radio scripts.

First of all, the public must have a tremendous respect for those materials, in one way at least. All in all, they are among the best produced materials in social-work publicity. They are well printed; the photographs are good, they are well laid out; they are, for the most part, well written. The public must have the impression that group work is very vigorous and thriving. The physical appearance of group-work materials give them an important head start over the materials of other kinds of agencies, because they are almost sure to make the prospective reader pick them up and open them. Now, having picked the piece up and opened it, what would the reader learn about group work?

Well, he would undoubtedly learn that "group-work agencies" are good places. They are wholesome and—like the church and the public library, but unlike the poolroom and the saloon—they are among the good things in the community. Second, the reader would learn that evidently athletics play a big part in group work. As a matter of fact, the literature of the "group-work agencies" would seem to say that practically the whole program is athletics because of the pictures of basketball teams, swimming teams, physical-fitness classes. In fact, several recent public-opinion polls concerning one large youth agency showed beyond argument that the public considers this particular agency a place to swim and take exercises.

A third thing our reader would learn from group-work publicity is that "group-work agencies" build good citizens. He wouldn't learn *how* they do it, but he would read that they *do* do it. By the same token, they prevent *bad* citizenship or juvenile delinquency.

He would, fourth, learn that group-work agencies are patriotic. He would learn this from pictures of youngsters saluting flags and pledging allegiance.

From much of the material, he would learn, fifth, that some group work agencies are built on a religious basis. He would get this from photographs, from descriptions of vesper services, services in the woods at camp.

On the sixth point, he might be a little confused. From some pieces, he would think that the objective of group work is to uplift the people from the other side of the tracks; from others, he would get the impression that the group-work agency's program is restricted to the middle class and has no place at all for the people from the other side of the tracks.

Finally, he would learn that everything is done in groups, classes, teams, troops, patrols.

His general impression, judged by this reader's, is, I would say, on the whole a pleasant one.

But it isn't a very deep one. And along about now, the lack of deep conviction on the part of the public is a very serious thing. There is no use denying, even the most optimistic of us, that harder times might come. No one knows just how hard, and we are hoping that they won't be too hard. But we have to prepare for *any* eventuality. If *really* hard times come, the things that are only pleasant, and not essential are going to have hard sledding. If they survive, it is possible that their survival may be based on such a wrong premise that it would almost be better not to have survived at all. Instead of developing the true objectives of the group-work program, group work in hard times may be allowed to survive because it prevents juvenile delinquency, provides cheap recreation, keeps the unemployed off the streets. That isn't what we want to build for. At the same time, we certainly don't want to be lopped off as just a pleasant thing, which is not among the things so essential that they must be preserved, in spite of hell or high water.

The true objectives of group work *are* essential in a democracy, but the public can't stand behind group work in the pinches if the public doesn't know what group work is.

As a background for thinking about the interpretation of group work, let's take a look first at the *strengths* we have to work with. From one point of view, the situation is really very cheerful. Group work has some enviable strengths on which to build. From another point of view, quite paradoxically, every one of these strengths presents also a hazard to which group work should be constantly alert.

From a public-relations point of view, probably the main criticism growing out of a list of the pleasant themes of present group-work interpretation is that they are lazy themes. Group work has been lazy in its interpretation. It has relied on a number of national patterns. Americans think that there is something salubrious in the trees and grass and flowers, so we don't have to explain much about camp programs beyond indicating that they will be carried on among trees, on the grass, and amidst the flowers. Americans—most of them—think that anything with the outward forms of religion must be good, so our picture of the sunrise services gets across without much trouble on our part. Patriotism, it goes without saying, is a national pattern of great strength, and "love of country" is a phrase that goes over big, with no need for explanation or discussion on the part of the group-work interpreter. In short, group work has been getting by on a lot of glittering generalities based on tried and true national patterns. May I repeat that, although these may be lazy themes, they are all positive themes; and if group work isn't made understandable by them, at least, for the most part, it is made *likeable*. That is our first big strength. It is also a hazard, because, as we discussed earlier, this kind of superficial idea of group work won't help the field to advance an inch, and it will not sustain the field when it needs sustenance. Pleasant, superficial things have a way of being considered non-essential.

Second, and closely allied to the strength and hazard of public approbation we have just discussed, is the fact that in "group-work agencies," unlike some of the other main fields of social work, the ticket of admission is not *trouble*. One of the principal problems in the interpretation of case work, unlike group work, is that one must be in *trouble* in order to command the services of the agency. The ticket to group-work agencies, on the other hand, has nothing to do with trouble. You aren't laboring under the public stigma of "relief," of "personal failure."

That is a very major strength and pretty unique in social work. You are the happy agencies. But here comes the hazard right along with this strength: happy agencies are not likely to be considered deeply by the community in times of stress, unless they interpret the real objectives of their programs.

Group work has another strength, and this is one that other kinds of social agencies would give their eye teeth to have. This strength is the fact that, laid end to end, your members and your volunteers would stretch around the world. What a potential army of interpreters of group work! The hazard involved in this strength is the hazard of confusion, from the point of view of public impression. As a matter of fact, as a member of the public myself I often find myself greatly confused about the group-work field. I speak glibly of group-work agencies, referring, I suppose, to the agencies that most of us loosely include under the phrase "group work," meaning that they are not health agencies or case-work agencies or Public Welfare Departments, and that their clients are served in groups rather than individually. This big group of agencies not only presents a tremendous range of types of activities, programs, and methods, but much of the work it does is not performed by professional group workers. In other words, the public-relations problem here is involved with the paradox of attempting to present professional group work to the public when, in many of the agencies that the public thinks of as group-work agencies there are few, if any, professional group workers. If group-work skills are highly professional, if the group-work process requires a high degree of training, then the picture of this profession is necessarily dimmed and confused if we present as group workers all the people who work in "group-work agencies." We won't dwell on this confusion here, because there isn't time to go into the question of the place of the professional and the place of the non-professional in social work. Anyway, our problem here is not the interpretation of a professional group itself, but rather the interpretation of the *objectives* of that group. *Nonetheless,* there is confusion, and this confusion presents a public-relations problem that we should at least mention here in our list of hazards to be dealt with.

But before we can really get into the interpretation job, there is a very major confusion that I want to discuss. And this time it is not a confusion coupled with a strength; it is the kind of confusion that is a real weakness.

Not so long ago, I heard the head of a settlement house say that one reason why her agency attracted people from all over the city, even though it was situated in a so-called "underprivileged neighborhood," was that, when it announced a pottery class, everybody knew it would be the best pottery class in town. When that settlement house has a play, it is a *good* play. Now, I know there is satisfaction for the individual in being in a *good* play; I know that, if you are going to study pottery, you want to be in a group that is making *good* pottery. But I get mixed up in whether that particular settlement house is teaching dramatics and pottery or whether it is doing group work. In other words, I don't know where excellence of activities ends and group work begins. Maybe that particular settlement house has a plan for the people who aren't good enough pottery makers to keep up with the pottery class, the head worker and I didn't talk long enough for me to ask about that. But it is puzzling, I suppose, to use another example, that it is a hard problem for a group worker to decide how to give a certain awkward child satisfaction and still not let her spoil the may-pole dance, which is so dear to the other youngsters' hearts. It must be a blow to have to decide not to have a may-pole dance at all.

You can tell, here, that I am not a group worker. Any group worker in the room could tell me in an instant how such in-dividual situations are dealt with. But I think the public shares my confusion between activities, programs, and group work. And certainly the money raisers are worried about it. Last year I attended a meeting on the interpretation of group work in a Midwestern city, and the problem came up there. Somebody was worried because, even with an excellent activities program, the children from outside the slum area in which his agency was located simply wouldn't cross the line and use the agency. Someone else said that this was because the agency had been publicized as an agency for the underprivileged and as an agency "doing good" to people. A public-relations director, when asked if he thought money could be raised on the basis of an activi-ties program, said "yes." He was hotly refuted by other people who felt that the community would never give money for anything but the relief of distress of one kind or another. (One newspaper man attending the meeting said that the prevention of juvenile delinquency was the best and the *only* story of group work.) The discussion ended in a shambles, and no wonder. Everybody was guessing, and the group workers themselves weren't sure about whether they should put the emphasis on activities or on the group-work process; they weren't very clear in their arguments to refute the man who said that group work must be interpreted as being for the underprivileged. These confusions grew out of the fact that, in a room full of group workers, we couldn't decide what group work *is*. Now, clarification of this confusion is beyond the scope of an outsider like me. It is within my sphere of competence, however, to point out to you that this confusion is a major stumbling block to the clear interpretation of group work, and that it must be cleared up before you go ahead.

It has taken me a long time to get to the real point of this article, because there were so many things that had to be cleared away first before we can really get into the subject of how group-work objectives shall be interpreted to the public. The reason for the delay is a simple, if perhaps tiresome, one, it is the fact that there are a lot of confusions and public misapprehensions about group work itself, which must be cleared away before real interpretation can begin.

Now, at the point of the interpretation job and how it shall be done, I am going to take a very definite side on a very controversial question. One of the most hotly debated subjects in social-work interpretation is the question of how much *process* the public needs to know. Some people feel that the public needs to know situations in which social agencies help and that, when possible, they should be told results; but that one cannot and needn't go too deeply into process. Well, I've never been quite of that school of thought. I think it is the failure of the case-work field to explain process that has made them retreat into the public position of being merely "good listeners." The public is still puzzled about what goes on in a case-work agency that helps to straighten out people's lives. And, most often, puzzled people are suspicious people. Now, it is a little different with group work. The public actually doesn't know enough about it to be puzzled. The public assumes that the camp counselor teaches the kids songs, takes his charges on nature trips, telegraphs the parents when their child gets sick, and maybe settles fights. The public doesn't know what goes on in a good camp; nobody has ever told them. And they aren't suspicious or questioning because, as we said before, camping is a good thing. It has trees and grass and flowers, and clean outdoor fun and sunshine, and—well, it's a good thing. Like motherhood, or bravery, or the Statue of Liberty.

It *is* a good thing. The public doesn't know *how* good. All right, how good is it? What happens on a nature trip, besides identifying different kinds of daisies and discovering queer-shaped rock formations? What happens in the discussion among the youngsters even before the nature trip, when it develops that some of them would rather use the time rehearsing for a play? It seems to me that if you are going to explain what happens on a nature trip, beyond what happens on any nature trip from any public school, then you have got to talk about the group-work process. Your only other recourse is to merely put it down as a nature trip and leave the public to draw its own conclusions about whether they want to believe in nature trips or not; or, you might indicate that nature trips make good citizens and let the public figure out if it can how in the world that happens.

That is what so much group-work interpretation does now; it makes good citizens on a nature trip, by some magic that will forever be a mystery. The development of personalities through such group experiences as the democratic method of choosing whether to go on a nature trip at all, the adjustment of the people who wanted to practice the play when the majority wanted to go on the nature trip, the feeling of being together, the mutual joy of discovery on the trip, the brief struggle about who got the credit for discovering the interesting rock formation that had everybody excited—all these things, to me, are thrilling. Why wouldn't they be thrilling—and revealing—to the public, if they were told well?

And, thrilling as they are, they come under the heading of *process*. When one describes merely objectives, which is what group work *hopes* for in its work with people, or when one describes only results, the public is still in the dark about what actually happened. It seems to me that only through the explanation of the group-work process—and that is what Miss Rowe has reminded us that group work is, a process—can the objectives of group work be made clear. After all, just on the face of it. It isn't possible to get the public excited about the objectives of a process when they have no notion of what the process itself is.

The telling of the story of process requires a great deal of skill. There is a vast difference between merely describing a home-making class, on the one hand, and, on the other, telling what really goes into making that class a meaningful group experience through which individual personalities grow.

One of the reasons why the interpretation of process requires great skill is the fact that it would be extremely easy to fall into the danger of making the whole thing sound like some sort of medical treatment. Just to show you what I mean, a couple of years ago I met with a committee in my little suburban town outside New York to set up a summer play school and recreation group. The chairman interpreted group work to the other ladies like fury. The whole thing got so therapeutic that you would have thought we were setting up a clinic. I was certainly glad that none of the kids was around. Even some of the women who were going to be group leaders began to have a drawn look about the eyes. We had certainly succeeded in taking all the fun out of recreation that day. And that is what you will do unless your interpretation of the objectives and processes of group work is very skillfully done.

That is what your army of volunteer interpreters will do if you, in your interpretation to them, fail to remember that group work is a happy, positive, satisfying thing. When the individual achieves social adjustment through group association, he has *fun* doing it. That's different from case work, from psychiatry, from the other ways in which we in other auspices of social work help people to adjust. These other methods are satisfying in the end, but the processes themselves don't even pretend to be fun. Let's not take the happiness out of group work too, by making it sound too therapeutic. Like a certain brand of cigarettes, let's keep it a treat, not a treatment.

By now you are saying: "Okay, Mrs. Bright, but a little while ago you said that, come hard times, communities aren't going to support 'treats.'" No, they aren't, or at least I think there is a danger they won't. I'm not saying here that we tell *only* the story of *fun*. That's where the subtlety and the skill come in. I'm saying that, by hook or crook—and mostly by just straight skill—we have got to tell the story of the process of group work and at the same time keep the tone of the whole thing cheerful.

One of the reasons why this is necessary is that so much of the interpretation of group work programs is directed toward actual members or potential members. This fact presents one of the most difficult of group-work interpretation problems. Into my office, every day, come invitations to young people to swim in a pool, to join the beauty class or the current-events group, to have a workout in the gym. When that material begins to sound therapeutic, when it begins to sound as if you are inviting people to participate in group activities because you think there is something wrong with them that needs fixing, then you are sunk. However, I think that the interpretation of

group activities to youngsters, even the invitations to participate, can carry a good deal more of the objectives and, yes, the
process, of group work than they do if you are skillful enough
not to make the message sound therapeutic. When you are
sounding the call to participate in a current-events group, for
example, why isn't it possible to say: "You see, fellows, it's a
tough job to make a democracy work. People who are going
to run a government intelligently—and that is just what you are
going to do one of these days when you are a voter—have to
know how to think through a lot of issues. They have to work
together, see the other person's point of view, get along with
a lot of different kinds of folks, have experience in taking the
lead sometimes and, other times, in following the leader. That
is what we are going to do in our Wednesday-night group.
We think you will get something out of it that will be learning,
but a lot of fun at the same time."

Maybe invitations to a plunge group or a drama class or some
of the other activities presents a harder problem; but I think
that if you keep in mind, every time you put pen to paper or
make a speech or write a form letter to a group, that you have
another opportunity to get something across, the ways of getting it across without making your specific piece of interpretation sound like a medical prescription will come to you.

Parents are part of the audience, too. If Johnnie is going to
join the Wednesday-afternoon current-events group, if he is
going to sign up for the Saturday morning gym group, if he is
going to camp, it is a pretty sure bet that the parents are going
to be in on the decision. Johnnie will pick the fun out of your
invitation; maybe he won't get the rest of it, unless you make
it sound like a dose of medicine that will taste bad but be very
good for him. Then, he'll get it and won't like it. The parents,
however, will get the whole message. They'll like what you
have in mind for Johnnie and his development; and what they

say in the neighborhood about the "group-work agency" may not sound professional to you, but it will be *good*. You have had enough experience with satisfied parents already to know that they are a powerful group of allies. Now they can be a powerful group of interpreters, too, if you give them the story.

We have already touched on the volunteers as an army of interpreters, and it doesn't seem to me that there is much problem here. It ought to be possible to give to volunteers the straight story of the objectives and process of group work; and I am sure you are already doing that, in some measure at least. I'll leave it up to you whether you, in your own agency, are doing as much with that job as you can, remembering other kinds of volunteers than just the adult group leaders to whom interpretation takes the form of leadership training.

It should be easy, too, to reach other groups in the community with the story of group work—the real story, the real objectives; and I am sure you know those methods as well or better than I do. There probably isn't a person here that hasn't made talks at the Rotary Club, to church groups, to PTA's, to labor unions.

The point on which I want to end this paper will not, I hope, sound to you like a pep rally. It is an old, old point, and one that group workers accepted a long time ago and are undoubtedly tired of hearing about. But it is by far the most important public-relations point I could make this afternoon, and to me it is the essence of the story of group work for the public. And it is the point that needs to be made to the public *right now*, in 1947, for particularly crucial and pressing reasons.

The point is that the fields in which group-work is practiced represent a laboratory and training center for democracy.

It is a very frustrating thing to live in a democracy these days. We sit in our living rooms and stew about whether it was right or wrong to by-pass the UN on aid to Greece and Turkey;

and even if we are lucky enough to know how to make a decision, what can we do about it as individual citizens? We worry about the housing situation; but having made up our individual minds that we just have to do something about it, who do we call up, to whom do we write a letter, what step do we take next? I repeat, it is a frustrating thing to live in a democracy, realizing that a democracy stands or falls on intelligent participation by the people, when there is so little chance for the individual citizen to make himself felt. In a group-work agency, there is an opportunity to learn how to participate, to learn how to live in a democracy. True, the settlement-house group may not be able to affect the Turkey and Greece situation directly; but a democratic nation is the sum total of democratic neighborhoods and communities, and what you are doing in group work is to give people a chance to practice the methods of democracy in their own back yards. And, from a mental-hygiene point of view in a frustrated nation, you are relieving the frustration of the citizen who can't make himself heard on a global scale by giving him a chance to make himself heard in the neighborhood. It is a thrilling thing to realize, then, that if the citizen can be heard in all the neighborhoods, his collective voice will, in the end, have global carrying power.

There is another important point in this business of living in today's democracy. We are a confused nation of erstwhile rugged individuals, Horatio Alger characters who are a little bemused and uncomfortable in a society devoted to the most good for the most number of people. Even the individual labor-union member who strikes for the good of the trade, but has to forego buying his wife a new spring coat in the process, wonders sometimes whether he is an individual or only a member of a group. Group work has an answer to that national dilemma in the very statement of its purpose: individual development within the group. That story will fall on the ears of a very grateful nation, if it is told well.

To sum up, the prospects of interpreting the real meaning of the group-work process are limitless. I would go so far as to say, at the risk of sounding corny, that the world is waiting for it.

COMMON OBJECTIVES OF GROUP WORK, PHYSICAL EDUCATION AND RECREATION
By Kenneth W. Kindelsperger

IT seems particularly appropriate to re-study a subject which involves the relationships between groups having common objectives in working with the problems people present in their daily living. Many others in our related fields have become sensitive to the fact of the absolute necessity today for the continual search for methods of helping people to understand one another and to learn to live with one another. It is for this reason that the subject of this article can be thought of as being related to the broader search of modern man to find common elements of relationship with his fellow man in order to be able to survive.

There are at least two elements basic in the social process today which make essential such a study. First of these is the obvious, yet fundamental, observation that life is continually becoming more complex. Many people still look with fond nostalgia upon the good old days as if in their dreams of the past they could find simple solutions to the problems which face us today and will harass us in the future. But we have learned enough about society and about the dynamics of individual personality to know that there are no longer any simple answers to the problem of human relationships.

The modern American family is being bombarded continually with all sorts of pressures which have an impact upon it. We are first of all living in a world with great uncertainty in relationship to armed conflict. Most young men finishing high school are faced with the problem of adapting to military life. The major share of our national economy is being focused on the production of military materials. Finding a job, getting married, raising children, providing for adequate housing, maintenance of health—items such as these no longer, if they ever were, are simple matters to be faced. Each phase of human existence has become so interrelated and interdependent upon other phases that one wonders how the ordinary individual is able to wander through this labyrinth of complexities to a happy life. The fact of the matter is that increasingly people are needing help in this attempt to find the secret of happiness. More and more community agencies are being asked to provide such help.

As a result of this demand for community service we have tended to develop the second basic element in the evolving process of social relations. This is the increasing degree of specialization that has been developed to meet the particular needs of individuals in society. It has become almost a maxim that, as needs become more complex, services to meet these needs have tended to become more specialized.

This degree of specialization has created many problems, of which we are aware. The medical profession which perhaps has achieved a degree of specialization not yet known to the other professions has now begun to focus its energies upon integration of the specialties. In a sense those of us who work in the various fields which serve the leisure-time needs of people are faced with this same dilemma. All of us are interested in relating to people and providing meaningful experiences for them and with them which will make it possible for them to achieve a happier life. Yet, in the process of developing our skills and knowledge we have become isolated from each other. This isolation is exhibited in the language we speak, in the separateness of our professional meetings, and in our relations to the general public. Now our field faces the direct responsibility for learning to share and to coordinate and to integrate our efforts for the common good.

It is therefore with the knowledge of the complexities of life and the realization of the problems that specialization has brought in meeting these complexities that we are approaching the task of finding the common objectives of recreation, physical education and group work which are words that describe our interests in our approach to human beings.

I became directly interested in the relationship between these three professional groups a few years ago when I participated in a study of recreation facilities and services in a relatively large populated county in upstate New York. This county had a large city almost in its geographical center and the purpose of the study was to discover the extent of services being provided in the county area outside the city limits by the recreation agencies with headquarters in the city. As the study progressed it became obvious that the county recreation program as a whole was really a collection of many separate bits of program. These were being provided by many different groups.

For example, in one rural community, there had been formed a community council made up of lay people and representatives from the schools and civic organizations. This council had sponsored a recreation program two nights a week during the winter and a program out of doors during the summer. These activities were held in the central school building. This community council was financed jointly by funds from the community chest of the county and by the public allocations that were made possible through the New York State Youth Commission. The director of the community recreation program in this little town was the physical education instructor of the local high school.

During the summer the council conducted a swimming program which utilized one of the nearby county parks. In this case the facilities were provided and maintained by the county government while the recreation program was conducted by a physical education instructor from the school. His salary for this recreation leadership was paid by the community chest and the State of New York through the New York State Youth Commission.

I was overwhelmed by the complexity and interrelationship involved in providing a simple program in this rural area. As a result of this study I became interested in exploring the interrelationship of these three areas of practice.

I tried first to define what in my thinking was the basic difference and similarity in these related fields. As part of this attempt I have asked people in various areas of responsibility what the terms "group work," "physical education" and "recreation" meant to them. Although there has been a great variation in definition there was a fairly common approach in that most people who are interested in these fields thought in terms of settings or facilities. Recreation is still generally thought of as a series of activities usually provided through the public departments of recreation in various city, town and county governments. Most people think of it as including facilities such as parks and playgrounds and swimming pools and activities such as special events, tournaments and parades. Physical education to most of the people to whom I spoke is thought of as an activity usually performed in a gym during school hours although sometimes including intramural events. Group work, on the other hand, in the common understanding of the people to whom I have talked, is work done with underprivileged youngsters in social agencies supported through the community chest.

These are, of course, oversimplifications of some of the comments I have received. But in general these are the feelings and attitudes of many people who can be expected to have some knowledge of the meaning of the three terms. I have a feeling that, if we conducted a general public opinion poll with the help of Dr. Gallup, we would be disturbed by the number of people who would not know what any of the three words meant.

In addition to my general questions to people, I have attempted in the past two years to examine the literature and to try and develop some understanding of the relationship of the three terms, "recreation," "physical education" and "group work." My own particular training was in the field of social work with an emphasis in group work and community organization. I point this out to indicate my own bias but at the same time to indicate that I consciously have tried to examine the total aspects of this relationship. The summary which follows has evolved from this examination and is focused particularly on the concept of interrelationship, rather than distinctiveness.

It seems to me, in the first place, we need to clarify the extent to which this concept of relationship is inherent in these three fields.

To me physical education and group work are alike in that they are both methods of working with people. Recreation is distinctive in that it represents a field of activity so planned and developed that it gives to the individual or the individual in the group a sense of satisfaction that is re-creative. Some people say that recreation implies the constructive use of leisure time through activities individually or group planned, others feel that there is nothing inherently good or bad in recreation but that the way it is used determines its usefulness to the individual and society. My own belief is that the root of the word recreation, meaning "to recreate," implies an individual and social goal which makes it possible for both the individual and society to benefit as a result of a recreational activity. Activities that do not meet these goals would not be considered recreation in my estimation.

Recreational activities are extremely varied from individual activities, such as golf, and more passive ones such as reading, to involved group activities such as team sports and games and also mass activities such as parades, treasure hunts, and dances. Recreation, therefore, is a field of activity which varies according to the way individuals participate. Some activities are performed individually, some of them depend upon the use of teams and clubs, and others require organization and leadership for the individual to achieve enjoyment and satisfaction.

Activities of the field of recreation are used by innumerable groups including social workers, medical workers, public school workers and by many social and civic groups which have recreational programs as part of their activities.

When a community organizes its tax funds and develops a Department of Recreation, it is saying that certain activities and facilities will be provided at governmental expense for the citizens of the community at large. In a sense, then, the Department of Recreation, utilizes these activities from the field of recreation and provides professional leadership and facilities for the common good. Recreation, therefore, becomes a vast field of activities which can be utilized by individuals or groups, in the broad area of leisure time services. Through the use of these activities a sense of enjoyment develops, a satisfying experience results, and from this an individual finds renewed strength in his adjustment to the world about him.

Physical education and group work, we have stated, are both alike in that they are methods. Physical education is a method of using the body as a means of expression whereby the individual achieves a sense of physical well-being through the process of either individual achievement or through participating in a structure of relationships to others. As a method of working with people, physical education plays an important role in the recreation services of a community. Because a large proportion of our public recreation activities are physical in nature there are many people with training in physical education who are on the staffs of recreation departments. The same is true of many of the social agencies of the community. The English have developed a term that they call "physical recreation," to describe this particular emphasis. The method of physical education, however, is not limited to the recreation field. The major contribution of physical education has been in the field of formal education and much of the preparation in college for work in this area places great emphasis on teaching methods.

Increasingly, however, there has been a growing emphasis on what might be called the informal method in physical education. This emphasis has stressed enjoyment, a relaxed atmosphere and has had influence in introducing new activities such as the modern dance, folk dancing and individual activities such as archery, golf, tennis and handball. There has been a resultant decrease in more formal gymnastics, marching and apparatus work. This emphasis on informal methods makes the total physical education method more flexible. Because of this flexibility we are finding that the method is being widely applied in numerous settings previously thought of as unrelated. The physical education method, therefore, may be utilized in the field of formal education when it is connected with a school system, in the social welfare field when it is applied in a Boys' Club, a YMCA or any other agency of this nature and in the medical field when it is related to a rehabilitation center or a physical re-training department. It may be adapted to the military setting as a method of developing bodily coordination and strength in connection with combat. We have found in increasing numbers physical education specialists in these respective fields. In general, physical education uses many of the recreational activities that we have described previously. Some of these are individual in nature, some of them depend upon a group or team and others are of mass nature. The function of the particular agency or sponsorship will therefore determine the extent or usage of the physical education method.

This does not imply that physical education has no goals or direction. The method is first of all geared to the development of orderly body processes and utilizes the knowledge of physiology and anatomy. It respects the teachings of psychology through its theory of individual differences. Its recognizes the use of a conscious process of relationships and it accepts the professional function of leadership to provide guidance to the method. Physical education, then, as a method, has a much broader horizon than merely the preparation for formal education. Many people in the physical education movement are stressing the greater possibility of this contribution.

Group work is perhaps the least understood of our three terms. It is only within recent years that we have come to an understanding of the dynamics of group process and have been able to utilize this knowledge in a constructive fashion. Group work is based upon the assumption that there is an inevitable process of social interaction that begins whenever a number of individuals are collected together around a common purpose. Each individual brings into the group a basic personality structure which has an impact upon the other members of the group. As a result of this impact certain observable group processes begin. From the studies in social psychology and from the field of social work we have been able to observe such factors as dominance, submission, elimination and compromise as being present in many group situations. All of these processes can be consciously changed or affected by injecting specific kinds of activities, leadership and goals.

Social group work utilizes the knowledge gained from the study of group interaction and becomes a distinct method in the field of social work along with casework and community organization. In the social group work method, individuals are helped to relate to one another and to experience growth opportunities by the use of a conscious process of relationships in which a leader, with the knowledge of individual and group behavior, utilizes program activities to help the individuals in the group move toward socially desirable goals. These goals in our society are those of the democratic life. In the process, maximum opportunity for decision-making is inherent for the individual member of the group. The activity never becomes more important than the individual, the leader is looked upon as an enabler who helps individuals to help themselves and the setting in which the group operates is consistent with the social goals of a democratic society.

The social group work method utilizes many recreational activities in its program, from team sports to group games and dancing and other activities. The social group worker is always aware of two simultaneous factors: the program or activity itself and the interaction of individuals who are participating in the activity. The small group is utilized as the most effective method of social relationships.

Agencies which utilize social group work methods are usually broad in nature. It is only within recent years that we have come to accept the idea that agencies may be multi-service agencies and that to use the term group work to describe them may not be the most exact or appropriate method of description. An agency such as the YMCA or Boys' Club or YWCA or a Jewish Community Center is a multi-service agency. It provides many activities through the use of small groups. It has many facilities open on an individual basis and it provides many activities of a mass or large scale nature. Most of these agencies utilize physical education methods as part of their program. They also use the social group work method in a large part of their program. In many cases these two methods are combined around a common goal; for example, a club organized on a group work basis may utilize physical education methods in the pursuit of its goal.

The agencies in which social group work is predominantly used are perhaps more appropriately called recreation or informal education agencies. The use of the social group work method, however, is not limited to the recreation or informal education field. Just as the physical education method is adaptable to other settings so we are finding the social group work methods adaptable in other settings. Many large hospitals have developed groups in relation to medical treatment of patients. Psychiatric clinics are utilizing the group method. Industry and business have found the group method as an effective approach. Let me make it clear, however, that there is a difference between social group work and the term group work. Group work is the much broader use of the small group in various settings. Social group work describes the application of the small group approach to the social welfare setting. The social welfare setting thereby establishes the goals of leadership and direction under which the group operates.

In all the foregoing, I have been trying to develop the principle that there is a distinct inter-relationship between the terms "recreation," "physical education" and "group work." In my estimation their goals are more alike than they are different. In conclusion, therefore, I would like to enumerate at least five common elements in the objectives of the fields of practice these terms describe.

In the first place, there is a common agreement as to the conscious use of a process of relationships. Physical education and group work and recreation leadership all are aware of the fact that planning and preparation are essential factors in developing the activities that they utilize in relating to people. This is not a hit or miss proposition. This is a conscous preparation of relationships. We are all interested in making facilities attractive and available and functional. We are all interested in the method of relating to people. We are all aware that it is essential to understand the way people learn new skills and to provide the maximum opportunity for the learning of such skills.

The term "conscious method of relationship" does not involve any negativistic principle of manipulation. We are not in the business of manipulating people. All of us are or should be continually studying the methods in which people relate to one another, and we need to share the experiences we have had in this process of relationship so that our contribution in the setting in which we work becomes increasingly more sensitive and effective.

In the second place, all of us use activities as a method of relationship. Therefore we all have a common interest in the development of skills, in the learning of games, development of new techniques, in the exchange of ideas of program materials and suggestions. The flexibility of both the physical education and group work methods make it possible for a great deal of interchange of ideas and experiences. The recreation field is constantly being stimulated with new methods of approaching and interesting individuals and groups. We need to increase our understanding of how we can utilize specific activities for certain goals; that it is not just a question of playing games with people but how these particular activities influence and consciously affect the people in them. Through this knowledge of the use of activities we can eliminate stereotyping, discrimination and points of conflict, and instead determine areas of use that are more conducive to wholesome human relationships.

In the third place, we are all interested in understanding more about the behavior of individuals. The fields of psychology and psychiatry have given us a great deal of insight in recent years and this material is equally available to all of us. All of us are, or should be, aware that the individual personality is more important than the performance of a single activity. We need to understand how to work with shy and withdrawn individuals, how the more aggressive individual can be helped through the conscious use of activities, what the impact of outside forces are upon participation in the group. We need to do constant research ourselves in the settings in which we operate, to use the advances which are being made in the understanding of the dynamics of individual behavior.

In the fourth place, all of us accept the role of the leader as a professional person who is consciously relating to individuals through the activities in which they participate. We all accept the responsibility of leadership and we need to study constantly the role and impact of this person in relationships. Already many interesting studies have been made. We need to share these constantly and to recognize the close relationship we have since we all fundamentally believe in the same goal of respect of the individual and the betterment of society. None of us accept the concept of dictatorial or manipulative leadership. We are all interested in finding ways of making the role of the leader that of an enabler, a person who helps people to help themselves.

In the final analysis, we are all very much involved in utilizing our contribution for the improvement of the community. None of us is in the business of making a profit out of the people for whom we work. Most of us are responsible to the community for our support, either through the tax dollar or the voluntary contribution of the community chest or other agencies. This, in a sense, gives us our goal and direction of constantly focusing on community needs rather than the development of any special interest. We need to be aware of community research and constantly integrate our efforts in attacking a general community problem. The treatment of juvenile delinquency or other maladjustments is not the special right or prerogative of any one of us. It is a common goal which we share with many other people in the community. We therefore need to work with and through other community agencies in this process of community development.

The three fields can come to understand each other if we can create more avenues of communication with one another and through them share our beliefs and experiences. Our training facilities must include the contributions of all of these areas. Our professional meetings and associations must relate more intensively to the topic of integration of our work. Our language must be kept simple so that we can understand each other; and, finally, we need to assume the responsibility of demonstrating on the level on which we work the belief that we all share in the basic ability of men to understand and work with each other. In today's world this is not only an ideal to be worked toward; it is a necessity to be accomplished.

DEFINITION OF THE FUNCTION OF THE GROUP WORKER *By Grace L. Coyle,* Chairman, Committee on the Function of the Professional Group Worker

The Committee on the Function of the Professional Group Worker was asked by the executive board of the A.A.G.W. to prepare a brief definition which might be used for interpretation to other organizations and with people unfamiliar with group work as it has developed. The Committee found this an extremely difficult assignment and spent many hours in writing and rewriting the definition. It has been reviewed and edited in several meetings of the Executive Board. The committee, in addition to the efforts of its own members, drew upon parts of the statements on group work written by 25 people in the field whom it had asked to submit 2500 word statements on the essential characteristics of group work. These in many cases, contained short definitions and also much background material. The result, therefore, while it undoubtedly will not satisfy many people in the field, represents a long collaborative process.

The group worker enables various types of groups to function in such a way that both group interaction and program activities contribute to the growth of the individual, and the achievement of desirable social goals.

The objectives of the group worker include provision for personal growth according to individual capacity and need, the adjustment of the individual to other persons, to groups and to society, and the motivation of the individual toward the improvement of society; the recognition by the individual of his own rights, limitations and abilities as well as his acceptance of the rights, abilities and differences of others.

Through his participation the group worker aims to effect the group process so that decisions come about as a result of knowledge and a sharing and integration of ideas, experiences and knowledge rather than as a result of domination from within or without the group.

Through experience he aims to produce these relations with other groups and the wider community which contribute to responsible citizenship, mutual understanding between cultural, religious, economic or social groupings in the community and a participation in the constant improvement of our society toward democratic goals.

The guiding purpose behind such leadership rests upon the common assumptions of a democratic society; namely, the opportunity for each individual to fulfill his capacities in freedom, to respect and appreciate others, and to assume his social responsibility in maintaining and constantly improving our democratic society.

Underlying the practice of group work is a knowledge of individual and group behavior and of social conditions and community relations which is based on the modern social sciences.

On the basis of this knowledge the group worker contributes to the group with which he works a skilled leadership which enables the members to use their capacities to the full and to create socially constructive group activities.

He is aware of both program activities and of the interplay of personalities within the group and between the group and its surrounding community.

According to the interests and needs of each, he assists them to get from the group experience the satisfaction provided by the program activities, the enjoyment and personal growth available through the social relations and the opportunity to participate as a responsible citizen.

The group worker makes conscious use of his relation to the group, his knowledge of program as a tool, and his understanding of the individual and of the group process and recognizes his responsibility to individuals and groups with whom he works and to the larger social values he represents.

3

Group Work and Case Work

Patterns of Case Work Services in Group Work Agencies
By Saul Scheidlinger

Referrals of clients from case work agencies to groups, and vice versa, have been a usual practice in the field of social work for some time. Other forms of cooperation between case work and group work agencies have been developed as well. However, the use of case workers in the setting of group work agencies, which I intend to discuss in this paper, is a more recent development. It attempts to bring about the coordination of the services of the two fields. Five representative group work agencies were selected for the purpose of examining the various uses they have made of the services of case workers and to see whether any distinctive patterns have been evolved in the way they functioned.

Agency A:

Agency A is a non-sectarian, progressive settlement house in a low income area of a large city. As one of the oldest settlements, this agency has had for many years a neighborhood worker who was also in charge of the adult club department. This worker offered her help to individuals on a "neighborly and friendly," rather than a professional basis. She had no training in social case work and her functions were not clearly defined. When necessary, referrals to special agencies in the community were made. The high degree of social pathology found in the neighborhood, however, was one of the chief factors leading to engaging a trained case worker with some group work experience to serve both as neighborhood worker and consultant to the House staff on problems of individual members.

At first the case worker's functions were not clearly defined. A Case Work-Group Work Committee composed of leaders in the field of social work was formed to help formulate ways in which the case worker could be most profitably used in the House setting. The Committee listed the following functions of the case worker: (a) to sensitize the group leaders to a better understanding of individual children which would lead to a more effective meeting of the latter's needs through group work channels; (b) to deal with the children whose individual needs were such that they could not be met by usual group work methods.

The case worker was to attempt to help this latter group of children either by referring them to appropriate outside agencies, or where this was not indicated, by short-contact treatment within the agency aimed toward enabling the individual to make better use of the group work services. In actual practice, however, the worker encountered a number of individuals where referral to a case work agency was either not possible—because of the client's inability to accept such referral—or where it was not practical. In some of these instances, the case worker would attempt treatment at the House, but this was the exception rather than the rule.

The problems of individual children were brought to the attention of the case worker by the group work supervisor or group leader, following which a social study of each child was made. After a joint discussion, plans were made as to how this could best be helped: either through referral or special treatment in the group. Some of the children presenting potential difficulties were detected by the case worker herself in the course of her association with various groups in the building. In instances where there was not a good relationship between the individual child and his group leader, the case worker tried to approach the child directly.

The worker was not known by any title to the House members, although they knew she was a staff member. A child to be referred to her would be told that she was the person who "helped kids get jobs," "talked to kids who were unhappy," etc. She was a recognized member of the staff, attending all meetings; she was consulted on any referral of a child to another agency. In cases of disciplinary measures, the case worker was used as a consultant. There was a highly aggressive group of boys in the building that refused to accept any of the limitations set down by the House. Instead of immediately expelling the whole group from the agency, the case worker made individual studies, following which a staff conference was held. As a result some of the boys were referred to appropriate social agencies for help.

In addition to acting as the interviewer for the birth control clinic located in the House, the case worker was also a camp registrar. Instead of the past policy of having a definite fee for camp, the worker determined how much each family could afford to pay. Prior to this the family's contribution for camp had never been determined on a realistic budget basis, with most mothers trying to bargain when told what the camp fee was.

There was a dual supervision of the case worker. She was

guided in the case work aspects of her task by a supervisor from a family agency. In regard to administration and function, the case worker was responsible to the Head Worker of the settlement house. The case worker was paid by the House on a 40-hour a week basis. Since many parents could not be seen during the day, the worker contributed two full evenings a week to the House.

In evaluating the case worker's performance, everyone in Agency A seemed to agree that she had demonstrated a need for her services on a permanent basis. The writer was told of a plan to engage an additional trained case worker to act in the role of the traditional "neighborhood worker," so as to limit the case worker's services to House members only.

Agency B:

The group work agency discussed here is a large, progressive settlement house and community center. In December, 1942, a worker was secured by Agency B under a special arrangement with a national federation of group work agencies and a local child guidance clinic. Each staff member received a memorandum explaining the set-up, purpose and use of what was to be called "consultation service." The worker was to be known as "consultation worker" to the staff and as a leader to the House membership.

The worker's functions were at first defined in general terms so as to make experimentation possible. Soon these functions were limited to observation and study of selected groups of children. Before visiting such a group, she had a conference with the group work supervisor and the club leader, in the course of which problem children were discussed and the group records read. After a clearing of these specific children through the Social Service Exchange, the worker visited the groups for observation.

Although some of the groups and their leaders reacted unfavorably to the case worker's presence, the Head Worker felt that the worker's presence was necessary nevertheless, because the group leaders were not sufficiently trained to detect children with problems. Each of the selected groups was visited at least three times, following which another conference was held at which the consultation worker presented written summaries on the individual children observed. At this conference decisions were made as to which of these needed the special attention of a case work agency and which could be helped through a more sensitive and understanding treatment in the group situation. In some cases a change of group was suggested. The Head Worker was emphatic in stating that no case work treatment was being carried on within the agency. Another function of the case worker was to act as a liaison person between her own agency and the settlement, which made for a more effective treatment of cases carried cooperatively.

In view of the fact that the case worker spent two half-days a week at Agency B, she was able to observe only a small number of the groups meeting in the building.

Known to the children as a "leader," the case worker functioned as a member of the staff and attended most of their meetings, and special group conferences to contribute her knowledge of individual children to the discussions. It is interesting to note that the group workers were more apt to recognize as behavior problems those children who interfered with group programs. Children who seemed to "adjust" superficially were often singled out only through the observation and study of the case worker. The latter placed most emphasis on developing a great sensitivity in the group work staff to behavior problems in children who are not especially troublesome and guiding them in making better referrals.

The referral of parents and children to case work agencies presented a great many problems. Almost invariably when a parent was told that the group work agency could no longer handle his child, a great many resistances resulted. In order to make these referrals easier, the parents of children with special problems were seen routinely, for a period of time, by the administrative assistant. They were told how the children were getting along in the House, and at the same time the parents reported about relationships at home. As a result of these conferences, they subsequently found it much easier to accept the need for referral to a case work agency. In actual practice the case worker dealt only with those referrals which were difficult and required especially skilled handling. Some preparations for referral turned out to be very lengthy. At one time it was decided that if, after a period of three months, the parents still refused to accept treatment for the child and the latter's behavior had not changed, dropping of the child from the membership would be considered.

The case worker was responsible to her supervisor from the child guidance agency. The Head Worker was consulted in all questions relating to administration and House functions.

In evaluating the program, it was the consensus of opinion of all people interviewed that the presence of the case worker had made the group workers more sensitive to the general matter of individualizing children in their groups. The case worker was also able to detect many potential behavior difficulties not previously recognized by the leaders. The Head Worker stated that in every one of the clubs observed and studied, the group work process was markedly improved as a result.

Agency C:

Agency C is a comparatively recently founded Community Center which puts most emphasis on special activities offered to children and adults. In addition to this the House offers various kinds of health services and has a personal service department. It was at the initiative of Agency C that the earlier-mentioned federation of group work agencies and local child guidance clinic undertook the experiment of assigning psychiatric case workers to community centers. The main emphasis at this agency was preventing the development of serious behavior difficulties in the Center, rather than on actual personal pathology.

A psychiatric case worker from a child guidance clinic was brought to Agency C under the same arrangements as at Agency B. In order to avoid the threat of a connection with the clinic's interest in delinquent and abnormal behavior, the identity of the case worker was here at first revealed to only a selected few. It was the Head Worker's plan that leaders and children should first learn to know the case worker as a friendly and sympathetic person before his purpose and affiliation was to be disclosed. It did not, however, take long before the case worker's identity in the House became known to all of the staff.

The case worker usually observed children as they participated in House activities, on his own initiative. In addition, children who seemed to present special difficulties were brought to the attention of the group work supervisor by the leaders, and plans for dealing with the individual child were jointly decided upon with the case worker.

There were also some children who approached the case worker of their own accord by virtue of the fact that he was known to the membership as "Children's Consultant." In very few of those short-range contacts was referral to another agency indicated.

After an individual child became known to the case worker a social history was gathered. For this purpose the case worker used the files of the personal service department, information from the Social Service Exchange, and reports from staff members. There was hardly any direct contact between the group leaders and the case worker. The Head Worker expressed the feeling that the untrained leaders might misuse the interpretations offered by the case worker.

In some instances, following a case conference with the group work supervisor, it was decided that the child could not be helped within the House setting and that referral to a case work agency was indicated. While the case worker usually undertook to prepare the child for a referral, the parents were sometimes seen by the personal service department of which the case worker was not a part.

The set-up at Agency C was the same as the one found at Agency B in regard to the worker's supervision. On the other hand, unlike the latter, most emphasis here was put on the careful planning of referrals and counseling services to children rather than on educating the leaders in a better individualization of children. All referrals at Agency C were carried out under the supervision of the case worker, while those from outside agencies to the House were handled by the Director of Activities. Later, the nursery school of the agency used the case worker to interpret behavior of individual children.

In the opinion of the Head Worker, the presence of the case worker at the House is no longer an experimental arrangement. Plans were being made to start a consultation service for parents where the latter could discuss with the worker problems related to the handling of the children in the home.

Agency D:

A case worker for Agency D, a community "Y," was made possible through an arrangement with a family social service organization.

In contrast to the earlier-mentioned child guidance clinic, the family agency offered people, mostly adults, professional help with their personal and family problems. A case worker was placed at the House for a period of three months to discover what contribution such a worker could make to the staff and program of a group work agency.

The primary functions of the case worker in this setting were related to the following: education of group leaders in handling children with special difficulties; familiarization with community resources for individual help; and training in making such referrals effectively. Children who seemed to require individual study were brought to the attention of the case worker by the group work supervisor. At a conference it was usually decided whether referral of the child to a case work agency was indicated. Most of the referrals were made by the group work supervisor with the case worker acting as a consultant. In selected cases the case worker would herself handle the preparation for referral. In cases of children under fourteen years of age, the mothers would be called to the agency by the group work supervisor and then introduced to the case worker. If the parents refused to accept the fact that their child presented a problem, plans for treating the youngster in the group situation were formulated. Furthermore, many older adolescents came to the worker dissatisfied with jobs, educational plans, or family pressures. The case worker did not visit any of the group meetings.

Staff conferences were also utilized to train leaders in a better understanding of individual behavior. In gathering information on children the case worker made use of reports from various staff members and of Social Service Exchange clearings. In cases of successful referrals of children to case work agencies, follow-up conferences were held with the case worker from the outside agency, the group work supervisor, and the "Y" case worker.

It is of interest to note that in this experiment, the case worker's presence in the House and her agency affiliation were made known to the members by means of a special poster placed in the lobby. In view of the fact that the case worker spent only one day a week at the House, her activities were necessarily limited. Referrals from other agencies to the House were handled by the group work supervisor. The case worker was responsible to her own agency in regard to functions and kept no records of conferences, except notes.

In evaluating this project, both the case worker and the group workers were of the opinion that it was fulfilling a permanent need. It was the feeling of the House Director that in view of the fact that all group leaders were people without professional training the case worker's services were not used as effectively as might be the case with trained staff members. The idea of using the case worker as an intake person for the group work agency was also advanced. In the opinion of the Director of Activities, the "Y" could use a full time case worker.

Agency E:

Agency E is a large settlement house in a community which comprises three different cultural groupings. Besides its interest in the various aspects of group work, Agency E emphasizes community organization and service to individuals through a personal service department.

Following a study by a psychiatrist of the basic needs of neighborhood children and to what extent they were being met by existing programs between 1941-1943, the agency manifested further interest in the general field of mental hygiene and particularly in its relation to social group work.

To deal with children in need of special help, two senior lounge leaders were engaged recently. They were practising case workers. The lounge groups had a number of adolescents presenting serious behavior difficulties. Using their case work skills, the two leaders were able to develop friendly relationships with a number of these youngsters in order to prepare them for referrals to a case work agency. The actual referral procedures in such cases were handled by the group work supervisor. The case workers were consulted also by other staff members on problems of individual children in their groups.

In general, the two workers were acting here more in the capacity of group workers than case workers.

According to the program director, most of the attempts to refer children to other agencies had so far not been successful. The reasons given were that most children and parents were unwilling to recognize that they had problems requiring special help. The group work supervisors did not have sufficient time available and also were too much identified with authority to be able to establish individual contact with children and prepare them for referral.

The Head Worker stated that there was a definite need for the services of a full time psychiatric case worker in the House. This worker would have to be very experienced in case work (supervisory level) and would be called upon to fulfill the earlier-mentioned functions and also carry on short-time treatment within the agency where advisable.

Summary and Conclusions

In reviewing the outstanding characteristics of the various patterns of case work-group work cooperation considered in this paper, some principles and problems emerge.

In all instances discussed, the initiative in bringing case workers to group work agencies came from the field of group work. The motivations were the recent increase in difficult behavior of children and the growing interest of group workers in the understanding of human behavior.

The exact ways in which a case worker can function most profitably in a group work agency are still in the process of exploration. The aims are to sensitize group work staff to individual behavior mechanisms; to act as consultants in regard to treatment and understanding of children and, where necessary, to institute referrals to other agencies; to act as liaison person between the group work agency and case work agencies, and to consult with individual members on personal problems.

There is some disagreement as to whether a full time or part time case worker is more desirable in the group work setting. For instance, the importance of further professional growth and additional training through practice in a case work agency is stressed by some. All seem agreed, however, that some form of supervision by a case work agency would be indicated even for a full time case worker at the group work agency.

The question as to whether some form of case work treatment is to be carried on in group work agencies is a moot one, to both case workers and group workers alike. In a sense, wherever there was preparation for referral or any contact between child and case worker, treatment in some form was taking place. Some people visualize long-term case work treatment in the group work agency of the future. They think that many who would otherwise be resistive would feel less fearful in accepting such service in the setting of a group work agency.

In addition, the question as to how the case worker's presence was to be made known to the House without his becoming a threat to either members or staff was also in the process of discussion.

The use of case workers in group work agencies is too new to permit drawing any final conclusions. There are still too many areas in which further thinking and exploration is indicated. Some of the questions needing clarification are:

Who is to handle referrals of individuals from other agencies to the House? What role, if any, can the case worker play in the establishment of special therapeutic groups? Furthermore, is it advisable to use case workers with little or no group work experience? In addition, should the case worker have psychiatric or merely generic case work training? Should the case worker, like a physician, be used as an occasional speaker for group meetings? How can the possibility of overlapping functions be avoided if the case worker is to receive dual supervision from both group work and case work angles? When a case worker is borrowed from another agency does he still represent this agency, or is he a part of the House? Only actual experience of long duration with a careful checking of results can give us the answer to such questions.

It is of great interest that most of the group workers interviewed were quite insistent that the services of case workers in group work agencies will be valuable even in the post-war world when there will be fewer individual problems (hopefully) and better trained group work personnel.

The whole subject of group work and case work cooperation presents many potentialities for further study and inquiry which could be of value to the total field of social work.

Some Developments in the Integration of Case Work and Group Work in a Child Guidance Clinic
By Mary E. Pennock and Grace Weyker

In 1948 when we added group work to the methods which had been in use in our Clinic for twenty-four years, we didn't know what we were getting into. We knew we would need a physical setting different from our usual small interviewing offices. We even knew we would need some play materials which might differ from those used in individual treatment of children. Little did we know the other complications such as the very simple fact that groups *always* eat. The much discussed "team process" took on new complications when we included group work. Scheduling coordinated appointments for one parent and one child is simple compared to scheduling groups of children and their parents. Procedures for exchange of information, coordinated planning between the team members, and methods of recording had to be experimented with. There were questions of grouping—which children should have group treatment? Which children should be together in a group? When should they begin group participation in relation to the over-all Clinic study and treatment process?

We believe we have worked out a few answers and methods, but there are many questions still confronting us. We know that many clinics throughout the country are working with the group work method and finding various ways of utilizing it and integrating it with the older clinic methods. Very tentatively, because we are in an early phase of integrating group work and case work service, we are offering some of our thinking and experience.

Obviously our questions and problems, as well as the answers and methods, are closely related to our particular setting. The Amherst H. Wilder Child Guidance Clinic is pretty much the orthodox clinic set-up. The director is the psychiatrist and is responsible for all direct psychiatric treatment of children. He does some of this himself and supervises others who may be doing it. The psychologist administers intelligence tests, school achievement tests, and Rorschachs, and carries on individual treatment in relation to remedial tutoring. The case workers handle intake, the continuing case work with parents, and the usual inter-agency responsibility. The referral may have been suggested by physician, school, court, social agency, or other friend. Reason for referral may be failure to function in relation to school, in relation to other children, disturbed relationship between parents and child, other evidences of anxiety, interruption of expected development socially or mentally, etc. Some children are referred by placement agencies with questions about prognosis for adoption or boarding home placement.

How did group work happen to get started in this Clinic? We would like to be able to say that we decided one day that we needed group work and then went about procuring it. Unfortunately we weren't that foresighted. Now it seems such an obvious and essential method in our study and treatment that we can't see why we didn't think of it sooner. Maybe it was because we hadn't really ever known professional group work.

In the fall of 1947 the University of Minnesota School of Social Work secured its first full time group work faculty member, Mrs. Gisela Konopka. The impact of her ideas and her portrayal of the group work method, based particularly on her experience in the Pittsburgh Child Guidance Center, convinced us that group work should offer a real contribution to our Clinic service. She helped us secure our first group worker, a person professionally trained in social group work.

The professional group worker, as we are using the term, has two years of graduate education in a school of social work with specialization in group work. This presumes social work courses such as study of physical, mental and emotional growth, personality development, dynamics of behavior, and study of physical and emotional illness. It includes an acquaintance with, but not necessarily skill in: methods of case work, administration, research, community organization, and public welfare.

Induction of our first group worker into the Clinic setting was accomplished partly through having her carry some case work responsibility during her first few months in the Clinic. By carrying cases she had an opportunity to know something of the feelings and expectations of parents in coming to the Clinic, to know the Clinic's place in the community as indicated by the attitudes of social workers, doctors and teachers, and to discover the limitations and complications of coordinating services in the Clinic.

Because this experience seemed to her and to us such a satisfactory way to begin the group worker's orientation to the Clinic procedures and philosophy, we have repeated it with successive staff group workers and then with field work students at the request of the School of Social Work and the students themselves.

Our present group work department is staffed by two social group workers, one working with pre-school children and one with school age children. Group workers participate in all referral meetings and case conferences. The number of school age groups active at any one time varies from six to nine. The pre-school unit is not organized on a group basis, but on a nursery school pattern and will be described separately.

School age groups meet weekly for one and a half hours in a fairly indestructible basement room that is provided with equipment for many kinds of activities. There are wood-working tools, a wrestling mat, boxing gloves, dueling sticks, bean bags and balls which provide good media for working out aggressive drives and for testing one's strength and skill against others. For more solitary and creative activities there are paints, clay, metals, leather and other craft materials. Using these materials, the passive, withdrawn, or fearful child can protect himself initially from a too close relationship with other children. As the children change, their needs in terms of program change, and different activities are provided. Dramatics, table games, active group games, cooking, picnics and trips become part of the group program as the group shows a readiness to work and play together. Food is always an important part of each meeting and is provided by the Clinic. To the child the giving of food may symbolize the giving of love. It serves the added purpose of drawing the children together for part of each meeting.

Program is not the only tool which the worker uses in group treatment. As in any therapy, the worker must use himself and his knowledge of behavior as helping agents. He must be able to play a varying role, as circumstances and individual and group needs dictate: active, passive, permissive, limiting or supportive. In order to make it possible for the child to express feelings which are ordinarily prohibited, the therapist must be accepting of all types of children and able to tolerate noise, confusion and aggression. He must not only be able to accept anti-social behavior, but to help a youngster understand why he is behaving in this way and why other group members react to his behavior as they do. The group worker keeps his focus on the relationship of members in the group with each other, and endeavors to help members associate with each other, trying to keep the relationship from centering upon the group worker himself. Group therapy is not therapy *in* the group, but *through* the group, and the professional group worker is aware of using the group structure—its bonds, sub-groups, leaders and followers, the conflicts and controls, and other social processes that grow out of group life—as helping agents. Herein often lies the difference in therapy done by the professional social group worker and other professional persons. Understanding the dynamics of the social process which group members create is just as important as understanding the dynamics of individual behavior if individuals are to be adequately served by a group.

Group treatment may be used concurrently with individual therapy or alone. It is not a universally applicable treatment method. Referral and grouping must be done selectively. Our experience has shown us that there are certain types of children for whom group treatment is especially valuable. Briefly, some of these kinds of children are:

1. The passive, withdrawn child.
2. The child unable to handle his sibling rivalry situation.
3. The child whose ego has been crushed.
4. The child who is suspicious of all adults.
5. The child whose aggression has not been allowed expression.

We have also found that there are certain children whom we cannot help in groups. Our experience closely parallels S. R. Slavson's in this respect.

The basic requirement for success in group treatment is that the child wants to be liked by other children, that his social hunger is strong enough that he will change his behavior to be an accepted member of the group. Therefore, the narcissistic child cannot respond to group treatment. Because of his effect upon the group, the provocative child and the child with strong sadistic components in his makeup are not good candidates for group treatment. The former keeps the group in a constant state of turmoil and conflict, and the latter so affects the role of the worker, who must constantly limit the child's sadistic impulses for the protection of the other children, that the worker cannot function as an accepting adult in the group.

The majority of our group members are between the ages of seven and twelve years. Therefore, the emphasis is on activity groups. We have had some experience with discussion groups with teen-agers, but because the teen-age population at the Clinic is small, it has been hard to find adequate groupings. An additional factor is that teen-agers have shown greater capacity to make good use of individual therapy.

The pre-school group treatment is set up as a separate entity from the rest of the group therapy program at the Clinic for several reasons:

1. There is very little development of any group feeling and real interpersonal relationships among such young children, and consequently the group itself cannot be used as a tool in working with these children. Treatment must rather be focused on the relationship between the child and the adult, using the group as a natural setting in which to observe the child and his relationships.

2. With small children, it is important that the therapy invade as large a portion of their lives as possible—that they be exposed to a health-producing environment for a substantial number of hours each day. Therefore, this unit is set up more like a nursery school, and children are seen three full mornings

a week for a total of nine hours of treatment. This allows an opportunity for children to have lunch together as part of their treatment experience.

Although all of the equipment provided for the pre-school unit is of the type found in most nursery schools, the use of it is often changed or intensified in treatment of these disturbed pre-school youngsters. *Blocks* are used not solely for the fun of building, but for the fun of destroying. A *punching bag* is not socked for the joy of being able to punch hard, but for the joy of pummeling little brother, or big brother, or the kids of whom one is much too afraid to ever attempt hitting back. *Clay* is not molded, but is reduced to bits by vicious pounding; *phonograph records* are not for playing music, but for spinning around on one's finger to alleviate some feeling of anxiety. While any of these activities may occur in individual treatment, the presence of other children gives the activity a different significance both to the actor and to the other children present. If it is one's first acquaintance with tempera paint, or if one has been limited and frustrated in all areas of investigation and experimentation so important to a young child, it may be necessary to pour paints from one jar to another, mix colors, taste the paint brush, and dab paint on book cases, walls, and woodwork, before gradually accepting the limits of a piece of paper. It is stressed that the playroom for the use of disturbed pre-school children should be so constructed as to weather any and all experiments, accidents, and results of emotional upsets which are likely to occur. This is the child's world and is geared to him and his needs. The furniture is sturdy, the walls, woodwork and floor are washable, as should be the group worker's dress, in order to provide a relaxed atmosphere in which the emotionally sick child may express his feelings and reorganize his ego.[1]

[1] The description of the pre-school unit is taken from a report by Janet Swanson Enquist, former group worker.

Although the pre-school unit is set up on a nursery plan, it is staffed by a group worker rather than a nursery school teacher. We have felt that the person trained as a group worker brings skill in the therapeutic use of materials and activities, an understanding of individual behavior and the effect of one child's behavior on another child, and a therapeutic rather than educational approach.

Before we had this pre-school group treatment unit we had usually not been able to do any direct work with children as young as three, four, and five years old. We were limited to counseling parents, often doing so on the basis of the parents' description of behavior, or at best on the basis of observation of the child in what is for him an unnatural and puzzling situation—alone in an office with a strange adult.

Now the case worker, besides discussing with the parents the meaning of behavior as it has been reported from the pre-school unit, may even take the parent to the treatment room. We have found that a parent and case worker can sit to one side of the large playroom or playground and observe what the children do and how the group worker handles situations. In the older age groups usually no observation or visitors are permitted, just as we would usually not permit observers or visitors in a case work interview. It is recognized that in either group work or case work the interpersonal relationships which are the primary tool in treatment would be affected by the presence of an extra person. In the pre-school unit this does not seem to be the case.

The on-the-spot discussion with parents has been most satisfactory in enabling us to communicate more directly with the background of a common observation rather than relying on one person's description of behavior which may frequently have different meanings to the teller and hearer. Since both case worker and parent have observed the same situation, differences in interpretation may reveal blind spots or other evidences of emotional involvement in the parent, which may then be used in further case work or as clues to limits in case work goals.

When it became known in the community that the Clinic had employed a group worker and was equipping space for group activities, this immediately led to many referrals for groups. *Some* of the children referred did have emotional problems requiring psychiatric study and treatment, but many needed only a place to play or the kind of group activity which should be available in all leisure time settings. Obviously our small facilities could never be expected to fill the gaps in recreational opportunities in the community. We stressed the policy that the Child Guidance Clinic groups were to be an integral part of our total treatment and diagnostic service, that it was distinctly not a leisure time activity even though we recognized that many children needed leisure time services desperately in the community.

As a way of stressing that policy we delayed placing any child in a group until after the completion of the diagnostic study of the child. If the findings of the initial conference seemed to indicate that the child could benefit from group treatment, and the group worker concurred in this opinion, the child was then entered in a treatment group. Subsequent treatment conferences pointed up the fact that the group worker had been able to gather a good deal of information about a child which increased the understanding of his problem. As the diagnostic value of the group became apparent, we began to see some of the children diagnostically in groups *during* the study period. This made the findings of the group worker available at the time of the initial conference and rounded out the picture of the child before treatment plans were set up. It also enabled the group worker to do a more intelligent job of grouping, if the child was later referred to a group for treatment, since she already had observed him and knew something of his pattern of behavior and how he reacted to different kinds of youngsters.

During this early period of our experience with groups, children were seen diagnostically in an on-going treatment group. It was soon evident that this was not a good practice from the point of view of the group or the individual entering it. The coming and going of new members interfered with the group development and often increased the anxieties of the insecure members and the aggression of the more hostile members. While the occasional addition of a continuing member can be tolerated and even be helpful to a treatment group, the constant addition and subtraction was most upsetting and slowed treatment measurably. We also had to look at what it meant to a child to enter an already formed group where patterns of subgroups and personal friendship were already somewhat formed. For the healthy child to enter a strange group is difficult. For a sick child it can be overwhelming and greatly affect the picture he presents.

Our next step, therefore, was to establish strictly diagnostic groups, in which all members would begin and end their initial group experience together. This not only made the experience less threatening to the child, but enabled the worker to establish the limits placed upon the group more intelligently, since limits change as groups and individuals change and grow more secure and more able to control themselves and others.

Our present practice is to see all children four or five times in diagnostic groups except when this is contra-indicated by the information we have at the time of intake. Group experience is an integral part of our initial study. In fact, we use the group as an introduction to the Clinic setting for some especially anxious children. Children who fear doctors, or distrust adults, or who are threatened because of their parents' attitude toward the problem, may be persuaded to enter the Clinic on the basis of a particular group activity. After several visits to the Clinic group, they may be able to keep an appointment with the psychologist or psychiatrist who is by now identified with a comfortable setting.

Diagnostic groups have been especially valuable, of course, in evaluating a child's relationships with his peers. In this area particularly we have found that the patient, his parents or the school may see and report a distorted picture of his ability to relate in a group situation. Perhaps a few case examples will serve to illustrate the contribution the group can make:

a. A nine-year-old boy was referred to the Clinic by his mother for his inability to work up to his capacity in school. She reported that this was the boy's only problem, stressing the fact that he had many friends and got along well with other children. Observation in the group showed him to be a child who related mainly to the adult, who was unable to compete with other children, and who avoided relationships in the group by withdrawal and play by himself. This information was used by the case worker to help the mother see that the school difficulty was only a symptom of a more general disturbance in the boy.

b. A twelve-year-old girl was referred by her mother because she was unhappy, unable to make friends, and socially inadequate. Group observation showed that she was a happy, normal child who was adequate to any situation in the group and that she soon was chosen by others for the leadership role. This information completely changed our concept of the problem, and the case worker now focused on the question of why this mother had to feel her daughter was socially a failure.

c. A delinquent, sophisticated, fifteen-year-old boy, living with his widowed father, was referred by the probation officer, who said the boy was "out of *his* reach." The boy was seldom at home, and a correctional institution was being considered as the only solution for him. In a special group of boys, all of whom had court records, the boy acted smarty and defied ordinary limits in his conversation about girls, but in small ways such as voluntarily helping the group worker clean up dishes, and in positive comments regarding a neighbor woman, he revealed that he actually did want to be a member of a home with a mother person in it. This boy's only Clinic service had been in the group, since he had steadfastly refused other contacts. Later when the case worker was asked to participate in a conference with another agency considering the possibility of a home or institution, the detailed information from the group record enabled the case worker to report evidence of the boy's readiness for a foster home.

We would have liked to include some case material to show the treatment value of the group, but our space limit makes this impossible. We have included illustrations showing the diagnostic value of groups because this is our most recent use of groups and because it has made such an outstanding contribution to our understanding of the child.

One of the early stumbling blocks was around the use and integration of group records. A particular case worker, psychiatrist and psychologist might be interested in finding out about only one or two children in a group. The group process record was unfamiliar to other team members, and plowing through the total record each week to find the pertinent facts about one child became an irritating and time consuming task. As a result, group records just weren't read. After many experiments with different methods of recording, we have developed a sort of hybrid form which seems to meet all our requirements. Briefly stated at the beginning of the record is information about who came, what the activity was and how it developed, and areas around which conflict arose. Following this is a summary of the group interaction, and then the record moves into separate summaries of each member's participation and the worker's interpretation of the meaning of the child's behavior in the light of what was going on in the group at that time. The individual summaries are clipped from duplicate copies of the group record and filed immediately in the case folder so that the records of all the work being done with a child are available in one folder.

Another problem has been around the coordinating of appointments. Since parents are often seen by the case worker during the time the child is having his group meetings, we try at intake to spread the cases of children who may be placed in the same group among several case workers. Scheduling a child's individual and group appointments also has to be carefully worked out. If he sees the psychiatrist immediately before the group, he is usually restless and pre-occupied with anticipation of the group. Immediately after the group he is often too stimulated to make full use of the individual hour. We have found that the child can utilize his individual treatment more fully on a day other than the one on which his group meets.

The group often serves to stimulate a child's participation in individual treatment. For example, a child may be picturing himself to the psychiatrist as a happy, comfortable person, although there is much evidence to the contrary. In this case the psychiatrist will stop seeing this child for a time, in the hope that group participation will reactivate conflict and bring into the open anxiety which can then be used in individual treatment, or at least to motivate the child to want help in individual treatment.

In the discussion of how group work has been integrated into our Clinic service and the advantages we see in this, we should offer two warnings. First, our experience would certainly dispel any vestige of the idea that there is a time saving in group treatment. Although the group worker sees more children at one time, the group meets for a longer period of time, and the group worker's expenditure of time for preparation, recording and case conferences brings the average time for each child to the same amount of time as the case worker invests in service on one case. We find that the number of cases carried by case worker and group worker are about the same. Our second warning is that salaries for group workers are high. At the present time the demand for qualified group workers so far exceeds the supply, that the group worker's salary may be higher than the salary for a psychiatric case worker of comparable training and experience.

Looking toward the future we have in mind several developments which we hope we will be able to work out soon.

We haven't yet worked with parents in groups. We have been interested in group treatment of parents as it has been reported from other clinics.

We would like to work out a plan whereby case workers and psychiatrists could have some experience in the group method.

Early, when we felt the necessity of proving our group work to be an integral part of the Clinic, we felt it must take place in the same building as evidence of its clinic connectedness. Now the integration is strong enough that we are talking of experimenting with Clinic sponsored protected groups outside the Clinic in a neighborhood house and possibly in a public school building. In addition to the direct benefit to the group members, we anticipate that having the Clinic group worker functioning within the school setting would give an opportunity to increase the school's understanding of: the child's personality and behavior; the philosophy of the Clinic regarding children's problems and how they are approached; the values of group treatment and some awareness of the group process as it affects children in other settings, including the classroom.

Two factors which have facilitated development of group work service in our Clinic are: (1) the *talent* of our director for maintaining an atmosphere in which all staff members have freedom and motivation to think and experiment creatively; and (2) the vision of the Wilder Charity Executive Secretary and Board of Directors in adequately financing the service.

In the attempt to describe our experience of integrating

group work and case work within a clinic setting, we find ourselves focusing primarily on mechanical aspects of the job—structure of groups, scheduling of appointments, materials and equipment, recording methods. Why this focus? Certainly not because these are the most vital aspects of our work. We believe it is because our primary problems have been mechanical ones. Why hasn't it been necessary for us to work toward integration of our underlying philosophy and goals? We believe that this is because we started out with a common philosophy, with same goals and same basic understanding of the needs of children and the sources of their emotional disturbances. As someone commented, we spoke the same language, and so our primary task in establishing an integration of the two methods was in the mechanical details. If case work and group work can come together with mutual respect, a respect which grows naturally out of equal professional competence, and a common base of knowledge regarding human behavior, it is fairly easy to achieve integration of the two methods of helping people.

4

Group Work and Recreation

GROUP WORK AS A METHOD IN RECREATION
By Grace Coyle

ONE of the purposes of this discussion is the attempt to clear up a source of certain confusions and some dissension in our field—namely, the relation of group work to recreation. The title of my paper sets forth the form of this clarification. Recreation is a function to be performed; group work is one method of fulfilling the function.

As we are organized in communities, recreation and informal voluntary education are often linked together within the purposes of the same organization. In fact, the line of demarcation between recreation and education is always an uncertain one. In addition to these two functions, awkwardly indicated by our hyphenated phrase education-recreation agencies, many of the private agencies and, to some extent, certain of the public agencies as well add to these purposes a third, the use of leisure time to prepare for and participate in "active citizenship."

In a world facing the urgent problems of today, it is essential

91

that citizens should inform themselves on public questions, create or join organizations expressing their views and so participate in the government of our society. Fruitful enjoyment, learning and the fulfillment of our public responsibility—these are the major uses to which all of us should be putting our expanding leisure. They become the functions in varying degrees and with varying emphases of the organizations set up by the community under public or private auspices to provide for that leisure. Some organizations claim to exist for one purpose alone, but familiarity with many such organizations will reveal that those engaging in what they call recreation are in fact often eager to learn, and those who come for learning begin to enjoy themselves in the process. Even those who organize and promote some cause of their own choosing find in it both learning and a certain enjoyment. In almost all our organizations all three of these functions blend together in the total program and often within the same activity.

Since this discussion deals with the field of recreation, I should like however to spend my limited time on the relation of group work as a method of the fulfilling of the recreation function, omitting from this consideration its relation to programs exclusively related to voluntary education or active citizenship. Even though in actual fact, as I have said, the three are often indivisible, for purposes of analysis it might be useful to attempt the separation.

The Group Work Method

For this audience it is not necessary to spend much time in defining group work. Group work arose out of an increasing awareness that in the recreation-education activities which went on in groups there were obviously two dimensions—the stream of activity—game, discussion, hike or artistic enterprise on the one hand and on the other the interplay of personalities that creates the group process. To concentrate on one, for example, the activity, without recognizing and dealing with the other is like playing the piano with one hand only. Program and relationships are inextricably intertwined. The group work method developed as we began to see that the understanding and use of the human relations involved were as important as the understanding and use of various types of program.

This same increasing awareness of interpersonal relationships and their significance is going on in several other fields. In formal education the progressive education movement grew from these same roots. In recent years significant developments in personnel management, especially those stemming from the work of Elton Mayo and his associates at Harvard, are revealing in similar fashion the importance of group relations in industry. The war served to heighten recognition of the significance of group identification as essential to combat morale and through the experience of the psychiatrists greatly extended the use of various types of group therapy. Discoveries always spring up simultaneously when their time has come. I believe we are seeing some such phenomenon in the widespread but as yet unrelated discovery of the significance of group relations in various fields. Group work, when it is used in recreation or education activities, is one part of a widening strand of consciously applied social understanding characteristic of our times.

The Function of Recreation

The function of recreation, as Romney defines it in his recent book and as it is generally understood, involves primarily the provision of enjoyment of experiences which are ends in themselves, the consummations not the means of life. As he states, "Recreation as one of democracy's ways dignifies human worth and glorifies the individual. It is then the individual seeks opportunities for adventure and experience, for self-discovery and self-expression. It is then he creates opportunities for doing and opportunities for appreciation. Recreation's incentive is gratification in the doing, its compensation is a satisfaction of human longings. Rich dividends in a variety of personal development accrue." [1]

When we provide recreation under community auspices whether public or private, we inevitably exercise certain judgments in our provision of enjoyment. Some forms of recreation obviously are dangerous, futile or trivial; some are anti-social. We cannot avoid the necessity for selection by merely asserting that we are to provide people with enjoyment. Under community auspices recreation agencies must and, of course, do aim to so select what they offer that enjoyment is derived from activities which provide constructive fulfillment to individuals and which contribute positively to the society which supports them for purposes of enjoyment.

Enjoyment, as we know, has not only many forms and many sources, but also many levels. John Dewey in a recent book has pointed out a significant difference between pleasure and fulfillment. "Pleasure," he says, "may come about through chance contact and stimulation. Such pleasures are not to be despised in a world full of pain. But happiness and delight are a different sort of thing. They come through a fulfillment that reaches to the depth of our being—one that is an adjustment of our whole being to the conditions of existence." It is, I presume, some such conception of "happiness and delight," rather than of chance pleasure, which underlies our recreation programs at their best.

The Contribution to Group Work

What contribution does group work as a method have to fulfilling of the recreation function as defined? I should like to

[1] Romney, Ott *Off the Job Living*, p. 52.

answer this in terms of three specific areas: first, its contribution to the increase of enjoyment by more satisfying human relations; second, the help it can be to individuals who are unable to enjoy themselves because of personal difficulties of some kind; and third, its contribution to the significant by-products of recreation experience.

Let us begin with the first and most obvious factor in recreation programs—the desire for fun. It is hardly necessary to point out that the fun derived from most activities arises in large part from the contact with the other participants. While we know that many people join clubs, classes or teams because of an interest in the sport, or the art or the subject to be discussed, there is plenty of evidence that sociability—the chance to make friends and to be with them—is a predominant factor in bringing and holding them to the activity. Many groups, notably our large collection of social clubs, arise and persist almost entirely on the enjoyment of sociability.

The opportunity for friendship, for the stimulating interplay of congenial spirits for the creative expression of powers that can come in an accepting group, for the personal security and expansion of the ego that arise out of belonging to a group— it is these and similar elements which make the group worker give pre-eminence to the aspect of human relations in the provision of recreation.

The recreation leader, of course, needs a full and adequate acquaintance with the recreation skills—music, drama, craft, sports and the like. With one hand he helps his group to use these resources to the full. With the other he needs equally to understand how to assist the interplay of personalities. It is hardly necessary in this audience to labor this point. We all know how much of what skill we may have in group work goes into the removal of those blocks in human relations which are spoiling everyone's fun in the group. These blocks arise out of such factors as the relation between rival subgroups, the vaunting ambitions of a domineering leader, the passivity or irresponsibility of a group of members. The skill of the leader consists not only in the preventing of unnecessary friction, but also in the channeling of hostilities into useful outlets or the control of the anti-social. One of the principles upon which group work as a method rests is its conviction that one of the chief sources of positive fulfillment for individuals lies in the deep delight available in the mutual interactions of a democratic and creative group. The group worker and the members, of course, at this point share the same purpose for the group. If it does not yield enjoyment, it has obviously failed of its purpose.

A second contribution which group work should be able to make to the recreation function is the assistance to those who, because of some personal maladjustment, have never learned how to enjoy themselves in play. It is, I think, significant that the Menninger Clinic reports that one of the symptoms characteristic of the emotionally disturbed people with whom it deals is their unusual lack of absorbing recreational interests. Many more people who do not need or will never get clinic service show in greater or less extent the same inability to relax, to give themselves up to play, to find outlets for unused powers or unconscious drives in acceptable recreation. The group worker in addition to his awareness of the group as a whole also should be able to distinguish within it those who cannot, though they would, enjoy themselves. These may be the isolates who wander disconsolately without friends, the wallflowers who suffer painfully through club parties, the bullies whose sadistic pleasures ruin the playground, the lonely aged going queer for lack of human contacts, the dependent and fearful child who shrinks from competing with others, the clinging adolescent whose only security lies in his emotional hold upon the recreation leader.

The personality problems behind these familiar types of behavior require skillful diagnosis. The treatment for them can sometimes be done by an understanding use of the group relations available. These may serve to bring out latent powers, to increase security by acceptance, to restrain aggression by collective pressure. In severe cases of personal maladjustment the group worker will, of course, need to seek individual treatment. He may know that the achievement of real recreation experience for them will come only with "the adjustment of the whole being to the conditions of existence," which makes possible the happiness and delight we all should get from life. He may realize that adjustment accomplished in a recreation setting will have its effect on the rest of life as well. If real enjoyment can be found, however tentatively at first, the compelling desire for its repetition is itself a powerful aid in necessary adjustments. Clinics and hospitals are revealing to us these days the healing powers of recreation activities and of accompanying social relations. Their value is equally great for the much larger number who do not need or will not get such care but who also can find more fun in life and more fulfillment than they do. Let me emphasize, however, that the group worker who is fulfilling the recreation function in such individualized ways is helping such individuals to enjoy themselves.

One final suggestion I should like to make—namely, the relation of group work to the inevitable by-products of recreation. If I may quote again from Mr. Romney's recent book in his chapter on the Education of Tastes, recreation's concern, he says, is "with the individual and his wants. . . . It must vitalize interests, improve skills, enrich lives. . . . It must use all its wiles to educate tastes." [2] Among such tastes Mr. Romney includes not only better levels of music, art and literature but also increased interest in public affairs. The dividends of sound

2 Romney, Ott *Off the Job Living*, pp. 85-86.

recreation, he declares, lie in "citizenship education, improved ability to express oneself and confidence in presenting views, faith in the democratic process, education of tastes, discovery of talents and appetites for work, joy in associating with people and an understanding of human nature." [3]

The Wider Implications of Play and Leisure

This is, I believe, a very clear statement of a fact with which we are all familiar—that while people play, they are also doing much more besides. As we begin, in every aspect of the social services, whether health, child and family welfare, education or recreation, to see the person as a whole, we come increasingly to understand that we cannot provide any one service by cutting a person up between specialists. Just as the doctor should not wisely prescribe without understanding the whole man and his social situation, and the teacher cannot teach without realizing the impact of the community on his students, so the recreation worker cannot provide recreation without awareness of the indirect and extremely significant results of what he is doing.

It was thirty years ago when Dewey and Kilpatrick first pointed out so effectively the fact that attendant and concomitant learnings, often highly charged with emotion, surround every direct and conscious learning. As our understanding of play as well as of learning has increased in recent years, we have begun to see more clearly why and how recreative experience inevitably has the wider implications to which Mr. Romney points. As we understand these attendant effects on persons and on society, it is clear that as professional workers we have to take them into account. Beyond and around the more obvious and conscious purposes, namely enjoyment, which we and the participants have in common, we cannot

[3] Romney, Ott *Off the Job Living*, p. 98.

avoid the responsibilities which arise from our seeing also the wider consequences which follow upon the community's provision of recreation. We are not here private persons enjoying ourselves with our friends. We are the community's agents providing one of the community's services to its members. Let me be more specific.

Much of the quality of any civilization obviously expresses itself in the way it uses its leisure. As that leisure expands constantly with technological change, it becomes ever more important that society find for its leisure more enriching and developing ways to use its time and its human resources. Art, philosophy, invention and adventure, the enjoyment of nature represent the ancient well tried and fruitful channels for the surplus energy of mankind. The types of activity sought and the level of taste attained in our expanding leisure will be one major test of the dominant values of our civilization. This concern we as group workers share with Mr. Romney and others in the recreation field.

If we have a contribution to make here, it is, I believe, in our belief and we hope also our skill in encouraging creative rather than imitative experience, in starting with existing levels of interest and taste and leading on through satisfying experience into the richer and deeper veins of our social heritage. I do not wish to make undue claims here. I think trained group workers are too often dull, unimaginative and stereotyped in their conception of recreation. But in purpose—and to some extent in practice—we, I believe, would like to unite our efforts with those in recreation who share the vision of its larger function for a richer civilization.

Let me illustrate in a different area our concern for the wider implications of the community's recreation program. From the way we organize recreation there follow certain effects upon the social life of the community. As groups form for activities they weaken or reinforce racial and nationality loyalties, they break down or build up class barriers, they separate or unite neighborhoods. The fact that recreation activities of different kinds give play to intimacy in varying degrees makes possible many different expressions of inter-group feelings. A careful and skillful use of various recreation resources, clubs, athletic leagues, classes or forums, inter-club councils, playgrounds or camps may be the means to build the bridges across our social chasms. As group workers we are concerned that the ways in which we organize, our methods of grouping people, will be such as to contribute to social understanding. This is a complex question upon which in this instance I can only touch. I believe, however, that it is another of these points where many group workers can join with those who think of themselves as recreation workers and in which our combined skills might yield fruitful results.

A third illustration as to the concern of group workers lies, I believe, in our interest in the democratic process within recreation groups. It is natural that a democracy should be concerned to establish adequate recreation facilities for all its citizens. It is equally true that the continuing vitality of that democracy depends upon the penetration of all the life within it with democratic values. If our recreation or adult education groups are autocratically directed, if they are full of corrupt politics or of minority controls, they will corrupt the larger social life about them. If in the way they are planned and led the participants experience democratic government, they will carry that over into other areas.

Margaret Mead has pointed out how strategic it is to the preservation of the humane and just values of our civilization that they be imprinted on the playground where so much of the cultural heritage is passed on to new generations. The group worker has long been concerned that we constantly examine critically our methods of organizing and conducting recreation groups to insure that their educational by-products contribute to democratic conviction and democratic experience. One final type of indirect but important result I should like to add as a further illustration. The professional worker whether coach, teacher or club adviser in the recreation setting has inevitably a significant relation to his group as a whole and to individuals within it. The quality of that relationship and its responsible use is of major importance if recreation is to yield all it should to the participants.

There are certain standards of professional relationship which the recreation worker shares with other professions that deal with people. Like the doctor, the teacher or the case worker, his interest must be in the service to the people with whom he works. He must know how to use his skill for their benefit—not his own—and he must consciously control his relationship to them to that end. Since he is dealing with a group, he has, I believe, certain opportunities and certain problems, arising out of his role in relation to the group. Unless he is aware of the potent influence which he wields, he will miss the chance to use it wisely—at its worst he may consciously or unconsciously exploit the group for his own ends. The recreation leader is demonstrating in every action his own values, is using his authority in helpful or destructive ways, is creating dependence upon himself or encouraging a balanced self-respecting relation. Such attendant learnings are inevitable. The question is shall they be dealt with consciously and intelligently on the basis of the best we know from modern social science? We are concerned that the responsibility of the worker in recreation be handled on the highest level of professional skill including both knowledge of the activity and understanding of relationships involved.

In this discussion, I hope we have reached a turn in the progress of both recreation and group work as separate strands of interest and endeavor. We in the group work strand make no claim to having found a panacea. If we think we have found a significant clue, we know we are only at the beginning of unraveling it. We share with others in the field of recreation the conviction that more adequate recreation should be extended under both public and private auspices. We believe that group work has a contribution to make to the extension of such recreation programs in ways which will enhance their value. It should make such enjoyment available to more people in fuller ways and it can, we hope, assist in using its deeper and wider social implications for the community's benefit. If this discussion can become the beginning of a more fruitful union of two streams of effort, I believe that many group workers would welcome the opportunity.

GROUP WORK AND PUBLIC RECREATION
By Marvin Green

NOT so many years have passed that many of us cannot recall the bitter arguments between recreationists and group workers and their constant destructive criticism of each other. This conflict, arising out of misunderstandings and competition for financial support and membership, wasted a good deal of time and energy that might have had more creative results. As recently as May, 1951, Grace Coyle called attention to the need for recreationists and group workers to work together as a team to provide a richer service to the community.[1]

For the past four years, the New York City Board of Education's Public Recreation Program has been conducting one of the largest group work experiments in the United States. Through an annual grant of $600,000 from the New York City Youth Board, the Bureau of Community Education which operates the school community centers in New York City has

[1] Grace L. Coyle, "The Group Worker in the Recreation Center," *Recreation*, May, 1951, p. 550.

developed thirty year-round centers in school buildings staffed by full-time recreational personnel. These "Youth Board" centers, located in areas of highest juvenile delinquency, are geared primarily for providing good general recreation programs using the method of fixed area activity programs (games, crafts, shop, gym, etc.).

The addition of trained group workers to this new program came about after the delinquency-conscious planning group took a realistic look at the problems of large public recreation. In recent years public recreation agencies have been subjected to strong pressures to serve large numbers of people. In New York City, the school recreation centers have tried to resist these forces and with the support of the community have fought to preserve the quality of their programs.

Nevertheless, small recreation staffs and greater numbers of membership have meant an increase in mass activity programs and with this four major problems which plague the conscience of the recreationist:

1. The lost child who never participates in the program;
2. The active energetic small group with apparent short span of interest;
3. The lip service to the goal of self-government;
4. The overwhelmed staff which sees its dark future in handing out equipment and keeping a watchful eye on the premises.

The planning group recognized that the group work method of working with people had a contribution to make to the solution of these problems. They felt that group workers trained in understanding individual motivations and the dynamics of group interaction could profitably supplement the work of the recreation staffs. At first a few group workers were assigned to individual centers. Today there are 22 graduate group workers in 20 of these full-time recreation centers assisted by two group work supervisors. The story of how the group workers became integrated into the recreation program is a happy one of successful human relations.

From the start the recreation workers were fearful; they felt that their skills were not thought equal to the task, that their status as professional workers was being challenged. On the other hand, the group workers were apprehensive. They felt at once like pioneers exploring a wilderness and like strangers come to live in a hostile town; for the group worker at the start was too self-conscious of his newness and too unsure of his knowledge and skills in this new setting.

The plan for integration started from a definition of job responsibilities. There were no basic changes in the recreation worker's job. However, the group worker's role in the center was carefully defined into three main areas.

First, the group worker would extend the program of the center by providing services to clubs on a sustained basis. Thus the group worker would help clubs to organize, recruit volunteer and student leadership and develop club projects out of the meetings to stimulate group life. There would be no competition with the recreation program of athletic and non-athletic activities which would continue to function as before.

Second, the group worker would work through activity committees and representatives of the clubs to stimulate the membership to strive for greater self-expression and self-government. The ultimate aim would be to develop a representative council which would reflect the program desires of the members and enable them to participate in governing the center. This would aid the recreation staffs by helping them to evaluate whether or not their programs were meeting the expressed wishes of the membership.

Finally, the group worker would focus his attention on the problems of emotionally disturbed individuals who could not adjust too well to the regular programs. Recreation workers have long pointed out that they do not have enough time to give to the problems of these people and that the training schools for recreationists have not devoted enough courses to help them to cope with the emotionally disturbed personality.

The basic premise of these three main areas of concentration for the group worker was that he had a method of working with people that could be applied in consonance with the ongoing recreation program. The recreation workers in general adopted a "wait and see" attitude toward the group worker. There was no question that if the group worker were successful he would be aiding the overall job of the recreation worker.

Many staff meetings were held in the individual community centers. At first these gatherings were used to air the hostile feelings of the recreation personnel against this new approach to the membership. However, the supervisory recreation workers turned them into educational and interpretative sessions which enabled the whole staff to take a fresh look at the methods and objectives of the general recreation program.

The group workers began to bring to the meetings record material of their activities with groups and individuals. The "gripe" sessions became case discussions of problems with recreationists and group workers attempting to solve them as mutual partners. One of the most important lessons that the group workers learned from the meetings was that there were many areas in recreation where their own training was inadequate. They began to look to the recreation workers for assistance and guidance in arts and crafts, dramatics, singing, games, and tournaments, and for a better understanding of recreation administration. In exchange, the recreation workers now freed from their anxiety began to get real help in understanding the hidden motivations of behavior and the complicated factors in the dynamic workings of groups.

New attitudes and enriched skills came out of this process of integration and mutual problem solving. Today after four years of cooperative effort the program is no longer an experiment. The group worker is an essential part of the program whose loss would be felt by the total community center. Some of the achievements of the group work staff have been:

1. Active club programs for small groups under supervised student and professional leadership where there had never been any club programs;

2. Membership councils participating in self-government where there had never been democratic representation from the membership;

3. Dances, festivals, and lounge programs coming from the members who had never before requested or participated in these activities;

4. Much, much more use of discussion and discussion techniques to solve problems and reduce tensions in centers where things were formerly first fought out and then talked about;

5. A special concern for emotionally disturbed individuals who could not adjust to the program before. This had meant new liaison with case work agencies to secure proper referral for treatment services in severe cases.

It can truthfully be said that in these community centers the New York City Board of Education is providing the best recreation services in all its history to the residents of the community. It has been well demonstrated here that trained group workers can function in a public recreation program and not only help to enrich the total services but in addition stimulate the professional growth of the recreation personnel.

What are the implications of this to the field of group work? First, it is proof that the multi-discipline approach where skills and knowledge from many of the social sciences are used provides more useful services than the narrow viewpoint of one functional area. No one field of work can adequately unlock the greatest potential stored up in groups and individuals. Today research is progressing in many fields. The task of discovering new skills and greater knowledge of activities and understanding of human behavior cannot be considered the private preserve of one discipline. Group workers must search for better means of communication between themselves and workers in these other disciplines.

Second, it is time that group workers recognize that recreation workers are not a kind of sub-professional who do not have a real body of knowledge nor standards of sound practice. The stereotypes of the enthusiastic muscle-bound athletic director with the whistle and the drowsy playground attendant are still unfortunately in some group workers' mind when they think of the field of recreation. Only by working side by side with him in a common endeavor will group workers learn that the average recreationist is a serious-minded individual who is proud of his calling and desirous of greater professional growth.

Third, it is apparent that group workers must pioneer in new areas where they have never worked before. While the private agency has seen money become scarce the public agencies in recent years have undergone great expansion. The community has begun to look to public support for total recreation programs serving the very young to the aged. The method of group work has a great contribution to make to these publicly supported programs.

The group work schools should gear their training toward providing skilled workers who could meet the needs of this expanding field. With a corps of trained group workers working in public recreation the day would not be far off when some administrative and policy making positions would be filled by people trained in group work methodology and philosophy.

Finally, it is essential that group workers strive to adapt themselves and what they learn in schools of social work to new settings. It is necessary that basic group work learning be in a protected environment. However, advance field work and beginning job experience should lead to comfortable functioning in unorthodox surroundings. Our program operates in public school buildings which were primarily designed to serve the educational functions of the day school. In this dual housekeeping situation it is a challenging experience for the group worker to adjust to this different setting and practice his profession.

Can the group worker measure up to the new goals that are implied in these four statements? The experience of the New York City Youth Board, Board of Education group work program is proof that it can be done and it is happening now.

5

Understanding Individual and Group Behavior

ON THE DYNAMICS OF BEHAVIORAL
CONTAGION [1]   *By Norman A. Polansky*

The purpose of this paper is to share with our practitioner colleagues the results of a series of studies which we have been conducting on the phenomenon of behavioral contagion. The material is offered not only for the content findings, but also as an example of research involving collaboration between practitioner and research specialists at every phase.

In presenting it, we shall start with a description of the area studied and our reasons for an interest in it. Following this, we will give data on the role of group position as a determinant of who is likely to be an initiator of behavioral contagion, and

[1] This research program was at the School of Social Work, Wayne University, and was supported by a grant from the U.S. Public Health Service, under the Mental Hygiene Act. Dr. Fritz Redl, of the School, and Dr. Ronald Lippitt, of the Research Center for Group Dynamics, were Principal Investigators. The author was Project Director.

the part played by the initiatory act, itself. This presentation will summarize the content of our work. The reader interested in the details of design, technique and statistical treatment will find appended a bibliography of our technical articles in the area.

What Is Behavioral Contagion?

"Behavioral contagion" is a term we have used for denoting a phenomenon very familiar to all who have worked in groups. One boy becomes interested in exploring the building, and others follow him into the activity. The club leader starts to sing and, with no urging, the other girls join in. Someone throws a pillow out of the cabin window . . . and so forth. In such incidents where behavior has been picked up without overt sign by the initiator that he wants to be followed by others, we say that it has spread, or has been imitated, or has "contaged."

There are two general reasons for being concerned with understanding this phenomenon. The first relates to group handling. Often when we think of contagion, we have in mind mass outbursts of undesirable behavior or mob hysteria. Many of the more restrictive methods of handling groups in, for example, delinquency institutions are based on an effort to prevent happenings of this kind. On other occasions, we hope for the occurrence of contagion as a vehicle by which involvement in program may spread spontaneously, or the people in a group may start to show more friendly behavior toward each other. The second general reason for interest in this type of interpersonal influence concerns attempts at differential diagnosis in the group. If, for instance, Pete calls his counsellor a name, does this mean he hates adults? Or, is he simply contaging this system from Johnny? Or both? When may such an act be seen as representing the basic personality; when, the current group situation? At the moment, we simply cannot know, and both for understanding and group handling our lack of knowledge about this phenomenon must be seen as serious.

What Causes Behavior to Contage?

I suppose the inclination of the average practitioner (as was mine) would be that this lack of knowledge is probably personal. He might suspect that a good deal is known about contagion, if only he had time to search the literature. His suspicion is misdirected. Here, as elsewhere with the problems he brings it, the "scientific" literature is not guilty. There has been almost no adequately controlled empirical study of the dynamic base of such incidents by sociologists or social psychologists.[2] This is not to say there has been no writing on the subject. But thinking about contagion as some sort of mystical entity or disembodied communication between people is not very helpful. Neither is reference to an "instinct of imitation" which fails to account for the many times contagion does not occur.

To us, it seemed more useful to make explicit two matter-of-fact assumptions and be guided by them: a. That the dynamics to be understood lie in the psychology of the person contaged, the "recipient"; b. That this is, after all, a behavior which like other behaviors may have a wide variety of different underlying causes. The research problem then became one of defining the various general conditions for recipients under which behavioral contagion is likely to occur. Our team has by now developed quite a number of hypotheses regarding factors which are probably relevant for predicting the likelihood of contagion of a given act. These can be grouped under the two main headings of: a. Relationship of the recipient to the initiator of the

---

[2] Significant exceptions are the early experiments of F. H. Allport on coacting groups (1), and the more recent work of Miller and Dollard (3).

behavior contaged; b. Meaning of the act, itself, in the psychology of the recipient. Let us examine a few factors whose significance we have thus far been able to demonstrate empirically

Likelihood of Initiation as Related to Prestige

The first question we set for study was this: In a group of children, which child is most likely to be an initiator of behavioral contagion—i.e., the child whose behavior is "picked up"? Our hypothesis was that children of high prestige in their groups, perceived by the other children as the possessors of admired characteristics, would be the most frequent initiators. To test this hypothesis it also seemed necessary to establish whether certain other behaviors towards children of high prestige—willingness to be influenced by them in direct attempts at influencing, behavior in which they are treated respectfully, etc.—would also relate to the measure of prestige.

The procedure which we employed for studying this problem has been described in considerable detail elsewhere. (4) Teams of three observers were brought into children's camps, and assigned to study four cabin-groups during the whole three-and-a-half to four-week period these groups were in camp. The children's behavior in which we were interested was recorded on precategorized observation schedules of the sort more familiarly used in laboratory studies of groups. On a time-sampling basis, the children were under observation from rising to retiring in the whole range of situations through which they lived as a group. From three to four thousand interactions were recorded between the children in any cabin studied.

The data on prestige in the group were obtained in individual sessions with the campers which were, in effect, near-sociometric choosing situations. We used pictures of the children being ranked which were placed in rows of boxes, or hung on arrows, to lend a game-like atmosphere to the proceedings.

Rankings were obtained of the children in the group by each group member on a variety of dimenions thought to be relevant to prestige in this setting—"Who is good at athletics? . . . Who knows a lot about the woods?" A final source of data lay in rankings by the counselors of the children in their groups on some personality variables not otherwise measured.

The study was conducted first in the summer of 1948 in two camps for "disturbed" children, one for boys, and one for girls. Eight groups in each were studied at that time. A subsequent duplication in 1950 dealt again with the camp for disturbed boys, this time contrasting it with a camp for normal boys. A total of thirty-two groups, then, has been studied. In many important respects, results were consistent throughout all three study populations.[3]

There now is little reason to question that in populations of the kind here studied a relationship exists between the average prestige of a child in his group, and the frequency of other members contaging his behavior. Our statistical results encourage a high level of confidence in this general finding.

It is of practical significance to list, however, on *which* choice scales this finding appears to be true. After all, in some groups being a good scholar carries a lot of prestige; in others, you have to be a ten-second man to be respected. A few dimensions which seem likely to relate to frequency of initiation in settings like these are: a. Ability in sports and athletics; b. Physical strength and/or fighting ability; c. Independence from adults; d. Sex sophistication; e. Having ideas for fun. Two dimensions which were found not to work in the groups of disturbed children, at least, were "being seen as helpful" and "attractive appearance."

[3] Our hospitable collaborators in these studies have been: Dr. William C. Morse, University of Michigan Fresh Air Camp; Miss Jean Wren, Camp Greybarn of the Community Service Society of New York; Mr. Elmer Ott, Camp Manito-Wish of the North Central Area Council of the Y.M.C.A.

In most situations, it is not feasible to conduct near-socio-metric studies to determine relative group prestige.[4]

Therefore, it is reassuring to have found that—on most scales —the counselor's prediction of how children will be ranked in his group by their fellow members agrees fairly closely with averages obtained from the children themselves. Better-than-chance prediction of who has, or will have, prestige should be possible for the group worker faced with localizing contagion initiation.

Prestige and Security in the Group

Having established that there is a relation between frequency of initiation of behavioral contagion and prestige in the group, another question arises. Is this because high-prestige children produce behavior differently, or is it that any act of one of these is more likely to be contaged than a similar act by a child of low prestige? Although the theory of prestige is in need of a good deal of overhauling, what we usually have in mind is the latter possibility.

We were led to raise this question in the first place from a finding which became inescapable in a study such as this: children of high prestige start more social interactions in the group. Our material has led us to believe that the reason for this is the security which they feel in the group situation, and they feel this security because the other group members give them overt signs of how they are regarded. It would take us afield from our present concern to give the evidence painfully accumulated in exploration of this basic hypothesis in group work. Assuming it is true, where does it leave us?

[4] We would like to enter a strong plea against the indiscriminate use of such methods. Often, for the child who is low on the totem pole, the sociometric has the effect of bringing into focus a situation which had lain implicit, and this proves disturbing. Such devices should be used only by persons conscious of what they may be stirring up, and never merely to draw pretty but meaningless diagrams.

One possible conclusion would be that the psychology of prestige, viewed from the standpoint of the recipient, has little to do with frequency of initiation of contagion in groups. Prestige enters in only indirectly by determining which children are likely to act frequently and hence provide acts which *can* be contaged. We have devoted considerable effort to seeing whether such a conclusion is tenable. Our finding (based on statistical manipulations in which activity level was "factored out") is that while the level of activity of the high-prestige children may account for a part of their frequency of being initiators, it does not account for all of it. Part of the relationship remains as due to the greater likelihood that any act of theirs will be contaged.

However, the net result of all this is clarification of the role of prestige in initiation of behavioral contagion. The degree of relationship is heightened by the fact that prestige in the group affects *both* the object of prestige and the person for whom he has it.

The Rotten Apple Theory

Few of us in this day and age come up with an expression like "The rotten apple spoils the barrel" if we are asked to explain our reluctance to introduce a very impulsive child into one of our groups. We have rationales which are more psychiatric and better defended. Nevertheless, we might be inclined to grant some credence to the old saw as describing what often happens, even if it does not explain it.

For, what do we mean by "impulsiveness"? We mean the degree to which a child operates in terms of his immediate urges. Otherwise put, it is the extent to which control systems in the personality are lacking or relatively helpless in the face of such urges. Our fear is that highly impulsive children will be found wanting in many of the situations of group living in which delay or frustration tolerance are called for. Not only will they break through their own or adult-imposed control but, in clearly and spontaneously expressing needs which the other children are also feeling, they may carry them along into uncontrolled episodes by acting as "triggers" for setting off the group.

We had, in our study of disturbed children, anticipated finding a relation between frequency of being a contagion initiator and the rating a child might receive from his counselor on a scale of impulsiveness. The relationship was *not* found, in general observations of the groups.

Although this is the frequent fate of hypotheses regarded as truisms when they are demonstrated, in this case we determined to explore the matter further by means of a little experiment.

This experiment was run with four groups from the camp for disturbed boys, near the end of one camp session. It consisted of bringing them, a group at a time, into a shack where they were to be asked to tell a story for us about a picture we would show them. As part of the setup there were treats to be had after the story-telling, and these were displayed enticingly on a table in front of where the group was seated. After the boys were settled, we announced that there would be a short delay, since the person in charge had the picture, and he had not yet arrived. No they could not have the treats until after the story, these were his orders. The "experiment" consisted of spending about eighteen minutes in this impasse while behavior was recorded by observers.

The dynamics present in the group were known in this situation to a large extent because we had produced them. There was a strong need to get at the treats which was being frustrated by counterpressures from the adults against moving in that direction. The need and the frustration were common throughout the group, and there were many clear signs of both, as one might imagine with this population.

The pattern of initiation of contagion which occurred during the experiment was very revealing, and especially when contrasted with patterns in these groups in the "general run" of observational situations. In the experiment, the factor of prestige as determining initiation became statistically insignificant; the factor of relative impulsiveness *was* significant.

We are, therefore, able to define with somewhat more precision the conditions favoring the impulsive child as a contagion initiator. These involve a need to act in a given direction which is common throughout the group and which is being held in check by social restraints against acting. The impulsive child, less able to tolerate such restraints, breaks through them. In so doing, he becomes what Dr. Redl has described as "guilt-bearer" for the rest of the group, who are then enabled to break through also.

In most contagion incidents the dynamics here described do not exist. A systematic recording of them makes one aware that relatively few are likely to be regarded by a group worker as hostile or "bad." Concerning most, he would have no opinion whatever. The dynamics involve other things than breaking through restraints. Further, there is reason to believe that the highly impulsive child often acts in response to needs which are not common to the other children at the moment or whose expression is unacceptable to them. Under such circumstances, his activity is more likely to lead to rejection than to contagion.

I believe that the familiarity of the trigger function of the impulsive child rests on the striking and memorable character of the incidents in which he is the initiator. Under normal conditions, so-called, the more relevant dynamic is prestige. Of course, where one has an impulsive or delinquent child who also enjoys high prestige the problem is more complex.

The Trigger Function of the Initiatory Act

The term "trigger function" has been used somewhat loosely. What, literally, is meant by the metaphor?

It involves the notion that here we are concerned with conditions in which the act, itself, rather than enduring relationship with the initiator, precipitates contagion. In certain cases the recipient is in a kind of conflict situation between wanting to do something and necessity for restraint against doing it. When simply seeing the initiatory act has the effect of tipping the balance and overcoming restraints, it does seem to act like "a trigger."

This was assumed to have occurred in the group experiments in the camp setting. However, since there are potentially so many variables at play in a group experiment, we determined to explore the hypothesis more concisely in situations involving "groups of two." This was done in experimental series in the observation room we share with the Merrill-Palmer School in Detroit. In all of these experiments, we used pairs of twelve- to fourteen-year-old boys who were strangers to each other. One of the boys, our Collaborator, was one of a rotating staff of children trained by us to behave in certain ways in the experimental setting so that we could vary the behavior of one child at will. The other member of a pair was a Subject. The object was to see whether the Subject's behavior in the experiment would be affected by the Collaborator's. In all experimental runs, the children were in apparently parallel but independent circumstances. No Subject ever recognized a Collaborator as in our employ. For the Subject, the situation involved conflict between a desire to act in some direction, and restraints which might or might not be maintained against acting.

The first experiment was one in which Subject and Collaborator were set at a very boring task (writing figure eight's), and asked to keep going as long as they could. Very shortly, the Experimenter left the room. In twenty-three cases (the Experimental) the Collaborator, on cue, made a series of "breaks" out of the working situation (e.g., wiggling fingers to rest them, getting up to sharpen a pencil); in the sixteen Control cases, the Collaborator simply continued to work. Our measure of the effect of the initiatory acts was the number of *Subjects* showing them in both situations. Differences were found between Experimental and Control cases which were statistically significant, although not great.

In the second series of experimental runs, the Subject was faced with a more ambiguous problem. The boys were asked to solve four block design puzzles, with a rest period after each one. During the rest period, the Subject had a decision as to whether or not to play with some attractive toys placed around the room. The Experimenter had told him that he might "lose points" for playing with some of these toys, but would not identify which toys these were. The issue was whether or not to risk play, in the face of an ambiguous fate. In the so-called Active cases, the Collaborator freely went and played with a different toy each rest period; in the Passive, he sat noncommittally at the work table.

Very large differences resulted between the thirty-eight Active and thirty-six Passive cases in terms of the numbers of incidents of Subjects' playing with toys. A third set of eight cases in which Subjects were in the situation alone fell intermediate between the other two.

Here we had a set of conditions controlled to resemble what we had abstracted as favoring the impulsive child in the camp experiment. The act of an initiator *was* able to tip the balance so that restraining forces were overcome. Not only that, but from the difference between the Passive and Alone cases in the second experiment we realize that by non-acting the Collaborator may also increase restraining forces.

Our theory was that in an ambiguous situation (and most situations of social restraint have this quality to an extent) the Subject's judgment would be affected by his perception of the Collaborator's. The Collaborator communicates his judgment about the extent of risk involved through his behavior. Other interpretations are possible, of course. In any case, we have had an experimental prototype not only of incidents in which a child decides he may attempt a bit of misbehavior, too, without fear of internal or external punishment, but also of committee sessions in which a reserved member acts as a damper on all free expressions of feeling.

Conclusions

Let us now briefly review our findings in terms of the aim we had set "of defining the various general conditions for recipients under which behavioral contagion is likely to occur." These conditions may be grouped into two sets: those concerned with relationship with the potential initiator; and those involving the function of the initiatory act, itself, relatively independently of relationship.

It appears that a child in a group situation is more likely to pick up the behavior of another child who has prestige for him in that situation. Since children of high prestige know they have it and feel more secure to engage in activity, their probability of being foci of contagion initiation is heightened further.

Contrary to expectation, highly impulsive children are no more likely to be initiators of behavioral contagion than less impulsive children in the general run of group situations—even in camps for disturbed children. However, situations involving the necessity for maintaining control against expression of a need commonly felt in the group seem peculiarly adapted to their acting as "triggers."

This "trigger function" may be seen as quite independent

of any lasting relationship between the initiator and the child picking up the behavior. Where the recipient is in a state of labile balance between an urge to act in some direction, and controls against so acting based on fear of consequences, the scales may be tipped in either direction by the mere visualization of whether some other child chooses to act or to play it safe. From this we may understand why it is that a child's impulsiveness rather than his prestige is the better predictor of who will be an initiator in situations of common frustration.

What are some implications of these findings for the group worker? These must be drawn conservatively since, after all, there is a long road between a few research generalizations and the full battery of laws we need for prediction in a complex, concrete case. Here are some which I would, myself, accept.

1. Although we still do not know how to diagnose when a child's behavior in a group represents his own enduring personality structure and when the influence of the current group situation, one thing is certainly clear. We cannot afford to overlook the latter. I should think group workers would be expected to examine it first.

2. Behavioral contagion is not a mysterious seepage of impulsivity from one person to another, but a process subject to detailed understanding and control. Where it initiates with a child otherwise of little prestige, for example, one would be likely to decide he was merely first to express a quite commonly felt need. In many situations (e.g., children kept waiting unnecessarily) the administrative problem revolves not around who started the destruction, but why there should have been such an urge in the group.

3. Ordered, effective and recognized hierarchical structures of prestige (and of power) appear to emerge spontaneously in a wide assortment of children's groups, in this culture. This

is a finding to which I, at least, have been forced by the data, and against my inclinations of how seriously to regard it. The evidence for this is not reported above, and the problems and opportunities it presents for us who work with groups are beyond the scope of present interest. However, the relation of prestige to contagion initiation is only one aspect of it. It is fairly safe, in observing our groups, to diagnose the prestige and power hierarchy present by watching simply who is most frequently an initiator.

Perhaps a final note on the current status of research in our field is now in order. For the present, the methodological difficulties of even the more primitive problems continue to be enormous. Any advance can only be regarded as the victory of the lawfulness of Nature over the awfulness of method.

BIBLIOGRAPHY

1. Allport, F. H., *Social Psychology*, Boston: Houghton Mifflin, 1924.
2. Grosser, D., Polansky, N., and Lippitt, R., "A Laboratory Study of Behavioral Contagion," *Human Relations*, IV (1951) 115-142.
3. Miller, N., and Dollard, J., *Social Learning and Imitation*, New Haven: Yale, University Press, 1941.
4. Polansky, N., Lippitt, R., and Redl, F., "An Investigation of Behavioral Contagion in Groups," *Human Relations*, III (1950) 319-348.
5. Polansky, N., Lippitt, R., and Redl, F., "The Use of Sociometric Data in Research on Group Treatment Processes," *Sociometry*, XIII (1950).
6. Polansky, N., *et al.*, "Problems of Interpersonal Relations in Research on Groups," *Human Relations*, II (1949) 281-292.
7. Redl, F., "Group Emotion and Leadership," *Psychiatry*, V (1942) 573-596.
8. Redl, F., "The Phenomenon of Contagion and Shock Effect," *Searchlights on Delinquency*, ed. by K. R. Eissler, New York: International Universities Press, 1949.

THE EFFECT OF CULTURAL VARIABLES ON
GROUP WORK PRACTICE *By Alan F. Klein*

FOR many years social workers and those in
allied fields depended almost wholly upon psychology for their
understanding of people. Behavior was interpreted accordingly and was related to human needs and drives that were
said to be inherent and universal. More recently, however,
the findings of anthropologists and sociologists have begun to
interest social workers and as a result they are beginning to
interpret behavior in cultural terms.

There are dangers in relying upon psychological factors
wholly or upon cultural determinants alone because behavior
rests upon a multi-casual base and is far too complicated to
be dismissed easily by attributing it to either the nature of man,
or to his specific culture alone. We know that all people have
certain basic needs and that failure to satisfy those needs results in differing but adaptive responses. Such behavior differs
from person to person but there are responsive patterns that
seem to be common within societal groupings. We also know
that much of behavior is learned. The principles governing
how people react to satisfied or unsatisfied needs can be found
in biology, genetics and psychology. However, the way people
satisfy their basic needs is often dictated by custom or their
culture.

As an example, all people must eat to survive. What they eat,
how they eat and how often they eat are culturally determined.
They all react to hunger, but how they react may be culturally
affected. Some groups might accept starvation with stoical patience while others become war-like and aggressive. People
learn how to behave, whether under frustrating or pleasing
stimuli by the way others in their society behave.

Some drives or needs are acquired. Many anxieties, appetites or frustrations are determined culturally. Man has learned to need many things which are not basic necessities but are acquired needs, yet the failure to satisfy these will often create the same reactions as deprivation in the area of basic need.

The culture in which a person operates conditions the way he looks at things, and the way he reasons. It forms the frame of reference within which he makes his choices, and affects the way in which he seeks to satisfy his needs. It would seem apparent that the knowledge of the conditioning to which individuals have been subjected shows the functional relationships of their cultural beliefs and often explains what otherwise appear to be unreasonable actions.

People living in close association for an extended period develop standard and acceptable ways of living. The activity or beliefs of such a group of people are related to the needs of the group to survive, and to be comfortable and happy. The culture provides a system within which members of the society can live together. Each individual must learn the patterns of behavior and attitudes that are acceptable to the other members of his group if he is to stay out of trouble, remain comfortable or happy, and succeed in the group.

How people react to life's pressures and problems will, in a large measure, depend upon cultural learning and cannot be explained, or modified, without reference to this causation. Moreover, seen in the light of such causation, the behavior may be perfectly rational. Behavior that group workers and others in the community may regard as delinquent or in need of change may in fact be realistic and adaptive within the systems of living in slum societies and may be, therefore, most rational within its own frame of reference.

It is common knowledge that persons brought up and living in different sub-cultural groupings have different ways of thinking and acting. For the group worker, each sub-group to which a member belongs takes on a different facet for assessing his personality, behavior, and needs. Persons from differing socio-economic groups, religious denominations, nationality backgrounds, and ethnic groups, therefore, have different standards of values, different ideas about democracy, sex, marriage, honesty, success and so on. Which one is right? What are to be the criteria for the group worker?

Each of the sub-groups has a mental image of the "approved" personality type, the kind of person most acceptable to it. For the group worker, which personality is "approved" as the goal to which to help members adjust? What does the group worker mean by his reference to personality and maturity? To which culture is an individual to be well-adjusted? In most communities there is a prevailing culture which is accepted by most "respectable" persons. It is generally middle-class and idealized. There are many sub-cultural groups within the community that differ more or less with the prevailing culture. Is it the function of the group worker to induct his group members into the prevailing culture? Can members learn to accept a world alien to that of their parents, their upbringing, and their immediate social milieu? Should they be asked to, and if so, why?

A word of caution is needed to avoid stereotyping persons by cultural generalization. The presence of common ways within any sub-group does not mean that there are not differences in behavior patterns within the same culture. There is a wide range of behavioral characteristics within any cultural group. However, culture does tend to limit the normal range of variation.

We know, however, that what is rational or normal behavior in some cultural groups may be regarded as delinquent or deviant by our standards. Some types of behavior are looked upon as indicative of deep emotional disturbance by persons reared in a different society, but within its own group they may be accepted and be essential to personal and group survival. This poses an important question for the group worker. The worker himself is a product of one particular set of cultural factors in each instance. The agency for which he works is an institution rooted in the prevailing culture. How the worker regards the behavior of persons from other cultural backgrounds is influenced by his own cultural bias and that of his agency.

It would seem that most group workers in this country are middle-class and subscribe to American middle-class standards. The usual criteria for maturity or normal personality are culturally colored and all our criteria are open to suspicion for cultural bias. It would seem also that we have not received the same training in understanding cultural determinants as we have in assessing psychological factors. We are open to criticism for diminishing emphasis on home visiting and community study in order to understand and appreciate the culture of our members and what that culture means to them. We have room for improvement in learning the language of our members so as better to communicate with them and also in learning to think in their language so as really to understand them. We have not learned too well how to bridge the culture gap that exists between our agencies and the segments of our communities which do not use our services because often agency culture is so foreign to them that they are uncomfortable within it.

Persons reared in sub-cultural groups whose patterns of behavior differ from middle-socio-economic groups do not necessarily want to be inducted into that way of life. They may not want to change their own patterns nor is it probable that they would be any happier if they did. If we as group workers regard the prevailing culture as normal and desirable we may tend to brand persons who do not conform as difficult, disturbed and delinquent and often refer them to specialized agencies for treatment. We often are wrong. To insist that prevailing patterns are correct or most rational, conducive to human happiness or mental health would be based upon a smug judgment. To assume that everyone who differs from ourselves is disturbed is to disregard the facts. To assume that the "other" groups are most desirous of entering the great American middle-class or would benefit from doing so is fallacious. It might be argued, however, that society in general would benefit if certain patterns of behavior were altered, or that every society has the obligation of transmitting the prevailing culture through its educational systems.

It would seem imperative that group workers examine and study their own culture and those of the members if the workers are to understand them and be able to work with them. It is not enough to understand the effect of cultural factors upon behavior but, in addition, we must weigh the effect of them on the use of group work method. We agree that we have no right to superimpose our standards upon our group. What, then, is the role of the group worker and the agency?

Condensed material is inevitably sketchy and bold principles tend to seem dogmatic. The limits of an article prevent supportive analysis and explanation. I can, therefore, do no more than suggest some general approaches to the subject.[1]

Social agencies are basically middle-class committed to the socialization of their members. They should:

1. admit that they are part of a middle-class American way of life;
2. develop sharper discrimination between behavior that is culturally different or psychologically disturbed;
3. adjust their standards to reflect more realistically the culture they do seek to represent;
4. select out of the community culture those practices more likely to be conducive to sound mental hygiene and reject those that are not;

[1] Klein, Alan F., *Society, Democracy, and the Group*. Whiteside, Inc. and William Morrow & Company, 1953.

5. preserve those aspects of the sub-cultures that are realistic, that make a valuable contribution to the general culture, and that are essential to survival within the particular culture;

6. refrain from holding out false hope for social mobility and opportunity;

7. adopt policies and programs likely to attract rather than repel children with delinquent and deviant values;

8. develop and foster social values around which all member groups can integrate;

9. teach about the complexity of our culture;

10. appraise values against the frame of reference of the individual and develop means of communication with and between members of different sub-groups.

The group worker may find the following general principles of some value in helping him to find his role.

In order for the worker to be able to work with persons from sub-cultures different from his own:

1. he must be mature and accepting and he would have to eliminate cultural bias from his interpersonal relations;

2. he will have to know and understand the meaning of their own cultures to the persons with whom he works; he will need to know the sub-cultures of their families, communities and social classes; he must accept the fact that cultural practices are relative (home visiting and intimate community involvement are indispensable to the achievement of real understanding and the acquiring of the language with which to reach some groups);

3. the worker must understand his own cultural background thoroughly and be able to view it objectively;

4. the worker must be clear as to his and his agency's objectives, especially as they apply to cultural transmission or change;

5. he should learn to use reward with children;

6. he starts where people are;

7. he must help people develop inner, emotional resources for personal security;

8. he can help people to understand the principle of the appropriateness of behavior;

9. he can help people determine their vocational futures by acquainting them with the varieties of opportunities available in our society, and the differing cultural demands within each;

10. he can help them to select goals realistically;

11. he can help them to see that total culture is man-made and can be changed.

Personal security requires consistency in training and workers can devise ways of minimizing the shock of cultural contradictions between home, school, and agency. Cultural contradiction and conflict, when met, can be worked through rather than denied or overridden. It would help workers to study and understand the emotional effects of learning to live in a world that is alien to that of the family milieu.

The role of the worker is not that of inducting members into the prevailing culture. It is a process of teaching them how to express their needs in a manner which is consistent with the welfare of the community; helping them to learn the techniques of living at their own cultural levels; helping to work out the problems that confront them, while exposing them to different cultural settings. It involves helping them to select their future based upon knowledge and a study of available rewards. It is a matter of helping members to acquire personalities that make them want to act as they will have to act to achieve their goals, and to cultivate a desire for the rewards that may be obtained as a result.

However, let us not forget that whether their psychological needs are being met will in the last analysis determine much of the behavior of individuals. The worker will have to insure that psychological needs, culturally oriented, are being met within his groups if he is to help individuals to adjust to the different social roles which they will have to fill.

RESISTANCE AND HOSTILITY IN GROUP MEMBERS *By Gisela Konopka*

JOHNNY was busily building a fire on the porch of the rickety old wooden building which housed the agency. He thoroughly enjoyed his work and called to two other boys to help him which they did with great satisfaction. I went to them and said that it was fun having a fire going, but it could not be done on the porch. How about moving over to the adjoining playground? No, this was much more fun. I explained patiently that they might burn down the building—their building where lots of things were going on and which they enjoyed using. No response. I said firmly that the fire had to be extinguished and I proceeded to do it. Johnny and one other boy jumped at me furiously screaming that they would not care if the whole "damn building" with all those "damn people" would burn down, that they did not like it anyhow and they would never, never return again! With that they left swinging their arms and continuing to tell me that I never let them have any fun, that they did not like me.

These were the two boys with whom several of us had worked intensely in the agency, the only place where they received any love and acceptance. Johnny was the same boy who at a recent club meeting had said softly to me, "Wish you were my mother. Wish I never had to go home."

A few years ago Hazel Osborn directed our attention to the fact that resistance is a phenomenon which is not known to case work agencies only.[1] She helped to dispel the notion that

[1] Hazel Osborn, "Some Factors of Resistance which Affect Group Participation," *The Group*, Jan., 1949, Vol. 11, No. 2.

people come to us full of happiness and positive feelings alone and showed the ambivalent nature of the emotions of our members as evidenced by broken windows and furniture, swearing, and, more subtly, by absence from meetings, sulking and even by sweet compliance to rules while withdrawing from any creative involvement in program.

This behavior must be understood with relation to the purpose of our work with people. This purpose exists in common for the settlement, the "Y," the Jewish Center and all the types of agencies through which group work is practiced. That purpose is to help people with their interpersonal relationships so that they can lead more happy, satisfying lives while being part of a mutually dependent society. We want to help people to grow so that they feel their own worth, and the worth of others.

This kind of pride does not grow by itself and it is much more threatened in the growing up process than encouraged. Most of us do not have this calm happy pride. Most of us carry many scars that have come from blows to this pride and the way we deal with those blows has determined whether our hostility or our acceptance of people becomes stronger. Every child feels alone and frightened, because he is dependent. If this feeling is not reassured, or is little reassured, fear, loneliness, resentment and guilt grow to a continuous circle ending as hostility directed toward self and others. Ann Porter's words in her book "The Day Before" have great significance:

"Hate needs no instruction, but waits only to be provoked. Love must be learned and learned again, there is no end to it."

It is the special task of our profession to support this learning process. It has often been said that the case worker does this when the situation shows a ready breakdown, while the group worker deals with the normal person to prevent such breakdown. That is only partially true. The group worker has the continuous task of helping the individual to gain this capacity to respect himself and others and deals with many aspects of this problem where difficulties have already arisen, because this is part of our "normal" life.

When we want to understand anti-agency behavior with which we deal we use very often the terms "resistance" and "hostility." It is important to know how these concepts differ from each other. Resistance is part of the general psychological makeup of every human being. Our whole growing-up process is a constant adaption to change during which we always want this change and we resist it. The child really enjoys being weaned, but he resists giving up the comfort of the mother's breast. The adolescent wants to grow up, but he fears the responsibility of independence. We want to learn about new ideas, want to know new people and places, but we are afraid of them, we resist. Resistance is part of the basic ambivalence of our emotional make-up.

Hostility has a different root. It springs from the cycle described earlier. All of us want to be loved, to be somebody special. All of us have to give up being the *only* in the affection of parents and of others when we have to share. This desire makes for resentment, for following guilt feelings, and, if not resolved creatively and positively through *some* expression, *some* suppression and a great deal of sublimation, will turn into hostility.

In discussing the manifestations and causes of anti-agency behavior, it is necessary to separate the thinking about children and about adults, since the reasons they come to our agencies are *fundamentally* different. Eric Ericson has described that clearly, when he wrote:

"What is infantile play, then? We say that it is not the equivalent of adult play, that it is not recreation. The playing adult steps sideward into another reality; the playing child advances forward to new stages of mastery."[2]

If we see the playing of the child as "advancing forward to new stages of mastery" and add our general knowledge that every learning experience involves enjoyment as well as resistance, then we begin to expect that necessarily in every "normal" youngster we will see signs of resistance, even in a setting that offers "play." The pre-school and early school-age child who comes to our agency is offered a great deal of gratification for his needs. He requires a place where he can move freely, where he can run and push and shout, where he can make simple things and gain the first feeling of real achievement, and where he can make friends, and drop them and pick them up again (the age of ever-changing friendships). He needs to find adults who are not his parents, but who are like good fathers and mothers, who are around for comfort when he gets hurt and for fun when he wants to jump on their backs or laugh with them or for teaching when he needs help in making something. Those are deep and important gratifications of the young child's needs and he enjoys them and shows it at this age by cuddling and kissing and wrestling and being happy. But there are other aspects of the same picture: If Jim wants to climb on the worker's lap or tussle happily with him, Joe and Dick want to do it too, nor will they leave, even if Jim pushes them. When the worker laughs and says they all three can tussle with him or says he can't take it, they had better come one after another, he just does not seem to love Jim enough, and Jim becomes angry at all the boys and the worker. Jim is struggling to meet one of the most difficult demands of LIFE, to share a person. It is hard enough to share toys and food, but sharing *people* is most painful. It started back home, when the new babies arrived, and it continues at a place where he just wanted to

2 E. Ericson, *Childhood and Society*, 1950, p. 195.

have fun. So Jim hits or kicks back or—starts the fire on the porch, and he thinks he "hates" them all.

Susan feels the same way, only she shows it differently by making almost every game impossible, by saying she does not like it and dissolving into tears as she complains that nobody does what she wants. She stands in the corner, finger in her mouth, not being moved. Susan is not only shy—as one would think looking at her superficially—but Susan is very, very angry and feels left out in the cold.

The constantly repeated demand that we share frustrates a basic need to be the unique and only one, and that frustration bears hostility.

Need the worker throw up his hands and accept as inevitable that we will have unhappy frustrated souls always? No, the point is only that we will always have frustration in life, that it was a stupid, superficial and harmful misunderstanding that led us to think that we must remove all frustration from a person's life. The basic principles in dealing with frustration are:

1. To avoid adding unnecessary frustration to that which is essential in the life situation; and

2. To try to keep the degree of frustration somewhat in relation to the capacity of the individual to cope with it.

When we, for example, make too many rules that can be broken, or ask eight- to ten-year-old youngsters to be quiet for too long a time, or expect teen-agers actually to sleep when they have a slumber party, we simply are asking too much. We have over-taxed the capacity to strengthen the ego through helping it to understand the necessity of the frustration. It does not make sense to tell Joe and Susan that as nice children they must learn to share, if that is all we do, because that is just what they don't want to do. It helps Joe and Susan to let them feel that they are loved, and to understand that sharing is hard, but is done anyway, and at points to let them also see where it is to *their* advantage. With such help, children begin to learn the basic art of human relationships, which has empathy as its fundamental factor. The small child can learn this, but better so when he is helped to learn this in a pleasurable moment, than when he is deprived. It helps more to say to a child who has eaten cake and ice cream and is very happy and full of good food, "You know that is the way the little boy in India would like to feel too, and therefore we are sending food," instead of telling him *before* he eats that he should feel guilty about having so much and must share his money with the deprived child.

The same feelings of hostility in relation to sharing are found in older children who have to interrupt their play in the gym, because the next group must come in, or the need to clean the room, because it will be used by another group, etc.

There are two other aspects of group work, which involve ambivalent feelings of satisfaction as well as resistance. They are the demands we make of group members to *participate* and to make *decisions*, both inherent in the democratic philosophy of life basic to group work. We believe that this type of participation is gratifying to human needs and therefore leads to the feeling of happiness in the individual. We have said, and rightly, that people prefer to participate in decision making, that only when they do will they really carry them out. Yet, we know that people also are afraid of such involvement. Schiller called it the "laziness of the heart" and he meant the resistance to make an effort that is in all of us. Dostoyevski, in his *Grand Inquisitor,* showed with the deepest of insight what "burden of freedom" means. It is therefore out of the strong ambivalence that is basic to human beings facing the demand of free decisions and participation that we find expression of resistance in our agencies.

A group of 12-year-olds, for instance, wants to prepare for a picnic. If the worker suggests an outing in the nearby park, he is turned down angrily, not so much because they don't like the place, but because they don't want to be told by an adult. So he settles back and suggests that they consider alternatives. The discussion gets hotter and hotter until at one point several boys begin to shout angrily. "This darn place never lets you do what you want to and the guy who is supposed to help us sits around doing nothing." The burden of decision was too heavy, and out of the anxiety regarding their ability to make the right choice grew anger and resentment.

How will the group worker help? No recipe can be given. He understands the youngsters' need for guidance not too strongly offered. He knows that their anger is not really directed at him or the agency but at themselves for feeling so fearful and insecure. He does not want to let them go with this unhappy feeling of being incompetent, so he may agree with them, that it *is* tough to find the best place, but what is it that they would like to *do?* This helps them toward a solution, lets them save face, and, hopefully, brings them one small step toward seeing decision making as something pleasant, not only a burden.

There are many other areas in which we encounter anti-agency behavior which relate directly to our specific program or situation in the community. Our agencies uphold a philosophy of the worth of all human beings and demand a basic respect for everybody. If this ideal is translated into reality in a community setting where tensions among minority groups are strong, we must count on hostility against the agency which does not conform to the mores of certain subgroups in the neighborhood. This resistance can take many different forms:

1. Membership stays away, boycotts the agency and spreads rumors about it.

2. The dissenting group comes to the agency, but insists on complete separation from any other group in the agency.

3. The dissenting group expresses their hostility through vandalism.

It is clear that we cannot discontinue our basic philosophy in the face of such resistance, yet we have to understand those who feel hostile toward our agency policy of accepting all people. Where does this hostility spring from? We go back again to the original ambivalence in the human being wanting to know something new and different, but also resisting it. If there is no protection in meeting the new adventure (if mother's hand is not there when we try the first step), the effort will be much greater. Many of the children who come to our agencies for the first time encounter other human beings strange or different in the way they look or in the way they act. It may be that some part of the usually comforting environment—their own family—shows the same fear and resistance to the new encounter. Are we surprised that they meet this new experience with fear and resistance or with outright hostility? Their fear is intensified by two other psychological factors:

1. The need to identify closely with the primary group, the family; and

2. The need to identify with the closest and most powerful individual who is in the child's life usually father or mother.

If both the general family pattern and the father or mother are against our policy, the child is thrown into a terrifying conflict that must engender guilt and hostility. This is not basically neurotic behavior, but the kind of reaction normal to everybody in a generally unhealthy community climate. Here is further evidence of how our better understanding of mental hygiene will lead us more strongly to the need for social action as well as intensive work with the individual. It is here that we in the informal agencies learn something that child guidance clinics have practiced a long time; that is, we cannot work successfully with children without also working with parents. Our work with the feelings of hostility must be related to parents and children at the same time.

In the life cycle of the comparatively normal individual

ambivalence becomes stronger, more pronounced, more difficult to handle in adolescence.

The struggle around the acceptance of sharing, of participating, of making decisions relates to coming to terms with other people. Yet the hardest struggle we face all through life is *coming to terms with ourselves,* to find out who we really are as different from anyone else, as an unique person and yet as part of the whole human race. The adolescent's struggle is around this problem and is not only a struggle for independence. It is the difficult struggle to establish himself as a person. This is development and it is work.

In adolescence, this struggle can carry the aspect of sickness, if it is not realized that this is an age of exaggeration and what is "abnormal" in another age period is "normal" in the adolescent. This finding of oneself becomes conscious in adolescence. Because of the fact that the self never measures up completely to the often very strong ideals of adolescence there is a great deal of self-hate. Because of the great discomfort of such feelings, we find much projection on others. The teen-agers' contemporaries are so close and so obviously in the same boat that too much guilt would be engendered were this projection directed toward other adolescents. Therefore the adolescent will project his negative feelings toward himself on the adult as well as projecting his feelings of wish-fulfillment of the ideal, on him too. This is the reason why we find the strange and confusing mixture of hero worship and crushes combined with violent dislike, resistance and hostility.

Often the individual worker will be the symbol for what is beloved while the agency as a whole will stand for all the shortcomings and restrictions. We find most "anti-agency" behavior in the adolescent. We find every form of it, described earlier in its most intensive expression.

One of our agencies reported a group of sixteen-year-old boys, who had already once been barred from the agency because of some damage they had caused. They had been rough with some of the teen-age girls, and they had distributed a newspaper containing offensive references to the girls. In this instance, adolescent boys used their newspaper in expressing their hostility towards the agency. In so doing, they were also exploring their own status as young males. They were expressing a real wish to understand better their own sex drives and to learn how to behave with girls, but they could not do it in an acceptable way. It was clear that if this underlying wish could be seen, good programming to help them grasp this understanding was much more called for than restrictive measures.

On the other hand, it is also at this age that we find the most constructive cooperative behavior, long hours of work for the agency, great idealistic acceptance of agency ideals (often combined with a complete rejection of parent-culture). At this age the adolescent begins to handle differences of values and can stand up more easily against conflicting values coming from his primary group environment. But he can handle them mostly in terms of complete acceptance or complete rejection. In our youth serving agencies the adolescent will often identify with the highest humanitarian ideals and be very scornful of those, especially adults, who do not live completely up to them. Their great need is for a much more accepting understanding of this period of growth. Given a great deal of trusted and early security and the stamina that helps withstand frustration, the adolescent, supported by understanding parents and workers, will come quite well through this period. Lacking all this, the self-doubt and hate will either turn violently against himself and we have the adolescent suicide or mental breakdown or strong withdrawal from or hate of their adult environment and we have the really delinquent child with many varying symptoms, destroying property, stealing or flight into genuine sex delinquency. It seems to me that when adolescent behavior in its depth is understood, it becomes impossible for the group work agency to be satisfied with the provision of superficial activities to pass the time. In imaginative ways, it must provide outlets for hostile and accepting impulses. At this time it can be a stronghold of mental hygiene in our society.

In young adulthood we will find many similar manifestations carried over from earlier ages since we never completely lose our struggle to achieve maturity. In addition, there are new pressures which often make for hostility. The choice of a vocation or profession is much related to the finding of oneself and every remnant of feeling of being pushed around or feeling too dependent or having no clear conception of oneself or over- or under-estimating one's capacities leads to new frustrations. This frustration, not tempered by understanding and acceptance, breeds resentment.

It needs to be pointed out, however, that anti-agency behavior of adults often has a reality basis in the way we deal with them. Group work agencies have so long worked with children and adolescents that they often deal poorly with adults and provoke hostility. It is not easy for one who has left childhood a comparatively short time ago to continue in a place where everybody knew him when he was that "cute" or "crazy" kid and where there are too many of that same kind of kids underfoot. I think we have seriously to consider whether there should not be separate, though not segregated, centers for adults. At a later age individual adults might again want to have a place in the same center where children are.

There is all too little work done with young adults and where service is given we too often carry over the form of our work with younger groups. In most younger groups the presence of a group worker, though received with ambivalence, is quite essential. This must and should be different in an adult group, with the exception of the group whose focus is on treatment. While the adult group will want a consultant at times to help with resources, a teacher to help with specific content or a personal counselor who will relate to specific individuals in the group, the mature adult group should not have a worker continually with them. This prolongs the idea of their immaturity and I think the resistance that adult groups show by not coming to our agencies or constant bickering over policy matters might have something to do with our way of infantilizing them.

Our efforts to achieve understanding of the behavior of our group members would not be complete if we did not examine our own reaction as individuals to the situations we have discussed. We are the same kind of people with the same kind of needs, and often react exactly the same way. When members frustrate our efforts to help them and give them a satisfying experience, we, too, feel guilty, because we did not achieve. This makes us angry and we find many ways of expressing our anger. We rationalize punishing behavior by saying one has to be "firm," because we know we should not be punishing. We run away from it by being completely "permissive," avoiding conflict and again rationalizing beautifully by saying that they must have an "outlet." We withdraw by finding reasons why the group should not meet, or by having violent headaches and being unable to come to the meeting and by finding it is the "best for the group" to dissolve entirely. Our anti-agency behavior is really not so different, though it usually takes somewhat different forms. We are human, yet if we let ourselves go this way, we are not fulfilling the purpose we accepted at the beginning of this article.

So—what can we do? The solution—never fully realized— lies in what we mean when we talk about professional knowledge and skill and a professional attitude. It has *nothing* whatsoever to do with coldness. On the contrary, it means, as Bertha Reynolds said: "The sensitivity of the layman raised to the nth degree." This sensitivity is raised by a great deal of knowledge of what makes people tick. The more we know about them, the easier we understand and the less frustrated we feel about their actions. This is the help which comes from professional *knowledge*. The *skill* comes by meeting those problems over and over again and meeting them for quite a while with some protection.

That is the secret of professional supervision. This protection gives us support and refuge while it puts demands squarely before us, helping us to apply theoretical knowledge and testing its validity over and over again.

The professional attitude means a conscious use of self. We begin to understand our own self, we learn about our own "frustration threshold" and by learning about it, we begin raising it, more and more. We not only can "take" more and more, but we begin to appreciate the human suffering and the human capacity behind the behavior with which we work.

> "Here we must qualify, at least in its simplified interpretation the statement . . . namely, that frustration leads to aggression. Man, in the service of faith, can stand meaningful frustration." [3]

We can add to this deep concern for others, that can help us stand frustration in the same way that we hope to help the people with whom we work, that they may not have always to fight the world and themselves. We have to achieve in ourselves a sense of creativity, freedom, and enjoyment of the other fellow with all of his obnoxiousness and all of his lovability. Ours is a profession based on science, but carrying it out is art. We can do it only if we are carried by a deep enjoyment of people.

> "Red Wine first, Jessie, to the passion and the power and the pain of life; and then a drink of White Wine to the melody that is in them."

—SEAN O'CASEY,
The Silver Tassie

[3] *Op. cit.*, p. 373.

6

Group Work With Different Age Groups

WORKING EFFECTIVELY WITH CHILDREN
By Monica Burrell Owen

O_{NE} of the greatest concerns of our times is
the improvement of human relations, and the urgency of this
problem underlines the importance of group work with children. It challenges group workers to a re-valuation of goals
and the way in which they are trying to achieve them. By
definition, we are committed to programming for growth
through group living, recognizing that, since children are social beings, they turn to the group for companionship and protection, for learning and growth. Now we are discovering that
the more we learn about children's deepest needs and desires,
the more we need to learn; and our concern has shifted from a
program of activities to a concern with the personality growth
and social adjustment of children. How, within a group setting,
shall we help children to live and work at their individual and
collective best; to gain self-respect, self-direction and a greater

capacity to live effectively in a democratic society? We have learned that no program chosen by the leader, however good it may be, can provide all of the experiences through which children grow. We recognize that when, in his "wisdom," he plans for rather than with the children, he is depriving them of the opportunity for growth that comes from the exchange of ideas, from the thinking out of plans together, and from experiment, with all its inherent chances of success or failure. Often the well-laid plans and careful programs of group leaders are like the bed of Procrustes in the Greek folk tale—that bed which was well and firmly built, and always ready for guests. But the guests were made to fit the bed; the tall guest was lopped off and the short guest was stretched, so that each fitted perfectly, no matter what the cost to his comfort or well-being. No bed, and no program is right for all.

Group Work Today

Group work must have been far easier two generations ago. Now, because of our greater awareness of individual needs and behavior, we are challenged to use all our imagination and skills, all our sensitivity, all our insight and understanding, if group living is to meet the needs of each child. We must remind ourselves constantly that the program is merely a means to an end, rather then end in itself. Theoretically, we know this very well; but when we are faced with a group of children, it is easy to think in terms of activity for its own sake. Too often a well-acted play, a neat picture, an accurate recitation, becomes the goal. Here we need to do some honest self-questioning. Are we afraid to risk criticism if the play is not perfect? Are we interested in outcomes because of our own involvement in them? Or are we sincerely and deeply concerned with helping children to use the play, the picture, the recitation, as a means of learning to solve problems, of developing new skills, of taking charge of their own minds, no matter how imperfect the final result may be? Which do we really believe is important: the growth of the children or the pageant at the end of the year?

Here is our dilemma: how can we focus our efforts on understanding individual children and at the same time assure a group life that will provide the maximum development for all? How shall we meet each child's deepest needs within the framework of group living? First, we must understand and accept these needs as valid and important. Although very little research has been done in child development beyond the youngest years, we already have enough guideposts to help us.

The Size of the Group

We know that the group must be small enough and warm enough to give each child that sense of belonging without which he can have no inner security. He must always feel appreciated as a person and accepted for better or worse on the basis, not of what he does, but of what he is. Here, too, we must question our own attitudes toward children. Do we really believe, and practice the belief, that conduct in children is a matter of behavior and not of morals, to be interpreted rather than judged? Do we believe that although he lies, he is not a liar; that although he uses bad language, he has not "a dirty mind"? Do we really like each child for himself and appreciate his unique contribution? Do we listen to his opinions with genuine respect, even when we think he is wrong? If we judge him rather than try to understand him, if we ignore or negate him, we are denying him his sense of belonging and thereby failing to meet one of his most basic needs.

Being accepted is fundamental, but it is not enough. Each child needs to have the consciousness of his ability to meet the demands made upon him. How shall we gauge these demands? How much and what shall we expect of him in order that he will be challenged to do his best, and not be devastated by too many failures? Objective standards—what we expect of eight- or ten- or twelve-year-olds—can no longer be relied on as infallible guides to the answers. We must really know each child as an individual—his strengths, his weaknesses, his potentialities. We must learn to evaluate and to accept every child's effort and achievement in terms of his own growth and development. Often this is difficult, both because of our own eagerness to see progress and our fear of being Pollyannas—of substituting sweetness and light for "character development." We need to remind ourselves that growing takes a long time and that it is never continuous. We must accept inconsistencies in children as readily as we accept them in ourselves. Looking at one day or one year in a child's life is like looking at a pool in a running brook; it is one small part of something that is continuously flowing and changing, growing as it goes. A child is always in the process of becoming; and he must have a sense of competency at each stage of his progress, although that progress may change its tempo and sometimes seem to have lost its momentum entirely. No set of inflexible, prefabricated standards is right for a group of children or for one child.

To meet children's emotional needs, we must provide not only the sense of belonging, of likeness to others; not only belief in their ability to meet with confidence the immediate demands that are made upon them. We must also give them countless opportunities for self-direction, in order that they will learn to accept success and failure realistically. They need to learn this through trial and error, until they can face the unknown with the courage that grows out of a long series of minor conquests. And, last of all, children need opportunities to experience the satisfaction of contributing to the group life, through which they feel themselves a part of a larger whole. Meeting these basic needs of children, helping them to create a serene inner life and to relate positively to others—this is one of our most important goals.

Group Leadership

Planning a program with these ends in view demands a type of leadership that is far from simple. Between the bed of Procrustes and the planlessness that has been described as "just looking in the children's eyes" there lies a middle course, often difficult to find and to hold. We know there must be content that is based, not only on our understanding of what interests most children, but on the interests of a particular group. As leaders, we must make a plan that grows out of the experience and needs of the group; but hold it in abeyance, rather than impose it, until we know the ideas of the group itself. Then, if the children's plan is better than our own, we must be ready to follow it, using our own experience to help us in adapting it, when necessary, to make it workable, at the same time utilizing the children's enthusiasm, their need to use their powers and their desire to grow up. We can learn to be imaginative about using every possible suggestion, incorporating each one into the whole. A program thus developed out of children's constant participation releases an immense amount of energy.

Sometimes, however, children are not ready for group thinking, and progress is very slow. This may be due to the regimentation of school life, or to over-protection, or lack of opportunity for self-expression at home. Here the leader needs infinite patience, working slowly, awakening interests through the enrichment of the experience and background of the group. Trips, discussions, increasing confidence in self and in the group—all these help. The children themselves give us clues to their own background of knowledge and their spontaneous interests, which we may follow. This calls on us to develop the techniques of discussion. It takes skill to accept each contribution, to use constructively the suggestions of all the children—not just the ablest and most articulate. It calls for self-discipline, if we are not to intervene until the group is ready;

and it demands the courage to stand by decisions that are at variance with our own. When, as leaders, we are co-workers, following a plan worked out by everyone—ourselves included—creative power results. This, held in check by the disciplines that are implicit in a joint enterprise, makes imposed authority unnecessary.

Of course, this ideal situation does not always exist—far from it. But when the plan makes sense to children; when each person can express himself, knowing that his ideas will be treated with respect; when disagreements are resolved through a sharing of opinions and a clear understanding of the issues involved —then we are going in the right direction. Often we fall back on "busy work" because we have not had the courage and patience necessary to work out a program that will provide the quality of living we want. Coloring paper doilies or making paper chains may or may not be busy work, according to the function served, the relatedness to a larger plan. But any job that is artificially created to fill the vacant spaces of a long afternoon should cause us to re-examine our goals for children. Sometimes a quick, relatively easy job gives needed satisfaction to a child. But when the group produces a series of unrelated small objects—often miscalled "creative work"—which do not fit into a broader pattern, we must recognize that we have failed to work out the kind of program that genuinely enlists the energies and abilities of individual children and of the group as a whole. We know that children enjoy hard work when they feel that what they are doing is important, when they identify with it, when they feel necessary to it. They wear themselves out in something significant to them. If we need to prove this to ourselves, we need only recall our own childhood and how we gave all our energies to building a club house, a dam, or a secret hide-away. Nothing is too disagreeable or tiresome for children when the end in view is really important. Their ingenuity and resourcefulness are endless, if adults will keep hands off, giving help only when unforeseen failure may occur. It is well to remember that when we substitute our desires for children's, their interest is killed.

Meeting Individual Needs

Organizing the group to meet individual needs is difficult and demanding. Certain rules must be made by the leader; but these must be reduced to a minimum, limited to the safeguarding of health and safety, and their reason for existence must always be discussed with the children. All other rules should be worked out jointly, as the need arises. This is a time-consuming process. But if we practice the theories of democratic living that we preach, we know that it is not only our obligation but is well worth the effort. It has been said that it is easy to make a Nazi child, but that it takes a long time to develop an American child who will know how to work with others while still retaining the independence that made a Valley Forge possible.

Organization should allow for maximum flexibility within the over-all pattern, in order that grouping may be based on interest, with freedom to move from group to group as jobs are completed, and with acceptance of individual likes and dislikes. Necessity for choice must be consciously provided, with a wide variety of things to do, both easy and difficult, in order that each child, according to his ability, will have a chance to succeed. In organizing, children are often able to see more clearly than we and to make suggestions more practical than our own. Certainly, organization as such should be reduced to the essential minimum necessary for effective group living. This means a clear understanding—an understanding based on their share in responsibility—on the part of the children, about arrangement and care of equipment and materials. They should have a chance to decide on their own jobs, recognizing their relationship to the whole plan. Even very young children are able to choose from among a wide variety of activities, help one another with smocks or aprons, get to work and afterward share in clean-up. With older children, the leader's job of organization is relatively simple if she helps children to fulfill their desire to help. Over and over again we need to strengthen our conviction that the program and its organization are only the framework for children's need for activity, for talk, for laughter and noise, their need to get dirty, their need to strive with one another, their need to experiment and explore, their need to grow.

Children Who Resist

And what about the children who resist? The need to rebel is a part of growing up, to be capitalized on in positive ways. Sometimes, however, it may arise from an inner and unsolved situation that has little connection with the immediate group life; and it helps to remind ourselves that "when a child is most unlovely, he is most in need of love." And what of the child who must always be first? If within the group we have developed a small social structure where co-operation rather than competition is the way of life, there are many chances for leadership for all, so that the need to be first can be partially satisfied. If this urge comes from a deep sense of inadequacy, individual help from the leader, outside of the group, in special skills—playing a game, or using tools or materials—is useful. We have an obligation to know more about each child than can be learned in a group program. Deepening our understanding through learning as much as possible about the many aspects of children's lives is imperative if we are to help them. We need to know parents and to welcome their help, being imaginative about finding ways in which they may share in the program. We must learn to listen to them, instead of telling them. They have known their children far longer than we and understand them better. We need to become acquainted with the school setting and the teachers, to learn about the community in which children live. Only so can we hope to have some understanding of what makes these children as they are and what makes them act as they do.

The problems of most children are the common problems of all human beings. We cannot do individual therapy; that is not our function. We cannot solve children's inner problems, but we can help them to do so by finding as many clues as possible to the causes of difficulty and by setting the stage accordingly. If we have continuously used all of our understanding and ingenuity, all of our insight and common sense, without result, it is our obligation to refer an unhappy child to one of the groups or individuals skilled in the techniques of guidance. Some help from a specialist often serves to solve seemingly insoluble problems of behavior, and through the solution the life of the group as a whole is enhanced.

Play and Growth

We know that the program is merely a framework for our objectives; we know that the content must be planned to meet children's basic emotional needs and urges; we know that leadership is a co-operative venture in which members of the group must have maximum self-direction. But what medium can we find that is applicable to many types of content? Modern children live in a world so confusing, so disconnected, that much of their experience seems unrelated and meaningless. The soundest and surest way of helping children to a sense of unity in their lives is through the medium of play. The urban environment in which many children grow up deprives them of opportunities for play, in its real sense; and we need to make up to them for this lack. In this country, play has been in disrepute since the days of our Puritan forebears. "Haven't you anything better to do than just play?" "Run along and play nicely"—meaning: "Keep clean, keep quiet, and don't disturb me." How often we hear this!

It has been said that "Play in its deepest and broadest sense is the great bridge over which children must pass in order to grow up, to make a satisfactory journey from childhood to adulthood." [1] It is the means by which a child digests and interprets his experiences, begins to understand relationships, and finds his place in his environment. Through play, a child learns about his place in his family, in his neighborhood, in his world; through play, children work out their fears, their loves and hates, their aggressions and confusions. Play in its widest sense makes use of the skills of childhood: painting, construction, dancing, games, rhythms, handwork. If we understand the meaning of play as learning for children, if we believe that it is their way of growing into adult life, then a program genuinely based on the play needs' of children can never slip into the superficiality and insignificance of busy work. We shall think not in terms of "activities" as such, but in terms of growth for individuals and for the group. Activities will become the medium of expression for basic needs and interests, not ends in themselves. We shall not only make opportunities for the development of skills and inner resources, but shall provide experiences that will give children a broader understanding of their world in which they must learn to live. All this needs space and freedom to be active. It needs a variety of equipment and materials. It demands constant growth on the part of the leader. And it brings endless rewards.

"No thing is so powerful as an idea whose time has come." And the time has come when we have the desire and some of the skills to make each of our groups into a functioning democracy, where wholehearted acceptance of each person in his own right and respect for individual differences are made real, and

[1] *School's Out,* by Clara Lambert and other staff members of the Play Schools Association, New York. Harper & Brothers, 1944.

where each unique contribution is used for the good of all. There is no better laboratory for the improvement of human understanding and human relations than group work with children.

PRINCIPLES AND PROBLEMS IN WORK WITH YOUNG ADULTS *By Laura Ault*

THERE is nothing esoteric about group work with young adults. Its aims and objectives, its techniques and methods are fundamentally those of group work in general. Any differences in program or emphasis are due to the basic social factors characterizing young adults—that group in our population between 18 and 35 years of age. A look at these social factors will reveal the origin of the principles governing, and the problems arising in, work with this group of constituency.

Foremost among these factors is employment. The largest group in any young adult program are the young workers, and that fact has a great deal to do with the kind of program offered them. What they do the eight hours a day they are on the job determines to a large degree what they need in their leisure time activities. The group worker needs to be aware of many facts about the jobs his constitutents do: whether they are monotonous, routine jobs or ones which call for some initiative or creativity; whether the jobs build up tensions or release them; whether they give the young worker any sense of importance or make him a mere cog in the wheels of industry. The staff member must know whether the jobs pay enough to give the young people an adequate living, including provisions for health, what hours and shifts they work, whether there are plenty of jobs for all seeking them, or whether the young adult finds his race or nationality or limited skills a restrictive factor in getting a job; whether the place where he works is unionized and if he knows how to function actively in that union to keep it a democratic institution. The staff member needs to be conscious of the caste system which exists in the job world and know how it affects the organization and the interaction of groups.

Marriage and Courtship

A second factor relating to young adults is that they are of the courtship age. Need I say that is an important fact? The group worker must know the marriage patterns among the nationality and economic groups with which he is working. He must be conscious of the effect of the larger social scene upon the attitudes of the group toward marriage such as the hasty marriages, the increased promiscuity and general lowering of standards of relationships between the sexes which result from the strains of separation and the uncertain future facing young people in wartime; the implications of the delayed marriages in times of economic recession.

The fact that most of the participants in a young adult program are of voting age is an additional one of which the group worker must be conscious. What help do his constituents need to be informed, effective citizens? Do they know what political democracy really means and how to be articulate about it and defend it against competing ideologies? In this atomic age, it is not good enough for an agency working with young adults to provide only recreation; we cannot dodge our responsibility for helping young people make their contribution as intelligent, participating citizens.

Another social factor characterizing young adults is their actual or desired emancipation from their families. Large numbers of them have left home in search of a job that interests them. They need guidance as they reject the old familiar mores and try to adapt themselves to new ones. They have to work out new moral values and a new pattern of social behavior. They frequently lose touch with the church they had known in their childhood and adolescent days. They have to learn how to live on the money they make and most of them need help on budgeting. Many of them come from the farms to the city for employment and have to make the great adjustment to urban life.

Cultural Gaps

Those young people who continue to live at home are not free from problems. They often feel that a measure of financial independence should warrant more freedom from family rules and regulations. In some nationality groups in particular, the gap between the social patterns of the older and younger generations is widened as the young people move out into the working world and form new associations and acquire new ideas. This clash between cultures is not absent for the adolescent, but it is intensified for the young adult as he goes to work, for most often he departs further from his neighborhood for a job than he did for school and usually works with a group which is less homogeneous in nationality and age. The young person finds a conflict of loyalties to his new associates and to his family resulting at times in personality maladjustments with which the agency must deal.

What do all these factors say to the organization offering program with young adults? What principles of operation do they reveal? First of all, they have some bearing on the kind of groupings used in the agency. Occupation, economic status, social homogeneity for purposes of courtship become important considerations for finding a basis for grouping. The degree of organizational consciousness among young people varies with their social and economic level. So the group worker must understand the habits of participation of people at various levels of society. Recreation leaders in war workers' housing projects along the west coast, for example, found that the idea of a committee was more foreign to a girl from the backwoods of the south than the intricacies of indoor plumbing! The most successful groupings allow for a measure of congeniality in the group but also for some upward social mobility. Most young people want fellowship with their own kind but they also want to "progress!"

Small Club Groups

The degree of intimacy implied by size or type of activity influences the variety of social differences which can be included in a group. Thus a second principle for group work agencies indicated by these social factors is the need for variety in the kind of activities offered. Small club groups are usually very homogeneous in their membership, and they form an important part of our program. The chairman of our YWCA National Industrial Council said to us recently that what industrial workers want is status, security, and knowledge and a chance to talk over their problems. Small club groups are ideal for those purposes. They are good for the person who works alone, such as a household employee, who needs the fellowship they offer as a place where she can feel important.

But for many young adults adjustment is easier in a large mass group which is less highly organized. If these, perchance, are co-ed dance groups, the agency may need more than one of them if its constituency is varied, for in any co-educational program the courtship drive is always present and there cannot be too wide a range of social and economic status in the group. Then, because the interest span of young people varies, there need to be short-term as well as ongoing, continuous activities. Because others are seeking new skills, we need the class type of activity or the special interest program such as an arts and crafts workshop or an outing club or a little theater group. If we are concerned with interracial or intercultural integration, programs of that sort are needed, too, for again experience has proven that such integration takes place more readily in activities where there is less social interaction. They help create the atmosphere which makes integration on the next step of more highly organized groups more possible.

Program Content

The third principle we learn from these social factors descriptive of young adults is that variety is needed in content of program as well as in organizational form. If they are young workers, is there anything in our programs that helps them to understand the economic order of which they are a part? Anything that will help them acquire more vocational skills or vocational guidance? Anything that will help them to live on the money they make? Do we know the health hazards of various occupations and build our program of health education with them in mind? Do we know what kind of physical recreation people who work at certain kinds of jobs need? If we are helping to plan program with a group of young workers who sit all day at their jobs, do we see that what is planned doesn't keep them sitting all night in our agency clubrooms?

Co-ed Activities

If they are of marrying age, what does that mean for our program? Certainly it means co-ed activities where young people of both sexes can meet each other. It means more than dances, too. Compatibility in dance steps might be an asset in a happy marriage, but it is not the most basic one! Perhaps the only things some young people know to do together for recreation are dancing, the movies, or riding in automobiles. We need to introduce them to the out-of-doors, frequently, which means taking our program out of our buildings. We need to teach them skills in the kind of sports they can enjoy together—tennis, golf, riding, badminton—rather than stressing competitive sports in our program and more "spectatoritis" in our constituents. We even need to help young people discover it is fun and stimulating to think together and talk over the questions that affect their lives. We need to include some good, sound programs of education for marriage.

If they are struggling to work out new patterns of behavior, our program and our buildings must be attractive enough to compete with the glitter of commercial recreation. We need to provide them good program in the fields of psychology and personality development and family relations and religion. We must include in our program some opportunity for creative self-expression and enlargement of their cultural appreciations. Certainly if we are going to help young people become effective citizens, we have to give them more than a chance to conduct a club meeting; we have to have some content in those meetings that will give them a sound basis of information for direct social action.

Self-Government

The last principle I would like to enunciate is that these young people need an opportunity for leadership and for developing their own policies as well as their program. If they are adults in their own minds, they want to be treated as adults, and we have to help them set up the mechanisms for self-government. We need councils for inter-group planning and for widening the chances for interaction of various economic and social groupings. We need to make it possible for them to function as responsible young people and I might point out that it is a bit difficult to encourage them to act as responsible citizens in the larger community if we do not give them the opportunity to do so within our agencies. If they are going to be interested in voting for the City Council, they should have the chance to vote for the Board of Directors of their agency; if they are going to see the necessity for voting on the propositions on the state ballot, it will help them if they have had some practice in voting on policies within their own organization; if they are going to have an interest in how government works, it is easier to demonstrate it if they have an opportunity to serve on the policy-making bodies in their agencies and learn in a small way what representative government means.

Work with young adults is not simple. Its problems are varied and numerous, so numerous it is difficult to know which one to single out first for attention. Perhaps one might begin with the fact that those of us who have worked with young adults know the job is not a sinecure but the community at large does not appreciate that fact. Where good interpretation has not been done, they do not see the need for the program and are inclined to think that young people are old enough to run their own program and that professional staff members to work with them are an unnecessary luxury. The only way around that one is more and better interpretation.

Related to that problem is the fact that there are not enough trained staff to work with this age group. Part of that is our fault in not providing the schools of social work with good recorded data to use as teaching material for training staff to work with young adults. Also, too few workers now in our agencies are equipped to supervise field work students in young adult programs. We are the only ones who can do something about that and we need to do it now and everlastingly.

Broadening Out

A third problem is the tendency for our agencies to attract only one status group. We need to attract and recruit young people across class and caste lines if we are going to create understanding and contribute to a richer whole. We must be aware that working on this problem will in itself create new ones. If, for example, we have been attracting largely a nice, well-behaved middle class group, and go out to recruit some upper lower class young people, we may find ourselves running into some difficulties in interpreting their different patterns of behavior. The new group is apt to be noisier, harder on the furnishings, cruder in their speech, to prefer beer to the "Unspiked" fruit punch, to smoke where they are not supposed to. But if we have the wisdom to handle these social situations, we will find that the group has also brought a refreshing new point of view, a frankness in discussion, a reality and "down-to-earthiness" that was missing before. If we want to thus broaden the base of our constituency, it means an examination of our recruiting techniques and publicity. It also means we need to look at our building, its furnishings (Are they too drab and staid?) and its location. Should we investigate the possibility of decentralized program? Is transportation a problem? Would we reach a wider variety of constituents if we took our program to where they live or work? Or is the lure of downtown always so great with young adults that only a downtown center will attract them?

Leadership Participation

Another problem we need to consider is how we set up channels for leadership participation. Do we sometimes push young people too rapidly into membership on intergroup councils or agency committees before they have had enough experience in leadership in more homogeneous groups because we are desirous of having these intergroup councils "cross section" in their nature? Do we sometimes get too many wheels within wheels or do we have too few channels for ideas and opinions to travel through our agencies? Do we have good organization for this among our constituency groups but not enough between constituency and adult lay leadership?

Then there are the problems in the area of program. The fact that a young person earns his living does not automatically make him interested in workers' education; or that he is old enough to vote in itself make him eager to fulfill his responsibilities as a citizen; or that the world is full of problems which his generation is going to have to solve or suffer make him desirous of thinking them through. Too often the young worker says, "I work hard all day; I don't want to think all night"; or the young voter says, "Oh, what does it matter who gets elected? They'll do what they want anyway and we'll have to pay the taxes." We want them to help plan their own program, but they have grown so used to the pattern of authority at home where their parents told them what to do, at school where the teacher did, on the job where the boss does, that they want us to do the deciding of what their program should be. Then at last they do make a decision—whether to take it or leave it! All of these situations are typical and can only be met by imagination, creativity and sensitivity to people and their moods on the part of the program director.

Social Action

Fortunately, many times there is a different reaction to program. Young people *do* get interested in their work problems and want to discuss trade unionism which sometimes disturbs some of the agency's patrons. Or they get excited about campaign issues and want to take an active part in political action, and this annoys the partisans of the side for whom they are *not* ringing doorbells. Or they decide if they are going to have to live in a world that is one, they should have some ideas and knowledge about foreign policy and to this the isolationists object. And all of the objectors tend to direct their criticisms to the whole agency, not to just the part of it which took the action.

There's more to this problem than that. When you get excited about saving the world, you want to get other people doing it with you, so our groups go out and line themselves up with Youth Councils in the city, or send delegates to World Youth Conferences. And when they begin to get really interested in social action of any kind, they have a magnetic attraction for other young people with definitely left-wing viewpoints, and Communist infiltration is no easy matter to handle if you are congenitally opposed to red-baiting.

Autonomy of Groups

What do you do about all these situations? I am no Answer Man but I have a few suggestions. First of all, you are genuinely glad you have these problems to deal with. The organization whose members never get into hot water are the dull ones! Then you keep a clear head and don't get rattled for these are the situations where procedures need to be well thought through. Those procedures should include a carefully developed agency policy on the autonomy of groups which has been developed jointly by constituency and older lay leaders. Then the staff member should be aware of the political mores of the community and give guidance to the young people in working in the light of these rather than flaunting them. He needs to train his young people in political astuteness and help them to be articulate about their own points of view so that the only spokesmen for the group are not the ones with ultra-liberal inclinations. He needs to be aware of the various techniques for social action; you don't always have to circulate petitions! Most of all he needs to be constantly at work in interpreting the thinking of the young people to the older adults in the agency and in bringing the two groups along together in their thinking or at least continuously informed of each other's points of view, so that crises will not be crises—or if they are, that they will not be catastrophes.

Work with young adults may not be simple, but it rarely is dull!

AN EXPERIENCE IN PROGRAMMING FOR
UNMARRIED YOUNG ADULTS OVER
25 YEARS OF AGE   *By Emanuel Tropp*

MUCH has been written in recent years of the special challenge presented in working with young adults in a group work agency. The experience described in this paper deals with the general category of young adults, but focuses primarily on single people over twenty-five years of age and up to about thirty-five. It is based upon four successive years of unusual growth in the development of a group and a program service, and it may have some implications for methods of operation in working with young adults in other settings. The experience took place in a Jewish Community Center in a middle-sized New England community. It was in the second year of the life of this activity that the writer became aware of something unique taking place in the process of this particular group experience. However, more time and experience was needed to validate this development, and the succeeding two years have been so rewarding that the first impression has been amply confirmed; namely, that this group's history has real significance for structure and method in programming with young adults, and possibly with other age groups.

"Club 25," as this activity was known, had its beginnings as a planning committee which met several times a month to organize a major social function one Sunday each month for all interested single young people over 25 years of age. It was started as a center-sponsored activity, in order to meet the needs of an age group that was not being served—a group that was not equated socially with the younger "young adults" nor with the general adult community. It was frankly motivated at first by the need to meet members of the opposite sex and possibly find a mate.

It was not actually a club in the usual sense, in that it did not have a membership as such nor membership meetings. There was simply a planning committee of about ten young men and women (nearly all women) and a monthly social gathering to which large numbers of local people of similar age, and many from nearby communities, came for the social contacts indicated. There were no dues and therefore no treasury. The center budget allocated a sum for program expenses and also showed an expected receipt of income from the dances. A staff advisor worked closely with the committee.

In its first year, this plan worked out fairly well. The active members of the committee were satisfied with the success of the dances, and these affairs were apparently meeting a real need of a hitherto unserved age group. In the second year of its existence, this "group" began to develop difficulties. Attendance at planning committee meetings became weak, and the committee members were expressing such thoughts as "we're tired of being the only ones who work for these affairs—sure they are good, but why should we always be stuck with the work." Actually it was a very weak group, both in numbers and in leadership potential, and the staff advisor (a graduate student in social group work) found himself "running the program" by default.

Not satisfied with this situation, the staff person began to draw more new people into the planning committee. He brought to a head the matter of electing officers, which the few original members had been delaying for fear of having more responsibility. He brought to their attention the need for regular bi-weekly meetings to give the group a greater sense of structure and continuity. *And, most important of all, he sensed that this was a group that found "business" and "planning" an insufficient reward for coming to the center on the evenings required.*

One week, the advisor asked the committee—which was now

becoming more of a "group"—how they would like to learn to play canasta at the next meeting. This gesture in the direction of program for the "committee" itself turned out to have more far-reaching significance than could possibly have been imagined at the time. By way of process, it was actually the key turning point in the development of "Club 25." The advisor taught canasta after the meeting that week; everyone was delighted and asked to have it continued next time. They also suggested refreshments to make it more congenial, and this was later approved as a center expenditure since the dances were producing enough income to more than cover the costs.

At successive meetings, canasta was followed by bridge, then party games. Refreshments were served by a sub-committee (a function that was a pleasure). New faces were attracted to these meetings. "Business" became interesting, even challenging. "We have a good club here and we want to plan dances worthy of our name." Yes, it had become a club—and through this strangely simple process, it also became an increasingly strong and effective "planning committee" for the monthly big events. Holding an office had meaning now, and prestige, and business meetings were important. Even those who came to join in the jolly social atmosphere that had been created, learned to find interest in the business and eventually to join the now-expanding sub-committee structure: program (for dances *and meetings*), refreshments, publicity, and others.

The membership was now about 25, with almost an equal number of young men and women. By this time, program planning *for meetings* had become an important consideration. A student from Israel, who was temporarily staying in the community, was invited to talk to the club about life in that land, and so much interest was created that this discussion carried over for three meetings. A friend of one of the members, talented along dramatic lines, presented several monologues at another meeting (and then decided to become a regular member). The interest and enthusiasm now generated in club meetings was carried over into a strong loyalty in making the monthly dances more successful.

Members visited other social functions in order to personally advertise their own affairs. Contacts with newspaper columnists were made. Programs by similar organizations were "scouted" to see if they were worth presenting locally. As a result, the dances became so well attended that they gained a very popular reputation. This, too, resulted in increased pride and loyalty on the part of members and a greater sense of the values of being a club member.

The programs at dances have been mentioned, and deserve some description. Actually a pattern had been formed, which consisted of hiring an entertainer (on a small budget) who provided about 30 minutes of program. The entertainers were usually humorists, with the occasional introduction of a variant such as a folk-singer. This was followed by dancing to records and the serving of simple refreshments. This pattern appears to have been hit upon for sound reasons, although perhaps unwittingly. Many of the people attending the dances did not get an opportunity to dance much, and some not at all. To attend a dance and sit the evening out without having danced can be a bitterly disappointing kind of experience. But to have joined with others in observing an entertainer means that part of the evening has been shared on an equal basis, and even at worst, the latter part of the evening can be spent discussing the program.

This second season ended on a high note of optimism, and elections took place for officers for the following year. This time there was an eagerness to serve, and a sense of importance attached to being elected to office in a successful organization. As the third year began, a number of the officers began to wonder whether they should form an organization that would not be dependent upon center support and financing.

They felt that there was something wrong in not being an independent body which could have its own treasury and would not be required to have policy matters "cleared with the center" through a staff advisor.

At this point, the problem was not directly dealt with by the staff, and it seemed to resolve itself with an informal understanding that it was best to stay on under the same arrangement. However, later in the season the heart of the matter came out into the open and required direct handling.

When the first dance of the season drew a tremendous crowd, and it became apparent that a good deal of money was being taken in and turned over to the center, the same members who were previously concerned about independence started to express resentment that the center was profiting from the hard work of the club. There were important matters of policy and procedure involved that had no precedent in the center, and therefore were beyond the scope of a new part-time worker to handle with the group. The program director arranged to visit the next meeting for a complete discussion of this problem. Before that, he had a full discussion with the executive director concerning the implications for the center in the matters of budget and the nature of sponsored activities.

First, it had to be recognized that the dances were bringing in sizable sums of money, even after all expenses were deducted (including the semi-monthly refreshments at meetings). On the other hand, there were hidden expenses which did not show budget-wise, but would become apparent if the club became an independent organization. As a center activity, there was no expense shown for room rentals, dance hall rentals, printing and postage. As a separate organization, such expenses would be mandatory and would, in effect, wipe out the "profits." However, was this the only approach to be offered to the members? Would it be better, after explaining this structure, to offer the group the privilege of earmarking the balance shown each year in their part of the budget, for some worthwhile center cause, such as day camp scholarships or building improvements? Would this better satisfy the needs of the members for achieving a place of importance which they truly deserved? It was agreed that this latter plan would be best. However, suppose the club did want to become independent —was it sound to hold this development back, or would it be better for the group to take this step? Staff felt that, although it would encourage the club to make a free and democratic decision, there were many values in having this activity continue to receive staff assistance.

And so, this plan was brought to the club—and it met with an immediate and warm response. The members were delighted at the opportunity to add "community service" to their achievements, by way of raising funds for scholarships. With this arrangement, there was also offered the authority of the club to decide its own financial matters, without having to "check" for approval for each expenditure. The understanding was that the concern of the club for raising the maximum amount for scholarships would become the conscience in determining how much to spend for refreshments or for entertainers. These changes were so satisfying that the matter of independent organization became academic and unimportant. In practice this plan worked out very well as time went on. Having the privilege of determining expenditures became a heavy burden, and the officers, no longer in the position of claiming financial restriction from the center, tended now to come to staff to ask for approval for fear of taking too much responsibility in spending money.

With this problem in center relationships out of the way, the club settled down to its program for the year—and this was the year to mark the most remarkable expansion. First, a number of the members began to express dissatisfaction with the name "Club 25." It so happened that a few of the active members were under 25, and some of those who were over 25 thought that there was no satisfaction in constantly being reminded of this fact. By common agreement, the name was left as a question ("?") in correspondence until a better one could be chosen. No other name was ever found, and the group remained "Club Question Mark" to this day.

Ambitious and optimistic, the club members decided to carry on sub-group activities in addition to meetings every other week and dances once a month. When the program director heard of their plans to start a dramatic group, bridge group, music appreciation group, and conversational Hebrew group all at once, he was frankly concerned about their ability to take on such a widespread program. However, the club turned out to have the vitality to carry out every single objective and, in one respect, to far surpass even their own daring expectations. The bridge group met in homes and thrived, with average attendance of 15 to 20. The music group also used private homes and produced even a larger following (although there was overlapping enrollment in the various sub-groups). The Hebrew class met at the center under a competent instructor, and had a small but steady following. The dramatic group was a development so truly "dramatic" that it is a story in itself.

In all of these sub-groups new members were brought in, and this in turn strengthened the club as a whole, so that club meetings were now busy, hectic occasions with 40 to 50 people attending. One of the new people brought in, had been sought out not as a member, but as a leader for the dramatic group, since she had some training and experience along these lines. This sub-group started with the simple intention of trying to prepare a few skits that could be produced for meetings. This was soon accomplished, to the entertainment and amazement of both members-at-large and the actors themselves. "Bigger game" was next in line—preparing a one-acter for the program of one of the monthly dances. Again, the dramatic group scored.

The other members seemed to catch the enthusiasm of this sub-group and it started to grow. "What about putting on a real production?" was the next question, and soon plans were set for the casting of "The Man Who Came to Dinner." Again, new faces were introduced to the club, including some talented actors, who had previously been members of a now-defunct drama group at the center (which, through lack of vitality, had disappeared from the scene). Over 25 people were involved in the cast and backstage work, and soon the entire club had an interest and stake in the success of "their" production. The event was actively promoted, a good advance sale of tickets was achieved, and the rehearsals brought about a wonderful new morale.

The play was a great success, well produced and well attended. The club had produced more than just another sub-group—it now had a large "Jewish Community Playhouse" on its hands as a going institution. The role of one individual figured very largely in the growth of this activity, and that was the dramatics leader, who possessed a combination of personal characteristics that spelled a kind of natural leadership capable of welding the group into an effective dramatic organization. Interestingly, a new part-time staff advisor this year played a passive role in his relationship with the club and its natural leaders.

Toward the end of the third year, proud of having an organization capable of such important accomplishments and more than ever interested in "community service," the club voted to increase the admission price to its dances so as to raise more money for the camp scholarship goal. The season was brought to a close in the flush of success, with a formal occasion provided for recognition at the center's annual meeting, when the president of the club officially presented a check for several hundred dollars to the center president for the scholarship fund. Still further recognition was granted when the club was invited to select a delegate to serve on the board of directors of the center.

During the fourth season, the pattern and structure of operation has continued in a similar vein. The volunteer dramatics leader has become a member of the staff, serving as Playhouse director and staff consultant with the club. There have been some variations in sub-group activities. A modern dance group and a current events discussion group have become the latest interests. Occasional week-end winter sports outings have been organized with a fine response. New members have been attracted as some old members drop out, and some attention has had to be paid to developing new leadership and committee personnel. Basically, however, the club is continuing along the same lines.

Looking back upon this experience, the writer tried to examine the implications for young adult activity generally, and possibly for other age groupings as well. Was this phenomenon peculiar to this particular age group? Did it depend upon a fortunate combination of circumstances in this particular setting at this particular time? Or did it find an important answer to the method of organization of activities?

In this light, certain problems might be considered:

a. It may be that this age group has needs that are more clearly expressed, interests that are more definitely established or easily formed, and personal lives less subjected to such immediate stresses as military service. However, this could hardly be the only key to the growth of the club described in this paper, since this group was on the verge of dissolving, *in a different pattern of organization.*

b. It might be maintained that a very effective staff advisor simply used his skills to develop more satisfying group participation. However, the facts show that the club reached the height of its operations during the following season, when a different staff advisor played a negligible role. Thus although the original staff "catalyst" did make a fine contribution, staff leadership did not appear to be the only factor in the continuation and further development of the club.

c. In our center, as in other group work agencies, a considerable portion of the programming on various youth levels has been accomplished through the medium of lounge committees, planning councils, etc. In the present experience, it was found that *the structure of a planning committee did not provide sufficient satisfaction to the members involved;* as a result, very little identification or loyalty was established.

In conclusion, it is hoped that these experiences may indicate the great opportunity for program service in group work agencies to single young adults in the "over twenty-five" category. Perhaps, too, there are indications that in working on a "planning" level with youth, young adults and possibly even adults, a certain amount of group satisfaction other than pure business may be valuable and even essential in order for the group to survive and grow.

THE OLD CRONIES *By Sidney Shapiro*

THE Old Cronies is one of the social clubs sponsored by the Group Work Department of the Friends Neighborhood Guild—a settlement located in the Poplar area of Philadelphia. The area, bordering on Philadelphia's famed "Skid Row," is high in disease, vice, poverty, mobility, delinquency, low-standard housing and social disorganization.

During my year of work with them, the Old Cronies had nineteen members on roll and an average weekly attendance of about fifteen members. They ranged in age from sixty to eighty-seven. Three or four of the men were married and lived with their wives in one or two rooms. All of the others were single men, mostly widowed, although some were bachelors and one was a divorcee. They lived in single rooms in missions, rooming houses, and overnight "hotels." Their club had been in existence for six years.

Except for a few dollars earned through some odd job, most of the men received their total income from one or more kinds of relief, including Old Age Assistance, Blind Pension, and Aid to the Physically Handicapped. They "saved" money by getting haircuts at the Veterans' Barber School, and by utilizing clinics of university dental and medical schools.

There were three Negroes in the group; the rest were white. About two-thirds of them were born outside of the United States, and many of them born elsewhere in this country just seemed to have "landed" in Philadelphia somehow. The majority of their time was spent listening to the radio, walking the streets, attending Missions, or just sitting in their rooms.

At least seven or eight of these members required crutches or canes. Many had audio and visual incapacities. For most, motor activity was considerably slow, and many suffered cardio-vascular difficulties.

There were two basic concepts of the social group work method that gave me direction as I constantly tested them in my work with the Old Cronies.

1. All people can grow and change—older adults as well as those in younger age groups.

2. There are dynamics for helping in the present reality of the group meeting.

I was able to acquire a beginning understanding of where this group was after a general discussion about the group with its previous leader, and my first meeting with them on the seventh of October.

About 2:30 I went into the lounge. Mr. Rose, last year's leader, introduced me to the members whom I did not know. All except Mr. King and Mr. Rutherford were playing dominoes very avidly. Mr. Rutherford spent most of the time at the piano singing, while Miss March, a staff member, played. Mr. King looked at magazines and then began telling me what he felt the club needed to do this year right away. "First of all, we have to get a camera." . . . I suggested to him that this was something that the group could discuss, and that he might bring it up. Mr. Rose and I prepared the refreshments, and just before we put them out, Mr. Young asked me if we could have a moment's silence ". . . for our departed brethren before we eat." I suggested he mention it to the group. He asked if I would get the group's attention for him to do this, and I said I would.

Though there was activity in this group, there was little that might be termed, "group activity." Rather, the first meeting of the Old Cronies in this program year was characterized by activities that were carried on by two or three men in various parts of the room. There seemed to be a minimum of group bond or "we-feeling," even considering the fact that this was a first meeting. In fact, most of the men were not familiar with the names of the other group members, despite the fact that they had been meeting together for some years.

The group had previously carried minimum responsibility in the meeting for the activities that took place in connection with games or food. This was consonant with their general activities in life; this dependency was also consistent with what the community expected of them in light of their social and economic position.

Recognizing the nature of this group at this time, what was there that I, as the worker, could deal with in their present experience that they could use to begin to find strength to help themselves? With my deep belief in the capacity and responsibility of people to share in their growth experiences, I was able to begin to formulate a focus in working with this group.

The worker begins with the group at their point of readiness. I identified five basic areas in which I felt the group might begin to assume more responsibility for group activities.

From the first meeting I felt that three of their activities— buying, preparing and serving refreshments, taking out and putting away the games, and buying the newspaper for their club meeting had enough meaning to the group members so that the members could, with help, begin gradually to share in the responsibilities connected with them. I noted that staff persons went to the outside door to open it for the members. It seemed to me that this, too, might be a logical spot wherein a particular member might function adequately.

There was one other interesting area. I had met the crippled men previous to the meeting and had arranged to pick them up. When I arrived at their homes, I went into each house, knocked on the door, and then waited for them to come out to the station wagon. It is especially important in work with the physically disabled to help them use the strengths that they do possess, rather than viewing their physical dependency in a total sense. With these men, I felt that they might well be responsible for being outside at a prearranged time, or in the hallway in inclement weather.

It was within the course of the next five or six weeks that the foci established at this beginning point, together with other program opportunities that arose within the group, were utilized by the Old Cronies to begin to discover within themselves their capacities for achievement.

At the following meeting a suggestion was made that the group acquire a camera. When I raised questions regarding the uses that would be made of the camera, they utilized this discussion to formulate their first program.

Mr. Kent said they might have a Halloween party. This brought smiles from the group. I enthusiastically said that this sounded like a wonderful idea. Mr. Franklin said that Mr. Rose, the former worker, had decorations for Halloween. I said I would check into it. I said that this would probably take more preparation than this meeting, and Mr. Kent suggested having the party in two weeks and having preparations next week. Everyone readily agreed.

In the meeting of 10/21/52, use of the marginal interview during the initial part of the meeting was effective in their movement toward beginning acceptance of responsibility for refreshments and games, and for future planning.

10/21/52   15 members present

Instead of putting out all of the games and papers this week, I opened the box and asked who was playing dominoes today. Mr. Young and Mr. King walked over to the box and began putting out the dominoes and checkers. I mentioned to Mr. Este that I had copies of the "Digest" this week, along with other magazines, and he came over and took out the magazines and displayed them on the table.

The group played dominoes and read and talked until 2:30. During that time, I talked with the rest of the members who were not involved in the games, and specifically with Mr. Randall, discussing the closeness of the national election. He went on to analyze the parties and their relative strengths. I said that maybe the group could have their own mock election and see how closely they came to the national results. He smiled, saying that might be a good idea. I left it there. With some of the others I discussed our forthcoming Halloween party. At 2:30 (earlier than usual) I brought down the refreshments. I lined up all of the coffee and cake at one end of the table, and rather than giving it out said, "Are we ready for refreshments?" Everyone agreed, and I said, "They're all ready." Mr. Este, who was sitting at the near end of the table, began passing them down and pretty soon, a few more people began to follow suit, and they passed out all of the refreshments. . . .

. . . I took a cup of coffee and sat down, asking if anyone would like a second cup. Mr. Kent said that he would, and so did Mr. El-gart. Mr. Zorch was standing across the table from me. I asked him if he would like to get them a second cup. "How about being a waiter, Mr. Zorch?" He hesitatingly walked over to the end of the table, and then looked back puzzled, to me. I explained how to use the powdered coffee, and he asked if that was all there was to it, and then said, "This is something new," and with a big grin, "I'll try it." He did, and with a beam of satisfaction, went around the table, all smiles, asking who else would have seconds. After filling about five requests, he smiled at me, saying, "I'm the waiter." I said he certainly was, and a good one, too.

I asked what preparations we had for our party next week. Mr. Este asked if the agency would provide the masks. I said that I hadn't thought about that, nor did I know if the agency even had masks. There was a moment of silence as the members pondered this problem. I said maybe we could improvise. Mr. Franklin said that we could use paper bags and crayon them. Mr. Rush added that we could use handkerchiefs, like bandits. Everyone started getting his own ideas, and the group agreed that this was good.

Again, in discussing supplies that were needed for the Halloween party, the immediate response was to turn to the agency for them. It was not until I questioned this that the members even thought of turning to themselves to meet their own needs. At the same meeting, the group attested to the validity of the committee structure and used its results for future planning.

I told the group that we were ready for a report of the committee which went to see about the camera. Mr. Young spoke for the committee, telling the group that the executive director had said that for the party he would take pictures, and that for the outings the Guild had a camera which they were going to overhaul, which the club could borrow. This brought a round of applause, cheers and banging on the table from them. I said, "This is what happens when you set up a committee, and the committee does the work. Everyone benefits in the group." I was trying to use this for something later in the meeting. I asked how we were going to get the refreshments. After a little hesitation, Mr. Young said, "The sponsor (leader) usually brings it with him to the party, and then we have it." I said that I could do that, but I wondered if, like the camera, we couldn't have a committee to go with me in the station wagon and get the refreshments, and decide what we should buy. I said I could buy it, but that it was their club, and I thought they might like to decide what they ate. I asked if anyone would like to help me. Mr. King said, "Not me." I smiled, saying that was one who didn't want to go, was there anyone who might like to go? Mr. Young said he would like to go if someone else also went. I asked Mr. Kent if he would like to go . . . he seemed to be wanting to say so, but looked as though he might need support. He beamed saying, "I sure would." The third volunteer was Mr. English, who said that because of his legs, he had trouble. When I clarified the station wagon situation, he agreed.

I said that I could leave the decorations at the lounge before I left with the food committee. I remained silent after this, and the group did also for a moment, until Mr. King said, "If someone else helps, I'll do the decorations." I said that that sounded like a good idea, and in an attempt to lessen the risks, I put in a few concrete suggestions as to how they might decorate. Mr. Dixon said he could come early. I said that we now had one person holding the crepe paper, and another pulling it to the other side, but that we needed someone in the middle to hold it up. Mr. Zorch laughed (he is short), saying, "If you get me a ladder, I'll hold it up." This made three on the decorations committee. I asked what they would do at the party. There was hesitation and silence.

I asked if they would like Miss March to come in and play. All agreed. I asked what they would like to do besides sing. Mr. King said, "Let's try to bob for apples." I saw some concern on the faces of some of the cripples, and I said that we could do this while sitting down, with our hands behind us, and a dish on the table. When Mr. Franklin agreed, I knew it was good, and the members agreed. Mr. Rush asked about "Pin the Donkey." I said that was good, and turned in Mr. O'Reilly's direction (he is blind), asking how that was.

He smiled, hesitatingly, saying, "Okay." I asked if we should have music. Mr. Franklin said to put Mr. Este in charge. I asked the group how they felt about this, and all agreed, saying he knew a lot about music. I reread the committee assignments and arranged to meet with the refreshment group about 12:00. Mr. King picked up on this, saying that the decoration committee should meet about 1:30.

Here, too, I laid stress on their right of determination in selecting what they would have at their party. I let them know that I, as the worker, might well do this for them, but pointed out the choice and decision that was theirs if they chose to accept the responsibility that went along with it. In Mr. English's case, it was necessary to put in additional support with the use of the station wagon, without denying his capacity to contribute in spite of his physical infirmity. Following this discussion, the effects of the interview with Mr. Randall began to take form.

I said that a few minutes ago, Mr. Randall and I had been discussing the election and the possibility of having a mock vote. There were smiles, and additional suggestions came quickly to include a speaker for each party, followed by a panel discussion and then, the vote. Everyone started imitating political orators, and Mr. Franklin said, "I'll bet the way we vote will be the same as the election comes out."

At the end of this meeting, the group took initiative in two additional areas.

I asked the group if there was anyone other than myself who might buy the newspaper for the club meeting. I said the agency would pay for it. Mr. Randall said that he always bought a paper on Tuesday, and could get an extra one for the members; and that he could afford the nickel. He said that he could buy the paper and still eat. Mr. Randall is on public assistance and lives in a mission house. . . .

. . . As everyone was getting on his coat, and reminding each other about committee assignments, I started to take the dishes upstairs. Mr. King and Mr. Dixon, who were standing nearby, saw that it would take two trips up the steps. They each took something (an empty kettle and a large plate) and started up the steps. With the dishes in my hand, I went last, standing in back of them in case of a possible accident, and they had no trouble at all. They came down saying, "Now it only required one trip." I said they were really very helpful, and I sincerely appreciated their efforts.

I believe it was the atmosphere engendered by their successful experience in acquiring the camera, and their assumption of responsibilities in regard to the party that motivated Mr. King and Mr. Dixon to think of helping with the dishes. At the end of this meeting, when I took the crippled men home, they were filled with comments about, "The club's doing things." It was during this conversation that I discussed with them the possibilities of having them meet me in front of their homes. They generally agreed to do this "because we'll be able to spend more time at the meeting," but raised some question about what would happen if they were not there when I came by. I told them that if they were not there, I could blow the horn, and if they were not ready, I might go up and knock, anyhow. This conversation ended in joking about the various kinds of signals I could give them on the horn of the station wagon. Since that time, the members have waited outside, or have responded to the horn. Periodically Mr. Franklin was quite sick and not able to make it, in which instances I always went up for him. It was this kind of support, of knowing that the worker would assume responsibility *if they could not* that enabled them to increase their own potential investment.

In some cases, it was necessary for the worker to be especially careful in gauging the amount of risk that the members should take. With older adults this is particularly true in regard to physical risks because of their generally declining motor and reflex ability. This was the case during the time just before the next meeting, when Mr. King and Mr. Dixon were decorating the meeting room for their Halloween party.

I permitted and encouraged as much creativity as possible, by just bringing in all the decoration materials and letting them carry it from that point. This action on my part—this trust in their capacity—was evidenced by Mr. King who said, "You leave it to us; just get us a six-foot ladder and we'll take care of the rest." While I wanted to be consistent in manifesting my belief in their ability, I had to distinguish between the risk of Mr. King's request for a six-foot ladder and the two-foot bench which I finally did bring in. I believed, further, that Mr. King, with his tendency to over-estimate his capacities, welcomed this limit to help him realistically assess his abilities.

The shopping trip with Mr. Kent and Mr. Young provided further opportunity for the members of this group, with the worker's help, to utilize strengths and abilities which they had, if the avenues of experimentation were open to them.

> I suggested several self-service markets, with the thought that this *type* of store would give them a chance to look around and change their mind if necessary, without the pressure of the storekeeper asking what they wanted and calling for rapid decisions. When we arrived at the store, I stepped to the back and pointed to a few things that were around that we wanted. They both looked toward me for a moment, as if to ask if I wasn't going to shop, and I said that they had the list and could get what they wanted. . . . They hesitated again, then looked at each other and Mr. Kent said, "Let's go." He started picking up cider. They went from item to item, and every once in a while I would suggest quantities. They had gotten everything except the "candy corn" which the members had suggested buying. I reminded them of this and Mr. Young said, "That's no good, let's get another kind of candy, like mints," then looked to Mr. Kent for approval. Mr. Kent remained silent, and Mr. Young again said, "They'll like this better." I said, "They might, but this is what they said they wanted, and

we're only the committee and have to get what the club said we should buy." I said if he and Mr. Kent felt the mints would be a good idea, that I guess we had enough leeway for another ten cents, and that they, as the committee, could decide to get this, but that they should also be getting the "candy corn." After thinking for a moment, Mr. Kent said, "That's right, they said they wanted it . . . if they don't like it, they'll know better next Halloween." I said, "Exactly." Mr. Young smiled and put the "candy corn" and mints with the rest of the order.

The group expressed justifiable pride in their accomplishments at this party. Of that point in the meeting, I recorded:

> There was a great deal of attention given to the fact that "the refreshments should look nice—at least until we start eating them."

We played a number of games and the group had its first experience this year with singing. One of these games was especially geared to illustrate that physical difficulties, though limiting, did not necessarily prevent equal capacity and participation in all cases.

> I had pinned the Halloween cat up on the wall and had a tail to pin for each member of the club. Mr. O'Reilly, who is almost blind, for the first time was on a basis equal with the other members. He declined the first two opportunities, and then, when he realized that everyone else had his eyes covered, he volunteered and came second closest to the tail . . . and I made the point for him that he had come in second.

Toward the end of the meeting, through partialization of the events, and individualization of the members who carried responsibilities, I helped them to recognize to what extent they had been responsible for the fun they were having. I took advantage of the happy feeling permeating their party to do this.

Again I reminded the entire group about the decorations and asked if they didn't think that the committee had done a wonderful job. They clapped in their agreement. I asked about the delicious refreshments and the committee's work on this, and they not only clapped, but also yelled. Each time I pointed out the individuals who had served on the committee. I then called on Mr. Ihle and asked if they enjoyed the cake which he had brought. Everyone gave him a pat on the back, and a round of applause. I told them Mr. Ihle used to be a baker, and he certainly knew good cake. I said that Mr. Randall had brought the newspaper today, as the group had agreed, and that we certainly appreciated that. Mr. Young suggested thanking Miss March for her playing. I said we certainly should. As they were in a very happy and clapping mood, I asked, "Are you having a good time at the party?" Everyone clapped and cheered. I then changed my expression from a smile to one a little more serious, and said, "Last week, we discussed the fact that the camera for the club was gotten because you did something about it, and again, this whole party was wonderful because each one of you made it wonderful. You decided to have it, you planned it, you decided on costumes, on which games you wanted to use, on what food to buy, and then you decorated it yourselves, and that makes it even more fun." Again, everyone cheered.

After discussing the forthcoming election meeting, wherein the group agreed there would be no "mud-slinging" by the speakers for the two candidates, they used the accomplishments of the decoration committee to manifest their changing relationship to "other people"; in this case, again, other members of the agency.

I said there was a request from the teen-age department to leave the decorations up for their party Friday night. I asked what they thought about it. Mr. King answered, "Okay, if they want it, they can have it." The group voiced approval. An interesting aspect of this is that it was Mr. King who, when he suggested using the lounge longer for meetings, had said about the children of the agency, "Put them all into the Gym. They don't need any more room." He was here accepting and fostering other members' rights to use facilities.

The process that took place in this movement was exemplary of my major focus with this group. I was well aware, by this time, of the antagonistic feeling which many of these men had against the society in which they lived. These feelings might well have emanated, in large part, from the deprived conditions in their lives. It was not surprising, therefore, that when they were first informed about the agency limit on space, which prevented their meeting longer, that they voiced their feelings against having to share the facilities with other members of the agency. "If we don't have, why should you?"

However, it was within the group experiences (here) and during this particular meeting (now), after they had been enjoying themselves by participating in group-planned activities, that they were able to share what they had with other people. When the situation first presented itself, I might have discussed with them, in a vacuum, the meaning of agency limitations, which might have led into a discussion and handling of the negative feelings against society, generally; but rather I had the reality of the group experience to help them deal with these feelings.

"Does such a focus on the present reality deny the significance of previous life experience of other areas of current relationship outside the agency? . . . The importance of extra-group relationships cannot be minimized. A person comes to the group with all of his life experience as part of him, but the worker's help, as well as his immediate source of understanding of his group members, must be focused on the spot where he had competence, and responsibility given him by agency function and his own professional skill." [1]

---

[1] Phillips, Helen U., Discussion of a paper by Dr. Alexander Martin, "Utilizing New Knowledge about Individual Behavior in Work with Groups in the Leisure Time Setting."

By the next meeting, the group moved into a formal assumption of the responsibilities connected with the regular jobs which were a part of every meeting. Mr. Zorch and Mr. Ihle were chosen for the refreshment committee because "Mr. Zorch is a good waiter" and "Mr. Ihle used to be a baker, and he knows how to buy good cake." Mr. Lawrence, who is deaf, and Mr. Young assumed formal responsibility for taking out and putting away the games and magazines, since they were two men who always used them. The affirmation of their ability to do this, rather than depending upon the worker, was expressed when Mr. Young, after a discussion of these various jobs, said, "That's a good idea, then we don't have to wait for you to do it, and we can get started earlier."

They had a fiery session around a discussion of the two candidates and their respective parties. An interesting reflection upon this discussion was to listen to these men reach back into history, into their own lives, and discuss conditions during the time of former administrations of fifty and sixty years ago. These comments did not come from history texts, but from personal experiences. Here is an asset which ONLY THIS AGE GROUP possesses—the ability to say, "I was there, and I know." This same capacity was utilized at their Armistice Day meeting, when the group discussed the causes of wars, and described their own experiences in them.

For some time, I had been going to the door to greet new members, and after a discussion about the possibility of one of them doing this, Mr. O'Reilly, who has only four precent vision, but who hears relatively well, beamed his satisfaction, as he was chosen to be the doorman. Their own feelings about their changing group were verbalized at the end of six weeks.

11/11/52

     When I came down, I received the tail end of some of their conversations. Mr. King was saying, "We've been having a better time this year than ever before. . . ." Everyone started saying the same thing. Mr. Randall said it was because we had activities like discussions and parties, where everyone took part . . . not where one or two did things, and the others sat around. I said I was happy to hear they liked that, because they made it for themselves. Mr. King said, "That's right . . . you work along with us, and we'll have good times always." I said, "That's my job, helping out where I can—but it's your club." They went on to talk about their last two meetings and how fine they were. Mr. English added, "Even the refreshments are getting better." I pointed to Mr. Ihle and smiled. He smiled in return.

It was about this same time that the idea for a newspaper was introduced into the group meeting by Mr. Franklin, as a project that had been mentioned last year, but out of which nothing had ever materialized. The publication of a newspaper, as an activity for this particular age group, was an excellent tool that was utilized not only to affect the movement and morale of the group as a whole, but to directly affect the individuals, by relating the various phases of newspaper publication to the needs and abilities of the individual members. There were jobs done by the lame person who could write, by the nearly blind who were able to feel and count, by the nonverbal members who could collate, by those unable to write, but who could remember events well, and by one member whose interest to date was only playing dominoes, who was author of that particular column for the paper.

At the end of November, during the week preceding the agency's annual Thanksgiving dinner, a situation arose within the meeting which provided the men with an opportunity to seriously affect a condition in which they had been living for many years. I had suggested bringing cans of food for a Thanksgiving basket. I was operating under the belief that, regardless of how desperate their own economic position might be, there was something enriching and self-respecting that could accrue to them as individuals if under their conditions they could still give to someone who was needy. This "giving" worked out quite well as most of them participated in this venture. But it began with a much different reaction which again enabled them to use a present reality experience for growth. The Old Cronies utilized their meeting to develop a changing relationship with the Philadelphia County Board of Assistance.

11/18/52   16 members present

I said that it had been suggested that they might like to contribute a can of food toward the basket for a needy family. Mr. Reidner said, "This is a good idea, but don't get caught having an extra can of food if you don't want to 'cut'." Mr. Franklin added that he was right. Mr. Reidner continued to storm about the way their D.P.A. checks were being cut recently by the "visitors" who came and found out that they had gotten a can of food somewhere, or that someone gave them a coat. These comments were affirmed and/or added to by several others.

Everyone became very excited. Mr. Franklin told a story about his wife and medical care, wherein she had never gotten the service she was supposed to, and asked, "Where did the money go for that? . . . into someone's pocket!" Everyone was screaming and swearing; the language that was used was demonstrative of their feelings. They were quite fiery, and I permitted this to go on, with them telling each other personal incidents. At the end of one of Mr. Randall's stories, I quietly asked, "What have you done about all this?" Then came a barrage of, "What the hell can you do about it?" . . . and a continuation of the indictments of everyone from the local visitor to Eisenhower.

As they retold their stories, the thing that I picked up was that according to the particular visitor, individuals in similar circumstances were being treated differently.

In this spontaneous outburst, they revealed their feelings, "They won't listen to us, they'll laugh at us." This represented their feelings not only of almost total dependency upon social forces and the whims of visitors for their very existence, but worse, beliefs and feelings of futility to be able to do anything to affect the *status quo.*

Several factors had to be considered in working with these feelings and attitudes. The feeling was put out in a total sense, and part of my role, right at the time that it happened, had to be helping them to break up their feelings where possible. Secondly, I had to help them constructively to find *themselves* in all of this, in contrast to their desire to want to put it all on the outside. Most important, the group had to determine wherein they could mobilize themselves to deal with this problem, utilizing their own strengths and the structure of the group, of which they were all a part. Some of this began to take place within that very meeting, right at the initial action spot, as I used that particular time in the meeting to enable them to recognize that, "Granted, these claims have validity, what can you do about it?" Part of this change is evidenced from a point at the beginning of the meeting, when they displayed their individual futility, asking, "What the hell can you do about it?" to a point much later, after I had accepted their right to complain, and helped them to focus on the potential strength of making use of the unique entity of their group membership. It was here that they decided to invite a representative from the County Board of Assistance saying, "Sure, let them see we have force."

I sought to help them re-focus their plan of action, and put in at the end the fact that this might lead to something beneficial for them, or it might lead to nothing. Mr. Franklin ended with, "Well, we got nothing to lose, it can't be worse."

I truly believed that these men possessed a force, individually and collectively, represented in the positive will to change, to become different; and that given help, this negative impulsive behavior with the utilization of their inherent strengths, could be converted into growth producing will action.

A letter-writing committee, which agreed to serve only after the reassurance that this was to be the work (and the responsibility) of the club and not only individuals, met and sent an invitation to the County Board of Assistance. I spoke with the prospective speaker, a public relations worker from the Board, and discussed with him the negative feelings which he might have to meet, and we agreed that the members ought to have an opportunity to verbalize their feelings and raise their questions, and that the speaker, in answering their questions, also had to give them concrete information on mechanics of Public Assistance, including how the state determined how much a particular individual could receive. We also discussed the fact that some of their claims to infractions might be valid, and if that were true, that he had some responsibility to accept the criticism. He felt he could handle the situation adequately and was grateful for the preparation.

With the group, it called for a different kind of readiness which emanated from the tone I had tried to set during the initial outburst. First, I had to act as a stabilizing element in the midst of their excitement and furor. Secondly, I had to help them clarify the purpose of inviting a speaker, and the function of the particular meeting which he would attend. This required parts of three meetings previous to the one which the speaker attended. Part of one of these discussions took place on 1/13/53.

11 members present

I said that the speaker from the D.P.A. would be at the meeting next week. I asked if there were any other questions they might have other than those they had discussed at the meeting at which they planned to have him. At that time they had made somewhat of a list of questions. Mr. Franklin said, "I'm all ready to ask him things which I know he won't be able to answer, because they treat people unfair." Mr. Randall said he was going to ask about a few things which have bothered him for some time. I said everyone seemed pretty enthused, and I wondered if the man who was coming would be able to take it. Mr. Franklin said, "He'll have to take it, once he gets here." Mr. King said, "Is he afraid to answer the questions?" I said I didn't know whether it was a matter of being afraid. I said that I had spoken with the man, and he told me that he would like to come to the meeting to answer the group's questions, and clear up any difficulties that might be present. I said, "Incidentally, I sent him a copy of the paper, so he could know some of the things the group is doing." Mr. King said, "That's a good idea, then he'll know that we do good things here."

They had to decide if they were just going to try to "put him on the hot seat" or whether they really intended to use this experience to help themselves. With these foci, or re-enforcing their rights and capacities, of clarifying the purpose of such a meeting, and setting realistic limits, there was a greater possibility for achievement of beneficial results.

I thought it important to help the group assume increased responsibility for a constructive meeting.

1/13/53   11 members present

    I asked if they thought that the speaker ought to be met at the door, as I had told him to come to the lounge. Mr. Lewis said, "He can't get lost." I smiled, saying he probably couldn't, but maybe he would feel more welcome if someone sort of met him, and introduced him around. Mr. Franklin said, "Well, we've got a doorman." Several expressions of agreement with this made Mr. O'Reilly the person who would greet him. . . .

The speaker came, was greeted and introduced, and the meeting took place. The preparation of both the speaker and the group meshed into a successful union of the strengths that each brought to this situation. The men, at first, had some difficulty expressing their real questions, but when I helped them to verbalize them, they plunged in with the list of questions they had prepared at the previous meeting. For the first time in many years they had been receiving Public Assistance, they were getting a clearer understanding of what they received, and how it was determined. At this very meeting, the Assistance worker shed a new light on the role of the visitor, which ameliorated the fear that the men felt in their relationships with their visitors.

They asked him if the visitor had received a copy of *The Old Cronies Review*, their club paper, and he said that he had, and felt that this group was really an active one. The speaker wisely picked up here to point out to the men how they could help change some of the laws they thought unfair, and explained the role of the State Legislature. After he had gone, the men expressed their feelings of satisfaction, but most of all, of enlightenment.

Since that time, the individuals in the group have received official correspondence entitling them to additional benefits under the act. Mr. Franklin, as the editor of the *Review*, receives a monthly bulletin from the Board of Assistance, telling of the various activities and changes, and he reports these to the group verbally, or through the paper.

In addition, through the efforts of Mr. Young, and Mr. King, the group is now awaiting the visit from a state legislator with whom the club has been corresponding. They have prepared a list of suggestions for legislation, which they want to make to him.

For the Old Cronies, their dim, disheartening view of the past was reflected in their current unsatisfactory existence, and entangled them in questioning doubt of the future. They hadn't had the heart to risk change.

It is valid to say, at the time of this writing, that since I first met the Old Cronies, there has been no appreciable decrease in their dependency in these areas. Maturity and growth, however, are not measured by the absolute factors of dependence or independence for dependency relationships exist in every age from birth to death. Rather, the criteria for measurement of growth is how this condition is accepted and handled by the individuals concerned.

The major change was not the eradication, or even the alleviation of their dependencies, but rather in their reactions in these relationships. As they risked and tested, they began to find, and affirm as right, strength and belief in themselves.

I had to accept and attest to the validity of this evaluation of their past and to agree with their uncertainty of the future. But I was not willing to accept immobility—and as my focus became theirs, we moved to a consideration of what they could do *right now—here*, to make life more worthwhile . . . how they could best utilize the time when they came together in the club to add more purpose to living.

7

Group Work in Specialized Settings

CONTRIBUTIONS OF GROUP WORK IN
PSYCHIATRIC HOSPITALS
By Raymond Fisher

W_{HILE} there was considerable experience with group therapy before the war years, it was the accelerated use of group therapy by the Armed Services that made most professional persons, who, in one capacity or another, work in the field of human relations, more aware of the therapeutic possibilities in working with groups. Psychiatrists were stimulated by these experiences, and shortly after the war opportunities began to be opened to group workers to expand their practice in work with psychiatric patients.

In Cleveland, group workers began some three years ago to practice in a psychiatric hospital, and, at the present time, are working in four such hospitals in the city. It is from these experiences that this paper will be drawn.

Those of us who entered this new field did so with considerable misgiving, with the purpose of exploring what kind of a contribution, if any, group work could make in this setting. Our explorations took considerable time and are still going on. We knew too little about mentally ill people, had to get acclimated to a new setting which involved learning about hospital procedure, and methods of working as a member of a team with other professional disciplines. We had to have enough experience with patients so that we ourselves could be comfortable in our relationships with them before we could proceed further. We counted on the fact that our basic concepts in working with people would be sound and applicable in this setting too, and indeed before too long, found that they were. We, of course, recognized that there would have to be adaptions in how to apply these concepts to this specialized setting to meet the particular needs of the emotionally disturbed individuals, but we were encouraged by the psychiatrists in our work and we learned as we went along.

I would like at this point to acquaint you with one of the group experiences with a particular group of patients. Prior to commitment, these patients had a long established personality pattern of being shy, timid persons, ineffective in their attempts to establish satisfactory relationships with others. In the first meeting of the group in the hospital, these patients seemed almost incapable of re-establishing relationships. Each removed himself physically as far from any other in the room as possible, retired to a corner, or leaned against the wall, head bent and eyes lowered. During this first meeting, the group worker was able to get only two patients to do anything—each played checkers with the group worker for a very short time. The others indicated no awareness of this. The group worker continued her work with these patients, and the group record of a meeting 3½ months later give us this picture:

"The group met in the kitchen for a waffle breakfast which they had planned at their last meeting. Bertha wanted to mix the batter,

Lucille and Hilda said they would make the coffee and set the table. They were enthusiastic and anxious to participate. Jacqueline seemed somewhat helpless. The worker suggested she play the piano. She played beautifully, and the music seemed to add to the warmth and good feeling evident in the group. Christine carried chairs in for the meal. Ralph was late because of his conference with his psychiatrist. He asked the worker to call the ward and tell them where he was, for he had been permitted to come to the meeting alone. He laughingly said they might think he had run away.

"There were not enough waffles for everyone at the first serving, so Hilda, proud of her skill, in a motherly way insisted that the others be seated so she could take care of the baking. Everyone was at the table when the meal was ready. Hilda finally sat down since the waffles were baking faster now and there was plenty for everyone. The superintendent of nurses and her assistant walked by the kitchen and came in to see what was going on. The members cordially insisted that they have waffles with them and the worker and Bertha got up and prepared places for them at the table. When the meal was finished, all the girls willingly took part in washing the dishes. Ralph went for a broom and swept the kitchen floor and carried the chairs out for the girls. In going back to their wards, everyone talked and laughed. This had been a festive occasion for them and their planning and working together had produced an esprit de corps not evident before."

The marked change in this session compared with the first one indicates the extent of growth toward ability to relate with others. It is always difficult to determine who is responsible for such a change in the patients. Any member of a treatment team may be providing that particular ingredient which the patient needs to show improvement. Actually, one of these patients were getting psychotherapy from a psychiatrist, though some were getting electric shock therapy and some were being seen by caseworkers. For the sake of simplification, we will consider only the group worker's role in enabling these patients to recognize and make more effective use of their environment. The role of the group worker was determined by the needs of these withdrawn, dependent persons and the help they needed to show movement. Any change was necessarily slow and involved a step by step helping process that began when the group worker first approached the patient on the ward to interest him in coming to the meetings. This initial approach was made with warmth and feeling and carried with it a respect for the individual and a belief in his capacity to feel and respond to this warmth. The group worker had something concrete and positive to offer the patients—a program of informal recreational activity, the very offering of which carried with it the reassuring implication that the patient had the capacity to make use of it. Thus, the group worker focused from the beginning on the patient's strength and the reality situation in the hospital; he did not deal with the patient's pathology. The inability of the patient to show any immediate response meant that the contacts needed to be continued so that the patient could begin to show awareness and recognition of the worker. The worker then stimulated the patient sufficiently to interest him in coming to the activity.

At the first meeting described, the worker tried to make all who attended aware that she was interested in each and trying to help each one as an individual. Because the patients were incapable of becoming, at this stage, involved in any program as a group, or of relating in any way to each other, the worker attempted to get each to participate at least for a very short time in some simple activity with her. She was actually successful with only two patients at this time. At following meetings, little by little, she was able to help them move towards participation in simple games and social activities with each other, first in small groups of two, and then in groups involving more members, and finally with the group as a whole involving all of the members. There were efforts made to expand their interests and to increase their ability to carry some responsibility for determination of their own program. Thus it is seen that the worker played a strong role in the slow process of leading these withdrawn, dependent persons to function at a higher level.

We have found from our experience that the group worker's ability to contribute to the patient's movement towards health depends on his skill in three major areas; (1) his ability to work with the individual patient and help him move; (2) his ability to work with the group. This involves his relationship to the group, his ability to involve the patients in helping each other, and his ability to affect the climate of the group so that it has warmth and congeniality that is conducive to growth; and (3) his ability to select program that is within the capacity of the individual at his particular stage of illness, and to use this program to stimulate interest and involve the patients in constructive, pleasurable and meaningful activities.

The way the group worker uses himself and his knowledge in each of these three areas to make the experience a helpful one for the patients is dependent on many factors and may serve a variety of purposes. In this paper, I would like to consider some of the factors in the first two areas.

In the first area, the relationship to the individual, the patient may be contacted once or many times; urged to attend, or casually invited; led by the hand, or allowed to come on his own. The approach would depend on his ability to respond, his particular needs, and the treatment plan. The objective might be to help him begin to be aware of and use his environment, to help him re-establish a satisfying relationship and/or to help him make use of a constructive group experience. Often the patient who has come to the group will need constant encouragement and repeated reassurance to be able to continue attending the group. This encouragement provides the help he needs to continue to take part in the group.

Sometimes the individual informal approach to involve the

patient in some phase of the program has value at the time it is made because it serves to penetrate the patient's immediate preoccupation with fantasy, or it may serve to substitute a constructive real experience for a distorted, hallucinated episode. The following excerpt will illustrate how this may sometimes work:

"When the group worker entered the ward, she was attracted by the sound of Miss B's voice talking loudly and constantly. As she approached the patient's room, another patient was standing in the doorway. She said that Miss B was now her roommate and that she was lying in her bed raving. The group worker went in and spoke to Miss B. She was looking at the ceiling and talking incessantly. The group worker asked if the patient recognized her. The patient looked at her and said, 'Of course, I know who you are.' The group worker said that they were going to get together in a little group to read this afternoon and asked if she would not like to join this group. Miss B said no, that she did not want to. She said that she did not want to do anything for anybody. The group worker asked her if she remembered the fudge party last week and if she had not enjoyed it. Miss B said yes, she did enjoy it, but that she participated only to be kind to other people. The group worker said that was a very good motive. Miss B then said she did not want to be kind to anybody. The group worker pointed out that this was a contradiction, since Miss B had said she enjoyed the fudge party because she was kind to other people, and now she said she did not want to be kind to other people. Miss B then said that she *did* want to be kind to other people. The other patient then interrupted her with 'If you want to be kind to me, you'll act nicer.' Miss B said, 'I don't want to room with you anyway.' The patient looked hurt and reminded Miss B that she had said previously that she did want her for a roommate. Then Miss B said that she did not know why she said things like that, that she did want her for a roommate and she did want to be kind to people. Again the group worker told her about the reading group and asked her if she had enjoyed it last week. She said that she had. The group worker then suggested that she might feel like getting up and coming down to listen today again. Miss B replied by insisting that she was going to stay in bed. The group worker told her perhaps if she rested just a little while longer she might feel like joining the group soon and that they would be looking forward to having her if she would come. She gave no response at the time, but did come to the group and for the greater part of the meeting was able to be involved in the program in a very real and constructive manner."

In this illustration we see how the group worker injects the reality into the situation, thus pushing aside the effect of the hallucinations. The group worker, too, helps the patient "get hold of herself," i.e., helps in the reintegration of the ego through clarifying some of her inconsistencies and helping her control some of her misplaced hostility. This enables her to function more effectively and realistically with the other patient with whom she shares the room, and later helps her decide to make positive use of the group.

In some instances, the group workers have found that through these attempts to involve patients in groups, some one patient who had previously not been able to relate to anyone in the hospital may show signs of reaching out to the group worker for a relationship. The patient may endow the group worker with the particular characteristics, such as the "good and accepting mother," he needs. In one such case, the patient, a very sick person, reached out to the group worker who worked on her ward. The relationship developed into a real transference; the patient used the worker as a mother person, repeatedly put her arms around her, her face on her shoulder, kissed her, and told her her anxieties and asked for help. It was the decision of the psychiatrist and treatment team that use had to be made of this relationship. This was done for a time on an individual basis because it was too difficult for the patient to share the worker in a group. The group worker played the role of the accepting adult, helped her in clarifying ideas and, to a degree, in differentiating reality from fantasy, and was able to help the patient move towards a positive and helpful relationship with the psychiatrist and later to share the group worker with other patients in a group situation.

The second area of skill, the way the group worker uses and affects the group for the growth of the patients, calls for sociological and psychological knowledge of group process. As group workers, we are familiar with the opportunities the guided group experience offers for creative activities which are pleasurable; for emotionally satisfying relationships; for status, responsibility and achievement; all of which can contribute towards a sense of well-being and a feeling of relaxation. These take on added significance in work with emotionally ill persons because they combine to add to the patient's sense of worthiness, his feeling of usefulness and self-respect. Schizophrenic patients have had so many blows to their self-esteem that they seek to escape additional harm by withdrawing from situations which will threaten them further. The form their protective armor develops may vary from complete withdrawal from contact with environment, to continuance of interpersonal relations on a superficial level with the substituting of intellectualization for emotional participation. With the emphasis in group work on the interpersonal relationships within the groups and the satisfactions to the individual of belonging and doing together, there takes place a natural building of self esteem. Therefore, this process becomes a counter-attack against escape from emotional participation and against tendencies toward withdrawal. The group members, too, provide a healthy pressure on the patients to give up their preoccupation. This is illustrated in the following:

". . . John seemed vague this evening and his attention had to be called back to the game on several occasions by the other players. At one point, Mary turned to him and said, 'You'll just have to stop day-dreaming now, John, and keep your mind on the game.' A little laugh accompanied this, which took the sting out of the words and John himself laughed."

Thus in the group we see that other patients take on the role of helping one another maintain contact with reality. They often are able, too, to help each other differentiate between fantasy and reality. This help coming from the patient's peers seems acceptable to the individual and does not carry with it the threat that it might, coming from an authoritative figure. It produces the desired effect without the intervention of the group worker, who encourages the development of this giving-receiving relationship recognizing that it has value for both. The patient who gives help gets the satisfaction and feeling of importance that comes with helping others; the patient who receives help responds to the interest in him and uses the help offered. From these beginnings, we sometimes see the early indications of leadership capacity in some of the patients, which can be encouraged so that they can function as indigenous leaders who may be able to hold a sub-group together.

The group worker in his relationship with the group attempts consciously to modify the group so that it has an atmosphere that is warm, accepting, understanding, and thus conducive to growth through a living experience in satisfying relationships. The group worker, like all therapists, cannot be expected to understand all of the psychotic patients' productions, but he can feel with the patients and learn to understand much of what he is doing and thinking. The impact of the group worker's understanding and feeling towards the patient can help infect the group so that it reflects much of this warmth and positive feeling. One of the values in the use of the group lies in this positive emotional tone and the use made in this warm climate of the ability of some patients to understand and feel with and help one another. In this way, within the group, a number of therapeutic agents in addition to the group worker become active.

Patients have many experiences in common. They have all had difficulties in their previous environment which has led to their hospitalization. They share similar frustrations in conforming to hospital routine and necessary limitations. Many of them are getting similar kinds of treatment and often they have similar anxieties about their treatment and their prognosis. These are bonds of identity that can be strengthened in the groups so that they act as another force operating to bring cohesiveness and a feeling of belonging. Identification with the group is helpful in removing some of the feeling of uniqueness which patients have, and may lead toward a sharing of feelings and problems, rather than a keeping to one's self. Thus there takes place a re-education through a living experience which may have considerable effect on the individual's growth in his capacity for developing satisfying social relationships. In these groups patients may find their first meaningful group experience.

The group too provides the opportunity at times to reach the patient who seems unable to respond to any attempts by the group worker, the psychiatrist or other members of the treatment team. This has been demonstrated repeatedly in our hospitals. There have been times when no member of the staff has been successful in establishing a satisfactory relationship with a particular patient and yet the patient may become involved in some activity by another patient. The following illustrates this point:

"A short travel film was to be shown on the ward. The group worker approached Mr. K who was pacing up and down the hall and invited him to come but Mr. K explained that he was too nervous to sit still this evening. The movie had been started only about 5 minutes when Mr. K came up to the door. The film was taken in New England where apparently Mr. K had been. He became quite interested and the group worker got him a chair and invited him to come in the room. Mr. K refused the chair and said he would just stand there for a minute and watch. At this point, Mrs. L, another patient, turned around and happened to see him. She was seated near the front on a divan and she invited him to come and sit by her. In about another minute he accepted her invitation and went up and sat with her. He remained for the entire evening."

The group worker then encourages this first reaching out towards a relationship as one of the earlier indications of change in the patient which may prove to be a beginning step towards recovery for the individual.

Some patients, because of previous life experiences are extremely wary of establishing anything approximating an intimate relationship with a worker. This may be because their previous experiences with authoritative persons have been consistently painful. In a group situation, the patient may maintain a rather casual relationship to the worker but over a long period of time, continue little by little in his own way to test the worker. The group worker then has the opportunity to prove to the patient that there can be an experience with an authoritative figure who can continue to be the good and accepting person, not the punitive, retaliating person he had known in his previous experience.

All the potentialities of grouping psychotic patients have not yet been fully explored. The traditional groupings used in our group work agencies, that is, groupings around an activity or common interest base, are a useful method in the hospital too, but one needs to take into consideration the patient's personality organization, his level of performance at the particular time and potentialities of achievement at any one time. The living group or ward group is another basis of grouping with which we have had some working experience. Here, the group worker has been able to have considerable success in involving heterogeneous patients in rather loosely organized but mean-

ingful program. Other groupings have been around the sharing
of a current experience such as insulin and electric shock and
some have been organized on the basis of the patient's stage of
illness, such as the withdrawn group mentioned. There has
been some experience in working with groups of patients who
are on trial visit and plans have been made to work with pre-
discharge patients and with groups of relatives of patients.
Whatever the grouping, we have found that work with relatively small groups is the most fruitful.

The group worker has found increasingly that his role demands more and more that he help clarify conscious and
pre-conscious problems of the patient. Patients have many anxieties about hospitalization, treatment and their own feelings
which they may not have been able to verbalize prior to the
time that they do so in the group. In this way they make use
of the group as a "sounding" board for testing and ventilation
of their ideas and feelings. The group worker helps patients
who become threatened by some situation in the hospital or
group. For instance, if some patient should become acutely
disturbed and thus cause the other patients to become anxious,
the group worker handles this through his own calmness and
by his recognition that this is upsetting to the others. He will
help them talk through their feelings and give them the reassurance they need. With increasing psychiatric knowledge and
guidance from psychiatrists, the worker is more and more able
to be helpful in these areas. Often when patients have indicated need for clarification and help which was better handled
on an individual basis, the group worker has been able to help
him go to the case worker or psychiatrist with these problems.
At times, psychiatrists have been invited to group meetings
when the group members have indicated that they seem ready
for a meaningful discussion and raising of questions with them.
These generally concern specifics of treatment, questions about
illness, and prognosis.

The patients themselves have had various concepts regarding the purposes and values of these groups. Some of them have looked upon the group meetings as purely pleasurable kind of activities which they have found helpful to occupy the time. Others have recognized that these were probably of a more therapeutic nature and have chosen such significant names for the group as the "Get-Well Club" and the "Random Club," the latter because the hero of "Random Harvest" recovered. One patient approached a group worker before Christmas and said she would like to make candles. The group worker suggested that this could be done in Occupational Therapy. "No, no! Not in Occupational Therapy, with you, around a table, all of us do it together." In another hospital a patient had this to say to the group worker: "You have a very important job. You're supposed to come and see us and talk with us and take us to the library, the club room and different places and make us friends."

Group workers cannot operate independently in a psychiatric hospital. The patient receives maximum benefit when the varied services are integrated. Because of this, the group worker has to be clear as to his own contributions in this setting. Some of these have already been discussed in this paper. One contribution that has not been mentioned but is very important is the material of diagnostic value which comes from the observations of the group and can be made available to the psychiatrist. Because in a group, the members are participating in a real life situation, the personality constellations become fairly clear. For instance, the relationship of the patient to the worker and the characteristics with which he endows him may be significant. (Does he use him as a parental figure? Does the patient become a dependent or hostile person?) The patient's relationships with the other members of the group are also important. (Does he relate to them as siblings? What is this relationship? How does he react to members of his own and the opposite sex?) In the group, he shows his strengths and weaknesses and ability (or inability) to function effectively in a social situation. As one doctor indicated after the report of a group worker in a meeting of the treatment team "the material that we have had up to this point has shown us some of the pathology of the patient, but we did not see the patient as a person. With the addition of the group worker's summary, we now for the first time see the patient as a live person."

Another psychiatrist has followed the record of the group worker in a setting very closely and has used these observations as a check on his treatment and work with the patients. He has found in many instances that in the group, the first clues as to the success of the treatment begin to be evident and is then assured that he is on the right track. In other instances, the group worker has been urged to involve certain patients in some small activity so that an opportunity for checking the reaction to the latest interview might be possible. One of the reasons that the group worker is able to be of assistance in this respect is the uniqueness of his relationship with the patient which is built around a friendly, informal role and is focused on involvement in pleasurable activity and the use of strengths. He sees the patient in a social setting which permits observation that may be helpful in determining a patient's readiness for discharge and the expectations in terms of social relationships.

There are times when the psychiatrist decides it is necessary for a patient to become sicker before effective treatment can be begun to make him better. At such times, the group worker as a member of a team may be asked to help break down some of the patient's defenses which at the time might aggravate his symptoms. He could do this by pointing out to the patient his unrealistic statements or behavior, of gently but persistently pointing out some of his weaknesses and giving constant reminders of illness. The group, too, might help break down some of these defenses and the group worker at this time would not act as buffer.

All this indicates that to function effectively, the group worker must work very closely with the case worker, psychiatrist, nurses, and other members of the team; that there must be a plan for the patient's treatment and that the group worker must be aware of this plan and clear as to his role in the total treatment process. The group worker must be aware of the dynamics of illness and what his role must be if he is to help patients move toward health. This, it seems to me, is one of the most difficult aspects of the job. It requires understanding of self, understanding of one's own limitations, and understanding and having conviction about the uniqueness of the group worker's contribution. It also requires an understanding of the contributions of the other workers. It involves an ability to share in planning and to participate in treatment, and it calls for a particular kind of personality. In essence this requires a noncompetitive person, who can continue to give, though even for long periods of time it seems that nothing comes back in return.

The group worker should be able to determine to a great extent the importance of his position on the treatment team. However, much depends on the other members of the team, and most of all, of course, on the psychiatrist who carries the responsibility for the treatment. Group work, as all social work, is rooted in concepts of dynamic psychology and psychiatrists who do not use these concepts in their approach to treatment cannot see the validity of group work. In the hospitals in which we have operated, considering the short experience which we have had, group work has been well recognized and received, and in all instances, has been definitely considered as making a therapeutic contribution to the patient.

Group workers are generally identified in the hospital as part of the social service staff. Group workers and case workers share a common base of knowledge which has become increasingly clear, both in practice and in training for practice. Case work has a longer and richer experience in the psychiatric field on which to draw. However, it becomes increasingly clear that the psychiatric knowledge required of both is equal. The difference between case work and group work lies not in the differences in psychiatric knowledge, but in the use of this knowledge to meet most effectively the difficult requirements of their respective functions.

The Special Contribution of Therapeutic Group Work in a Psychiatric Setting[1] *By Marion B. Sloan*

THE group work program is a unique part of the Social Service at Cleveland Veterans Administration Hospital, Cleveland, Ohio. It was orginated in the fall of 1946 as an experimental project. Now it is recognized as one of the professional services of the hospital, and is considered an important part of the total treatment plan for patients. In spite of a very limited group work staff, consisting of one full-time trained group worker and one or two graduate students in group work each year, we have achieved interesting results in social group work with psychotic patients. During 1951 we added a unit of group work with paraplegic patients in two of the medical wards of the hospital. As our major efforts to date have been concentrated on developing techniques for helping in the treatment of psychotic patients through social group work, this paper will deal with that part of our experience.

Before describing our practice in this treatment setting, I should like to share with you some of our thinking on the application of group work philosophy and techniques in hospitals.

[1] Published with permission of the Chief Medical Director, Department of Medicine and Surgery, Veterans Administration, who assumes no responsibility for the opinions expressed or conclusions drawn by the author.

Outside of hospitals, social groups are constantly being formed, with or without the help of trained group workers, because of man's universal need for association with his fellows. Man has always sought the response of friends, the security of accept- ance, the sense of personal importance that result from meaningful group associations, and the opportunity for new experiences and skills that may result from doing interesting things together with friends.

Hospitalization breaks off these normal associations, and de- pendency develops. This is natural in a hospital setting, where most of the patient's daily activities are determined for him by those in authority, and where his illness often prevents his per- forming socially as a free agent. Here there is a very real need for help in forming interim social relationships.

This is particularly true of mental patients, many of whom have never made normal or satisfactory social adjustments. In addition to the usual regression and dependency that accom- pany hospitalization, there may be severe emotional malad- justment that has prevented the patient from having warm human relationships. This may cause him to withdraw even further when his social failure is recognized as severe enough to necessitate sending him to a mental hospital.

The psychotic patient feels inwardly disorganized and has withdrawn from people in an effort to reorganize himself. He needs a great deal of very direct and understanding help be- fore he is able to venture out and dare to try establishing friendly relations with other patients around him. In many ways the mental patient is like a child. He is able to meet new demands only if he has the security of a familiar parent nearby. We find that the group leader, and the group itself, can often carry along a patient whose insecurity would otherwise leave him isolated and resistant.

It is here that the special competence of the group worker comes into play. She is able to make a professional contribution to the combined efforts of the medical team who are carrying out the treatment plan for the patient. A large part of the group worker's professional skill lies in the flexibility and resourcefulness with which the needs and interests of various patients can be met through group experience.

The trained social group worker in a hospital makes conscious use of group experience in order to help individual group members to create sounder social relationships. The worker's focus is determined according to the social needs of individual group members.

We understand the group worker's role in a Neuropsychiatric Hospital as helping the patient mobilize his ego strengths, through concentrating on the things he can do, rather than trying to work through the unconscious conflicts which have led to his disorganization. The group worker, therefore, seeks to know what the patient's interests are; what have been his previous strengths and successes. Some of this information is contributed by the doctor and the case worker from their contacts with the patient and his family. The patient is very likely to indicate some of his interests and skills in his first individual contacts with the group worker. We know that even in periods of severe disturbance there is a fragment of the patient's personality which remains in contact with reality. The group worker then seeks to strengthen his ties with reality by working with these positive aspects of his personality and seeking to extend them.

Through a number of carefully planned and supervised small group experiences, referred patients are given the opportunity to participate in a program that satisfies some of their personal needs and helps them to be more accepting of the difficult period of hospitalization and treatment. These small groups vary in intensity according to the treatment plan for the patients and the skill of the worker. In our hospital there are usually five to seven different groups in operation at a given time, meeting regularly with the group worker or the group work students.

Program activities also vary, according to the interests of the group members. In the hospital, as in other group work settings, the trained group worker draws on a variety of activities to meet the needs of the group. She sees and uses these program tools in terms of their effect on individuals.

These various means of helping patients share in group experience are always used as tools, never as ends in themselves. As Grace Coyle says, "The test is whether the group leader is aware of the contribution which a particular group experience may have for given individuals, and helps them to get that value from it." [2] The group is thus consciously person-centered, rather than activity-centered.

In our hospital patients are referred for group experience by psychiatrists whenever it is felt that a planned group experience would have therapeutic values to the patient. Other professional personnel (case workers, nurses, etc.) may suggest for referral; the group worker then discusses the suggestion with the patient's doctor. Whenever a patient who is not yet referred indicates his interest, the worker is responsible for suggesting a referral to the patient's doctor.

The group worker, in consultation with the director of group therapy, a staff psychiatrist who directs and co-ordinates all phases of treatment of patients in groups, determines which social groups seem likely to meet the particular needs of the patients. The organization of groups to meet specific needs involves through consideration of the patients' needs as evaluated through conferences with the doctors and case workers, and as seen in the group worker's personal contacts and observation of patients. In establishing groups for which the need has been determined, the group worker must give due con-

2 Coyle, Grace L., "Not All Group Activities Are Group Work, *The Group,* November, 1944.

sideration to avoid overlapping of services with any other department. She must clear on all administrative details related to the organization and functioning of the groups; use of equipment, facilities, space, scheduling of group meetings, etc. This requires an understanding of hospital routine, so that group meetings do not conflict with the operation of other departments or interfere with other forms of treatment.

The steps following referral are usually based on this plan: The group worker, as a friendly, non-competitive, non-possessive individual approaches the patient and establishes a relationship with him on the basis of continuous and consistent contacts—all on a very friendly and informal level. This may continue for several weeks before any suggestion is made to the patient about joining a group. From this beginning, the worker is able to help the patient move out gradually until he can tolerate association with one or more other patients—and on further, as soon as he is able, into a guided group experience.

We find there is some variation of approach, depending on whether the patient is reacting to his problem with aggressive or withdrawing behavior. He may be approached at several different levels, according to the severity of his illness and the degree of his recovery at the time he is referred by his psychiatrist for group experience.

An individual patient may be approached at any one of four distinct levels, or he may progress from one level to the next. The group worker may follow the patient through the four levels, or he may be referred to other therapists at Level I, and later be referred to the group worker at Level II, III, or IV. This is decided in consultation with the director of group therapy. In relation to social group work, the four levels are as follows:

Level I.—The very seclusive, withdrawn patient is encouraged by the group worker to respond to her individually as a preparation for future participation with others. We call this the "warming up" process. It may consist of paying the patient a friendly visit every day in his ward, at the Occupational Therapy Shop, or in the ward dining room; chatting with him about current events in the hospital, his hobbies, and interests; answering realistic questions he may have about hospital life, etc. The patient begins to recognize the group worker as a friend and to look forward to seeing her. The worker is alert to opportunities to include other patients in these informal contacts, thus gently moving the Level I patient into non-threatening associations with his ward mates.

Level II.—The patient who is in closer contact with reality is able to use his relationship with the group worker as a link to lead him into a group experience that is not too demanding of him, where he can share with others a common goal. This process helps him to emerge from his general withdrawal. Such a patient may be encouraged to join a very informal recreational group, where the patients choose the activities they enjoy doing together, or an interest group, such as a social dancing class for patients who want to learn how to dance.

Level III.—When a patient is getting better, he is able to take his place in a group where he plans with others, helps the group make decisions, and carries his share of responsibility. This opportunity to help make decisions is invaluable for the mental patient, whose self-confidence has been badly shattered by the experience of being mentally ill. A carefully planned and guided group experience for a patient at this level affords him the opportunity to test himself in reality situations, to develop latent capacities for participation or leadership, and to receive the recognition of others for his accomplishments. For the past five years, we have had a Patients' Dance Planning Committee, composed of seven to nine referred patients, who carry responsibility for planning the bi-weekly social dances for the closed wards. This group meets at least three times weekly under the leadership of the group worker, or a graduate group work student. The group has been a continuing demonstration of the positive therapeutic values of such group experience for psychotic patients during hospitalization.

Level IV.—Here we place those psychotic patients who, for the most part, are oriented and in good contact, but whose inter-personal relationships are strained, fruitless, and super-ficial. For patients at this level, a combined program of group psychotherapy, social group work, and corrective therapy is offered. Group psychotherapy sessions are held two to three times weekly with a group psychiatrist in charge. These dis-cussion meetings give the patients a chance to express them-selves verbally in an atmosphere of tolerance, and help the patients develop an understanding of their method of adaption to reality. Frequently these patients have begun their "group life" while undergoing insulin coma therapy. The group pro-gram includes a variety of activities selected by the patients and carried out under the leadership of the group worker. A corrective therapist is assigned to direct part of the activity pro-gram for the group, especially active games and sports. The group worker sees the patients daily in carefully planned in-formal group activities, discussion, and individual contacts, all related to the total treatment plan worked out for the group and for each individual patient member. There are six to nine patients in each such group.

The average "life" of Level IV groups has been six months. This includes the period from the formation of the group until the patients are discharged from the hospital, for the group is transferred from the treatment ward, to the convalescent ward, to the open ward, carrying with them all the original group members whenever possible, and meeting regularly with the same therapists. The functions of the doctor, the group worker, and the corrective therapist seem to complement each other very effectively in therapeutic values with such a group because of the intensive integration achieved. Weekly conferences are held where the group psychiatrist, group worker, and corrective therapist report and discuss in detail their impressions of the group and of the participation of individual members in all phases of the combined program. The director of group therapy acts as consultant in these conferences, which is also attended by the supervisor of psychiatric case work. Our experience with this integrated approach has clearly indicated the value of such coordination in leading each member of the clinical team to a better understanding of each patient and his needs.

The greatest values have been found in that part of our group therapy program which provides intensive, continuous work with groups of patients whose membership remains fairly stable. Here the group worker plays the role of the familiar, stable parent person, helping the child-like mental patient to meet new experiences in a safe, non-threatening way. Our experience has been that success (in group treatment) with psychotic patients depends on the quality of the human relationship which is developed. With such thin threads holding psychotic patients to reality, the sustained relationship becomes the important one. Consistent schedules and many hours of direct relationship with patients are needed.

The most interesting development in group work in our hospital has been the combination of intensive, long-term group experience with group psychotherapy. (Level IV.) The first such group was developed for seven months in 1949, and included six extremely ill psychotic patients. It was a special study project set up at the suggestion of the Chief of Neuropsychiatry, to observe the effects of an intensive program of social group work with a very carefully selected and limited number of closed ward patients. The initial plan was to use the group experience, through daily informal activities with the group worker, as an opportunity for the patients to express them-

selves, develop self-confidence, and practice group living together.

From a list of patients whom the various psychiatrists wished
to refer, the Chief of Neuropsychiatry and the group worker
chose the six patients who became the members of the group.
These patients all had a diagnosis of schizophrenia, and were
very ill at the time of referral. Four of them were receiving
electric shock therapy. Two began a program of insulin shock
therapy soon after referral.

All of these patients were considered to be in need of group
experience. There was no attempt to hand-pick the group for
any theoretical social compatibility. At the time of referral
there were no known human relationships between any two
members of the group, and they were living in different wards.

In order to promote association and help foster group feeling,
it was decided that they should live together and engage in
daily activities together. They were, therefore, all placed on
the same closed ward, and thus had the same daily schedule
of meals, occupational therapy, gym, etc. Episodes of daily life
in these activities, as well as in the planned group experiences,
played a large part in the inner-action of the group members,
and made it possible for group feeling to develop to the extent
that they acted as a unit in many situations.

In addition to sharing a ward "home," the patients had an
attractive and comfortable room for their meetings, and the
familiarity and relaxation of their "clubroom" helped to
strengthen group ties.

For the first two months of the life of the group, the patients
were seen individually and in group experience by the group
worker each day. She visited them in their ward, as well as in
the Occupational Therapy Shop, where she became interested
in each patient's individual projects. She attended the regularly
scheduled parties and dances with them. Three times weekly
the group worker spent the periods immediately prior to and

following electric shock therapy with the four group members who were receiving this form of treatment. Through these consistently friendly contacts the group worker was able to help these very sick patients establish relationships with her, and then with each other. The patients came to look upon the group worker as their friend. One of the members, Tom, defining group worker's role in the presence of a wardmate who was not a member of the group said, "Yes, I know you have a very important job. You are supposed to take some of the fellows to meetings and to games and so forth; to visit us in our wards; and to *make us friends*." Another group member, Bert, interpreting her role to a patient in the group who questioned why the group worker came to see them and arranged various activities with them said, "She's just trying to help you. She wants to help make things more pleasant for us while we have to be here in the hospital." In another meeting where selected patients were invited to describe their group experiences to a visitor from another agency, Tom described the activities of the group with enthusiasm, and gave as his understanding of the reasons for the group meetings: "It helps us to get to know each other better, and we can get along better in the ward." Of group worker he said: "She's our Social Woman, she goes along with us on all of these things. She fixes it so we can have rides in a station wagon, etc."

Six weeks after the first group meeting, a doctor was introduced to the group, by mutual agreement of the group members and the group worker. The patients had indicated in several ways that they wanted to be able to refer their problems to a doctor who could "answer our questions." Bill said, "I never see that damn doctor." Bert remarked, "The doctor keeps us here to earn his pay." So the doctor was invited to meet with this group.

Then followed, concurrently with the daily informal group activities and discussions, a series of group psychotherapy meetings, twice a week, in which deeper emotional material was handled through discussion with the doctor. The group worker was present at the group psychotherapy meetings and continued to carry on the activity program with the patients as well. This arrangement marked the beginning of an intensified coordination between psychiatry and social group work. For the group itself, the entry of the doctor completed the family picture, with a group home, and a father and mother figure with which to identify.

The resulting group life was studied for the period of seven months. The observations made by the doctor and the group worker during the development of this Special Group Project were used as the basis of study and discussion by the entire psychiatric staff. Material about the various group members, and the progress of the group as a whole, was presented to the weekly psychiatric seminars by the doctor, the group worker, and the psychiatric case workers. We learned many things about the treatment of psychotics in groups through the very rich and interesting material produced in the continuing life of the group. We found that basic group work principles and philosophy can be applied even to a group of extremely withdrawn and isolated psychotic patients.

The advantages of combining social group activity with group psychotherapy were shown very clearly. The group psychiatrist felt that the continuous group association of the patients in activities paved the way for their very lively participation in the group psychotherapy sessions with him. They were a group with established positive feelings about each other and about being members of the group at the time when they started the psychotherapy sessions. The doctor noticed that their shared experiences in the various pleasurable activities selected by the group made possible recognition for each member in the group. Some could gain recognition through ability to participate in discussions on an intellectual level.

Others, who would have been most uncomfortable had their group experience been limited to discussion, were able to participate actively and with skill in games, hikes, and other social group activities. This seemed to indicate that recognition for each group member is possible only where the patients are provided with a variety of modes of self-expression.

A very strong group feeling was evident and supportive relationships among the patients and between the patients and the group worker were observed in the psychotherapy sessions as well as in the informal group activities. There seemed to be a very definite positive transference toward the doctor and the group worker. As anticipated, sibling rivalry was clearly demonstrated. Although the patients found much satisfaction in their group activities, they were able to express their hostility toward each other, and also toward the authoritative figures, the doctor and the group worker. For example, they criticized the group worker very severely when she was unable to secure tickets for a baseball game they wished to attend. The patients seemed to have had a much richer and more satisfying group experience from the combination of psychotherapy and social group work. They showed some awareness of this and mentioned in the meetings that they were "the envy of all the patients in the ward." In their ward relationships, the patients in the Special Group, with one exception, showed definite progress in social relationships and in their ability to understand and get along with other patients.

We have been able to make application of similar techniques and co-ordination of services in six other groups formed since the conclusion of the Special Group Project in 1949. In three of these the group worker has had the responsibility of preparing the group, through shared experiences and consciously motivated friendly relationships, for the entry of the doctor to direct the group psychotherapy.

The last Insulin Shock Therapy group is still active with eight of the members now on open ward. This group was organized in January, 1952. At that time the group worker was specifically assigned responsibility for formation of the group and for discussion leadership with the patients until such time as they seemed to be ready for the psychiatrist to come into the group. This occurred two and one-half months after the group was formed. Meanwhile, the psychiatrist had been in charge of the daily insulin shock therapy treatments for the group members. He was clearly identified by the patients as their "insulin doctor," and in spite of their resistance to treatment, they had shown many evidences of positive feelings towards him.

The group worker was also very closely associated with the insulin treatment for she was with the patients every day in the period following treatment, and during their late breakfast hour. The group worker's presence in the daily "breakfast club" period was found to have many direct values in developing group feeling and establishing a positive social climate for the growth of friendly interpersonal relationships within the group. In these breakfast club meetings and in several of the group discussion meetings, the patients turned to the group worker to discuss their feelings about hospitalization and treatment. One day a patient said, "Why don't we have the doctor come in and talk to us about these things?" Other group members agreed and said they never had a chance to talk with the doctor except "right after treatment." A lively group discussion followed in which the patients exchanged ideas about some of the questions they wished to discuss with the doctor. Two members had some reservations about bringing the doctor into the meetings, saying they would rather have private interviews, but the majority favored inviting the doctor. Two days later, in the breakfast period, a patient asked, "Could you come to one of our group meetings, doctor?" The doctor agreed, set a date for his first meeting with them, and the series of weekly group psychotherapy meetings was begun.

Once more, this time by decision of the group through democratic discussion methods, we have been able to reconstruct for the patients a "family group" where they have been able to express themselves without fear. The group worker has been very clearly recognized by the patients as a "mother" and the doctor has become the "father." The doctor feels that this attempt to set up a pseudo-family group has accelerated the "healing" of the schizophrenics' disorganized regression. In his analysis of the use of this method in treatment, the doctor states:

"Schizophrenia seems to result from a loss of significant love object, with a consequent disorganized regression along the course of psychosexual development. The distortion of reaction pattern seems to start very early when the only possible love objects are the basic family group. Therefore, in group therapy, we attempt to reconstruct a more favorable 'family group' for the enfeebled ego to deal with in its reapproach to reality testing. By being loving, understanding, encouraging, permissive, and gently controlling, we attempt to make it far less difficult for the damaged ego to reassert itself and to grow to maturity. Since the mother is the usual primary love object outside ourselves toward which the first reality testing takes place, it was felt that we should duplicate this early phase in group therapy for our present insulin group. With the common experience of insulin treatment as a background, our group worker made individual contacts with each patient, then fostered group spirit. Clinically it became apparent that she was a 'mother' to the group and this feeling was carefully nurtured. In a sibling relationship, the group was able to find mutual support. Thus, they were able to organize and progress without recourse to the psychosis as a defense. The role played by the mother group therapist is a primary one and makes the greatest demands in time and understanding on the therapist involved. It would seem that this method of reliving family relationship may be a significant contribution to group psychotherapy in schizophrenia." [3]

In this paper I have presented, in very abbreviated form, some of the understanding we have developed concerning the place of social group work in a psychiatric treatment setting, and a glimpse at our practice. We are convinced that the group worker can and does play a significant role as a member of the treatment team.

REFERENCES

1. Halle, Louis and Landy, Arthur, "A Plan of Group Psychotherapy for Psychotic Patients," unpublished paper.
2. Halle, Louis, and Ross, Jack F., "A Therapy Program for Schizophrenic Patients," Department of Medicine and Surgery Information Bulletin, Psychiatry and Neurology Division, Veterans Administration, IB-10-13, July, 1951.
3. Coyle, Grace L., "Not All Group Activities Are Group Work," THE GROUP, November, 1944.
4. Perlman, Bernice T., "Group Work With Psychotic Veterans," *American Journal of Orthopsychiatry*, Vol. XIX, No. 1, January, 1949.
5. Wilson, Gertrude, "Hospital Group Work," unpublished paper.
6. Fisher, Raymond, "Contribution of Group Work in Psychiatric Hospitals," paper presented at A.A.G.W. meeting, National Conference of Social Work, June, 1949.
7. Konopka, Gisela, "Similarities and Differences Between Group Work and Group Therapy," paper presented at National Conference of Social Work, May, 1951, published in *Selected Papers in Group Work and Community Organization*.
8. Sloan, Marion B., "Social Workers Share the Job in a Veterans Hospital," unpublished thesis, Western Reserve University, April, 1948.

[3] Strate, Gerald, memorandum re treatment of schizophrenia through integrated approach of psychiatrist and group worker at V.A. Hospital, Cleveland, O., May, 1952.

9. Sloan, Marion B., and Wagner, Esther O., "Report on Social Group Work in the Neuropsychiatric Section of Crile Veterans Administration Hospital," unpublished report, January, 1949.

GROUP WORK WITH CEREBRAL PALSIED
ADULTS *By Robert M. Armstrong, Joseph*
B. Pyles and Mary E. Crawford

DURING the past year, 1952, the United Cerebral Palsy Association of Cleveland has sponsored a young adult group for the Cerebral Palsied at the Cleveland Rehabilitation Center. This has been the first attempt by this organization to provide group work services to adults, most of whom have had extensive medical experience with speech, occupational and physical therapy. Many members have had vocational counseling provided by the Bureau of Vocational Rehabilitation but few have had work experience in a regular job. How can the group worker be of service to them? What are their problems as young people? Are their problems different from those facing other adults? These are all questions on which we can make some observation on the basis of a year of experience in working with this group.

According to John F. Pohl, M.D., "Cerebral Palsy is the term used to designate a group of neuromuscular disorders in which there is an impairment or loss of muscular control due to a lesion of the brain." [1] This damage can occur at any period of life. As a handicap, cerebral palsy places various kinds of limitations on the physical, intellectual, and emotional growth of those afflicted with it. When we think of the simple but important problem which we all face in learning as children to feed ourselves, we develop appreciation for the kind of limitations which the cerebral palsied person must face. The cerebral

[1] Pohl, John F., M.D., *Cerebral Palsy*, Bruce Publishing Company, St. Paul, Minn., p. 1.

palsied person from the very beginning faces additional frustrations in the basic struggle for life. His learning is also difficult. Children learn through playing with blocks and toys, through picture books and through sight and auditory stimuli, but the cerebral palsied child may not be able to pick up blocks or to play with toys.

As a cerebral palsied child grows up he becomes increasingly sensitive to the feelings of those around him. Dr. Earl Carlson gives this account of his feelings as a spastic: "A normal man finds no difficulty in walking along a narrow plank which lies on the ground. If the plank is raised 20 feet in the air, he will go through the same motions painfully and hesitantly, granted that he can perform them at all. He is experiencing the difficulties which beset the spastic at all times. 'To be scared stiff' is no empty figure of speech, but a singularly exact one when applied to the spastic. Fear destroys the concentration which enables him to control his unruly muscles." [2]

With this brief knowledge of the handicap, let us look at the composition and makeup of this group.

By and large this group consists of members of middle- and lower-class background. They range in age from 17 to 34 years and are almost equally divided between men and women. At the end of the year there are 10 female and 14 male members of the group. The median attendance index for the group is .795. (An index of .70 is considered high.) The group members have a variety of types of cerebral palsy according to medical records and are diverse in so far as school grade completed is concerned. From a physical standpoint, six of the members rely completely on the wheelchair for locomotion and five of the members are unable to feed themselves. These figures include some duplication, since of the six who rely on the wheelchair for locomotion, four are unable to feed themselves.

[2] Carlson, Earl R., M.D., *Born That Way*, The John Day Company, N.Y., 1941, p. 68.

The fifth person who is unable to feed herself can walk around, speak, and is otherwise unhampered except for the use of her arms which have to be locked together in order to be controlled.

The high attendance index for individual members and the high median for the group is one indication of the strong interest on the part of the members in this activity. No member is absent except in the event that he is sick or is unable to get the needed transportation. What accounts for this high interest? What holds together such a group which is so diverse in physical ability, school background, class background and age?

Analysis of the bond between the 24 members of this group reveals the following facts which may help us to answer these questions. Only one sub-group of four exists in the entire group. This is made up of two co-ed pairs of members who date each other. The rest of the group is made up of individuals whose heterosexual interests more nearly resemble those of the early adolescent than of adults. This is due to the lack of opportunity for social experiences of this type. There is one strong friendship between two men and one between two women members. In an entire year of close relationship in the program at the Rehabilitation Center, no appreciable change occurred in the structure of relationships in the group.

We found, in addition, that the group members as a whole were held together by an identification with the local executive of the UCPA and with the group worker. This identification operates because of the strong drive of the members to want to do the so-called "normal" thing for their stage of development, such as dancing, going on a hayride and other co-ed programs. Consequently, they try to be like the worker and like this executive. The bond between the members and the executive is stronger than that between the worker and members, partly, we believe, because he is cerebral palsied himself and provides an easier person with whom to identify as an "ego ideal."

An area of great concern to the members is that of finding a job. The drive for independence along with the struggle against dependence constitutes one of the main social problems of these young people. The discussion about jobs in the club came about when a volunteer worker suggested that the club members might enter into a project of making Christmas tree decorations for sale. He showed them the model and explained about the labor required and what the sales value would be. A work project was contemplated by the group at one time. Here was an interest that meant a great deal to the members. In evaluation of the plan there were many unforeseen obstacles that the group could not surmount due to their varying degrees of physical handicap. Resource people on employment were brought in at the request of the members. One of the main questions asked by these resource people was: "Can you compete with others on the labor market?" The thought was conveyed to the members that they must be able to compete against the labor market and that there were not too many amends for their handicaps. The members did not receive any encouragement as to their being employable in a competitive market. They were helped to face the fact that their degree of handicaps made them unemployable in regular industry. This created great emotional problems that the group worker had to be aware of and help to alleviate through club programming.

Of a membership of 24, only three are employed. One is a cabinet maker by trade, but sort shoes in a salvage industry; another is employed as a janitor in a large manufacturing concern; and the third sells greeting cards for himself. The remainder of the members are not employed which means as adults they must depend on their parents to provide them with support.

The conflict around the independence-dependence struggle can be seen in who is permitted to join the club. Members have repeatedly brought up their feelings that polio victims, who also participate in the program of the Rehabilitation Center, should not be invited to join the group because "they take over" clubs. Whenever any handicapped person applied for membership in the club, the first question that would be raised was, "Is he a cerebral palsied person?" If there was any question as to whether the applicant was a "CP," immediate action would be taken by the Membership Committee to check with the Rehabilitation Center or the local UCPA concerning his status.

Another incident concerning a common feeling about the club was when one member suggested that the members have a camp of their own because they "understood each other better." The camp period sponsored by the Cleveland Rehabilitation Center for handicapped adults has always included all persons who have physical handicaps.

This group has an interesting pattern of relationships to the worker. While we do not wish to create the impression that the independence-dependence conflict is the only concern of the group members, it is a striking phenomenon in this group and recurs again and again and with much greater intensity than the workers have experienced in other groups. The members keep constantly directing feelings toward the worker by calling him the "boss" or "our director." Incidentally, these adults call themselves the "kids." This sometimes occurs in adult groups but is very much emphasized in this group.

We found in working with the President of the Club that he felt threatened when the worker stood up to make an announcement to the group during business meetings. He expressed this insecurity by pounding loudly with his gavel in order to attract attention. The President himself was in a wheelchair and consequently felt rivaled by the ability of the worker to stand up. While he expressed this rivalry he found it difficult to accept the help from the worker which he needed in learning how to conduct business meetings. The worker established a relationship with the President by taking special pains to help the President to get transportation for a group trip, to get together with him prior to the meeting to plan the agenda, to sit behind the President during the meetings so that he could help support the President and yet not be in a position so that he would have to stand up and threaten the President's leadership. The result of this approach was to modify the feelings of rivalry of the President and to help him to feel more secure and competent in his leadership in group meetings.

In their relationships with parents which we pointed out as being so important, we have found that most of the members have some conflict over their dependence.

Mary, who is 32 years of age, is typical of this type of dependent adult. In preparation for her trip to camp, her mother registered her with UCPA. Mary's mother was very concerned about whether she would be able to do things for herself at camp such as dressing, fixing her hair, tying her shoes, etc. Her mother said, "I don't see how Mary can go to camp because she can't do anything for herself. Maybe I had better go along." She was assured by the camp director that there would be adequate staff to look after Mary. After the first day at camp, Mary had begun to dress herself and near the end of the period she was fixing her hair alone. Group pressure in the camp situation often helps to foster a desire for independence which is not necessarily present in the home situation.

Mary also had an intensive problem in heterosexual relationships. She often suggested to one of the staff that they should have games like "Post Office" and "Spin the Bottle" (kissing games). She often remarked, "Why don't the boys ask me to dance?" When she caught her "husband" on Sadie Hawkins Day she acted out many of her feelings about men in attempting to live through a "marriage" relationship. She lavished her "husband" with affection. The great display of affection was more than the "husband" could accept so he ended the relationship with a "verbal divorce." The rejection caused Mary to revert back to her everyday role of being passive in her relationships with male campers. Mary's problems required the help of an understanding staff so that she could accept to a limited degree why she was having difficulty in relationships such as this. Her adjustment from a heterosexual standpoint can be materially aided by case work or psychiatric counseling along with her group experience. The social and sex education of cerebral palsied persons such as Mary is often neglected.

Earl Carlson recalls this account of his first love experience which indicates how much help one of these young adults might need at this time. "He who has thought of himself as being cut off from the rest of mankind by his handicap suddenly discovers that the barrier has vanished, and he idealizes the girl who has released him from isolation. This avalanche-like emotional reaction makes love a serious problem for spastics because it is difficult for them to choose the right mate when they are apt to be swept off their feet emotionally whenever anyone takes a personal interest in them." [3]

Our experience with parents of these group members confirms the observations of other contributors to this field. E. M. Denhoff makes the point that the recognition and treatment of emotional difficulties due to psychogenic factors should be considered as important as the correction of the motor impairments. The entire habilitation program is wasted unless the emotional needs and problems of the child are adequately met. Disturbance in the child's emotional life, psychosexual development and social experience are often the determining causes of behavior disorders and neurotic patterns of adjustment. [4]

This kind of behavior we have observed in the exaggerated

[3] *Op. cit.*, Carlson, p. 71.
[4] Denhoff, E. M., Smirnoff & Holden "Cerebral Palsy," *New England Journal of Medicine*, Vol. 245, No. 8, 1951, pp. 728-735.

dependency needs of Mary. The relationship which the worker builds with the members of the group, the group projects, and the cooperation which all of these involve in so far as parents are concerned, makes the group an ideal place around which to build better understanding between parent and adult member. The sensitive worker can observe the adjustment of the handicapped adult in a variety of social situations and can be extremely valuable in helping these adults learn to relate to one another as well as being an aid in psychiatric and case work diagnosis and treatment. We have found that the worker as well as the parent needs to have as complete an understanding of the nature of cerebral palsy as is possible. Before he "gets his understanding in his muscles" he may have a tendency toward a feeling of rejection of the handicapped person. This may show itself in a variety of forms of behavior such as over-solicitation, denial of the handicap, a desire to change the handicap, a physical revulsion or sickness at the sight of the cerebral palsied person, or impatience with his slowness.

The program of the group itself seems merely to be a means to an end. This end is a co-educational social experience in an informal setting. Types of program activity are square dancing of a simple variety, games, singing, hay ride, dramatics, planning and having parties, putting out a newspaper, having guest entertainers, discussing job opportunities, engaging in some craft activities and listening to records.

Earlier in the day's activity, the members have an opportunity for swimming, public speaking, speech therapy, and English practice under trained leadership. After this they have a break during which preparations are made for them to eat together, before the meeting. They spend a long time talking and visiting over the meal. During the business meeting they raise many objections if adequate time is not provided for them to get together in small groups to talk, relax and enjoy each other's company. The recognition of this need by the workers has resulted in a very flexible schedule. If the members enjoy talking with each other, rather than working on a phase of program, the worker supports this activity since group members have little real opportunity to meet each other socially. During these periods the workers have an opportunity to become more intimately acquainted with individuals and their problems. At one meeting the worker helped Mary to begin an interest in learning how to sew and helped a volunteer to instruct her. In another situation the worker learned of a member's problem in getting public assistance and enabled him to work out a program to explore the possibility of getting this assistance.

Many members say that people are always reminding them to relax and, of course, all of them are constantly striving to do this. Channeling efforts at control toward constructive ends has been possible through games and group projects. An example of this use of program occurred when the worker came upon a member who was making an attempt to drink coffee out of a cup without spilling it. The young man said that he could control his arm if he really concentrated on it. The worker asked him if he had ever played "Pick-Up-Sticks." This group member was interested in learning the game. Since he had difficulty in relating to women, the worker suggested that he might play with one of the most understanding women volunteers. He began to play the game with her and seemed to have a happy experience while working at the same time on this problem of control of his arm.

This type of group experience has both social and educational value. From the standpoint of social experience these sessions offer an opportunity for the adult to work through some of the feelings of competition, rivalry, dependence, and independence with an understanding worker and to find his place in a social group of his peers. The group offers the member support and courage which he gains from social contact with other persons faced with similar adjustment problems. This group offers the sensitive worker an opportunity to help with problems around individual adjustment, education, employment, public assistance, and an opportunity to know the problems which each member faces in his family situation. There is a great deal of opportunity for interpretation and education of parents through the relationships built around the group.

We have found that with this group the same methods are used as in working with any group. The differences, however, are important in that the worker has to learn to "shift gears" and to allow much more time for decision making and programming. He may have to exercise a great deal of leadership in decision making and may even have to make some decisions for group members in order to help them achieve and accomplish a particular project. The frustration tolerance of this group is rather low and extensive discussion is quite difficult since most members have some degree of speech impediment.

On the basis of our observation of the lay person's relationship with a group such as this we are convinced of the value of the contribution of the trained social worker to this program. The group worker must possess self-awareness and must have a clear understanding and acceptance of his own feelings about the physical handicap. The role which the worker plays with this group has less of the social action focus and more of a focus on social relationships. His job is to help the individuals and the group as a whole to use this experience to increase skill in relating to other men and women.

While this emphasis is part of the major purpose of the group, it does not differ from the purpose of group workers in other settings; so we can say that the same principles apply but they must be adapted to the limitations of this particular handicap.

BIBLIOGRAPHY

1. Abel, M., "Feeding the Child with Cerebral Palsy," *American Journal of Nursing,* Vol. 50, September, 1950, pp. 558-560.
2. Bakwin, R. M., M.D., and Bakwin, H., M.D., "Cerebral Palsy in Children," *Journal of Pediatrics,* Vol. 39, July, 1951, pp. 113-122.
3. Bice, Harry V., "Psychological Services for the Cerebral Palsied," *Nervous Child,* Vol. 8, April, 1949, p. 191.
4. Bice, H., and Holden, S., "Group Counseling With Mothers of Children With Cerebral Palsy," *Journal of Social Casework,* Vol. 30, 1949, pp. 104-109.
5. Bice, H. V., "Two Steps Toward Improvement of Psychologic Services for Cerebral Palsied," *American Journal on Mental Deficiency,* Vol. 54, October, 1949, pp. 212, 217.
6. Carlson, Earl R., M.D., *Born That Way,* The John Day Company, New York, 1941.
7. Deaver, G. G., "Life Adjustment for Cerebral Palsied," *Nervous Child,* Vol. 8, April, 1949, pp. 222-225.
8. Denhoff, Eric, M.D., "Needs in the Field of Psychologic Appraisal of Children With Cerebral Palsy," *The New England Journal of Medicine,* Vol. 243, July-December, 1950, p. 524.
9. Denhoff, E. M., M.D. and Others, "Cerebral Palsy," *New England Journal of Medicine,* Vol. 245, November 8, 15, 1951, pp. 728-735, 770-777.
10. Denhoff, E. M., M.D., and Holden, R. H., "Pediatric Aspects of Cerebral Palsy," *Journal of Pediatrics,* Vol. 39, September, 1951, pp. 363-375.
11. Dowd, H. L., "Pediatrician Looks at Cerebral Palsy," *Nervous Child,* Vol. 8, April, 1941, pp. 244-245.
12. Egel, Paula F., *Technique of Treatment for the Cerebral Palsy Child,* The C. V. Mosley Company, St. Louis, 1948.
13. Elledge, Caroline H., *The Rehabilitation of the Patient,* J. B. Lippincott Co., Philadelphia, London, Montreal, 1948.
14. Fay, T., M.D., "Cerebral Palsy," *American Journal of Psychiatry,* Vol. 107, September, 1950, pp. 180-183.

15. Gesell, A., "Development of Diagnosis and Guidance for Palsied Child," *Physiotherapy Review*, Vol. 28, May-June, 1948, pp. 128-129.
16. Giden, Francis M., "And Descant on Mine Own Deformities," *Nervous Child*, Vol. 8, April, 1949, pp. 234-243.
17. Greenwood, Edward D., "The Psychiatrist's Role in the Treatment of Cerebral Palsy," *Crippled Child*, Vol. XXIX, No. 4, December, 1951, pp. 6-7, and 28.
18. Kinoy, Sarah Jane, "Camping for the Cerebral Palsied," *Nervous Child*, Vol. 8, April, 1949, pp. 203-213.
19. Kessler, H., and Abramson, A. S., "Symposium: Rehabilitation; Rehabilitation of Paraplegic," *New York State Journal of Medicine*, January 1, 1950, pp. 43-47.
20. Little, S., "Investigation of Emotional Complications of Cerebral Palsy," *Nervous Child*, Vol. 8, April, 1949, pp. 181-182.
21. Mason, Mildred A., "Social Service Coordinates Community Program for the Cerebral Palsied," *Crippled Child*, Vol. XXIX, No. 2, August, 1951, pp. 19-20, 30.
22. Menninger, William C., M.D., "Emotional Adjustments for the Handicapped." Reprint from the December, 1949, issue of *Crippled Child*.
23. Norfleet, G. M., "Mental Hygiene Program for Palsied Child," *Physiotherapy Review*, Vol. 27, March-April, 1947, pp. 101-106.
24. Phelps, W. M., M.D., "Cerebral Palsy Problem," *Postgraduate Medicine*, Vol. 7, March, 1950, pp. 206-209.
25. Phelps, Winthrop, M., M.D., *Rehabilitation of the Handicapped—A Survey of Means and Methods.* Edited by William H. Soden, The Ronald Press Co., New York, 1949.
26. Phelps, Winthrop M., M.D., "Description and Differentiation of Types of Cerebral Palsy," *Nervous Child*, Vol. 8, April, 1949, pp. 107-127.
27. Pahl, John F., M.D., *Cerebral Palsy*, Bruce Publishing Company, St. Paul, Minn.
28. Roe, F. Hall, "I Face the Future," *Crippled Child*, Vol. XXIV, No. 3, October, 1944, p. 89.
29. Severns, Emma, "Social-Emotional Factors in Cerebral Palsy," *Crippled Child*, Vol. XXIX, No. 6, April, 1952, pp. 8-9.

30. Sirkin, J., "Five Years' Work With Cerebral Palsy—Critical Analysis," *Psychiatric Quarterly*, Vol. 14, January, 1940, pp. 185-193.
31. Soden, William H., Editor, *Rehabilitation of the Handicapped—A Survey of Means and Methods*, The Ronald Press Company, New York, 1949.
32. Strauss, A. A., and Lehtinen, L. E., *Psychopathology and Education of the Brain Injured Child*, Grune & Stratton, New York, 1947.
33. Usher, E., "Integrated Approach to Cerebral Palsy," *Delaware State Medical Journal*, September, 1946, pp. 196-199.
34. Ware, Louise E., Ph.D., "Parents of the Orthopedically Handicapped Child," *Mental Hygiene Series No. 3*, Association for the Aid of Crippled Children, 580 5th Avenue, New York 19, N.Y.
35. Weymouth, Edna E., "Medical Social Work-Aid to Adjustment," *Crippled Child*, Vol. XXVII, No. 5, February, 1950, pp. 14-15.

8

Group Work and Social Action

THE PLACE OF AGENCY STRUCTURE,
PHILOSOPHY, AND POLICY IN SUPPORTING
GROUP PROGRAMS OF SOCIAL ACTION
By Helen Northen

HELPING members of groups to achieve together socially desirable goals has always been considered an integral part of the function of every social group worker. It is through education resulting in collective social action that people move out beyond their relationships in intimate, primary groups and program geared to meet their own personal needs and interests to ever-widening circles of relationships and program of greater social significance. When there are social issues and community problems about which the agency-as-a-whole is concerned and where there are official channels within the agency and between agency and community for effecting appropriate action in relation to these issues and problems, primary groups within the agency may move further and more

236

effectively because of the support provided by such structure and agency-determined goals.

The Y.W.C.A. is one agency which has set forth officially, through its regular membership channels, a program of Public Affairs and other emphases to achieve the societal goals which it deems desirable for carrying out its commitment "to help bring about a more abundant life for the women and girls it serves." Currently, the statements of its national Public Affairs program and Interracial Policies[1] give direction to its efforts in this area. One specific section deals with intercultural-interracial relations and pledges the Y.W. to work to insure equal opportunities on a non-segregated basis for all minority groups. Local associations are committed to move forward as rapidly as possible in implementing these policies through practice. This article will describe how one Y-teen club[2] worked for a year and a half on a social action project in line with the agency's interracial policies on a local community level.

Hiland Branch is one of five geographical branches of a large Metropolitan Y.W.C.A. It serves sixteen neighborhoods which have Negro populations varying from one to ninety-six per cent of the population. It has been working in a purposeful way for many years toward achieving complete integration of minority groups into all phases of its program.

The Hi-ho Y-Teen club was a group of sixteen senior high school girls, all Negroes, ages 15-18, who have been affiliated with Hiland Branch for three years. It has carried out a varied program to meet the needs and interests of its members. Included in its program have been sports—swimming, basketball, roller skating; social events—parties, dances, picnics, suppers,

---

[1] National Public Affairs Program (A program of study and action), The Woman's Press, 1946, 600 Lexington Avenue, New York, Introduction Interracial Policies of the Y.W.C.A.'s of the U. S. A., Edited by Dorothy Height, The Woman's Press.

[2] Y-Teen clubs are groups for girls 12-18 years of age affiliated with the Y.W.C.A.

teas; discussions of teen-age concerns—boy-girl relationships, sex education, jobs, marriage, colleges, current events; service projects, including participation in activities around the Y's "World Fellowship" program. It has participated actively in interclub council meetings, interclub activities, and events for the entire membership of the branch.

The question of racial discrimination in the local community has come up many times in discussions and informal conversations. The adviser, who was aware of the members' ambivalent feelings about racial backgrounds and discrimination, recognized that the group was ready to move from "talking" to "doing something" about community conditions affecting them. When there was an opportunity, she picked up on the girls' expression of interest:

"After the business meeting, the girls were preparing to go to the gym to roller skate. Mary Lou said, 'It's a darn shame there isn't any other place where we can skate.' Julia said, 'Oh, the gym's all right, but it's just not the same as a rink.' Marjorie remarked that every time she passed the Wellington rink, she became mad, and felt like giving the owner a piece of her mind. Jackie asked, 'and what good will that do?' Marjorie retorted, 'No good, I guess, but it makes me mad anyway.' Jane asked if Marjorie really thought the owners of private rinks should admit Negroes if they really didn't want them. Marjorie said she didn't know but she sure wished she could skate there—just once. Adviser asked if the girls thought there might be something they could do about it. Jackie thought they would have to find some Negroes who would be willing to start and operate private enterprises of their own . . . The general feeling was that getting some rinks of their own was the most logical answer. Marjorie said we could talk about it further next week."

The next week, in the supervisory conference with the volunteer adviser, the group worker helped her to think through some of her own feelings about segregation and whether or not working to establish segregated rinks for Negroes was the answer. The adviser was helped to think about possible alternatives to meet the girls' desire to do something about the situation, and was given specific help with program resources. At the next meeting,

"The girls were reminded by Marjorie about their discussion on roller skating and thought maybe Miss Roberts (the adviser) would have some ideas about something they might do. Adviser said she had been talking to Miss Parsons (the supervisor) about this and that Miss Parsons thought it wonderful that the Hi-hos were interested in doing something about discrimination. Perhaps segregated rinks weren't the answer, and it might help if they had someone talk to them who knew how to go about these things. Marjorie asked if the others would like to do this. There was enthusiastic response. Mary Lou asked, 'but who could we get?' Adviser said that Miss Parsons had made a suggestion of a minister who was chairman of an interracial action group in the city. Marjorie called for a vote, and it was unanimously decided to invite Reverend Castleman to a meeting in the near future."

When Reverend Castleman spoke to the club about prejudice and discrimination and the work of the Interracial Action group in combating them, the Hi-hos were enthusiastic. With some help from their adviser, they brought out their questions about discrimination at the Wellington and Roxford skating rinks.

"Reverend Castleman was asked by Marjorie about the possibilities of doing something about this discrimination. He explained that it would be a long, hard fight and that a club like ours would be a good group to start the project if the girls felt they really wanted to do something about this. He told them about the hardships they would encounter in such a campaign. This did not seem to deter their ambitions and everyone talked at once about what could be the first steps. Reverend Castleman stressed the importance of getting other groups to work with them from the beginning and that this would mean having accurate information and ideas to present. Marjorie asked, 'are there groups in Hiland Branch who'll help us?' Adviser asked if they wanted to consider writing a letter to the interclub council—perhaps they would give some time to a discussion of this at the next meeting. They decided to write such a letter and also one to the adult committee for Teen Age Work, telling them of the plans they were making, and asking for their support."

When the letter from the Hi-hos was read at the interclub council meeting, many different points of view were expressed. After thorough discussion, the council voted to support the club and the chairman appointed an interracial committee of girls to work on the project. After consideration of their letter, the Committee for Teen Age Work, officially voted to support the project and referred it to the Committee of Management so that it could have the full support of the branch as a whole. The Committee of Management, believing that this project was clearly in line with the Public Affairs program and Interracial Charter of the Y.W.C.A., voted to make the project one of their major emphases for the year. Four members were appointed to a special committee on Interracial Roller Skating to pursue the project, and it was suggested that two members of the Hi-hos and the committee of the senior interclub council serve on such a youth-adult committee. Later, the Metropolitan Public Affairs committee agreed to serve in a consultative capacity, endorsed the project, and stimulated other groups throughout the Metropolitan Association to begin work on similar projects in the community.

The special committee discussed ways of proceeding and decided to (1) get further information about other roller skating rinks, particularly one in a neighboring community which has interracial skating; and (2) discover if other groups in the Y.W.C.A. and Hiland area might be interested in working on and supporting this project. Members of the committee, both girls and adults, were assigned to interview representatives of other community groups to enlist their support. At its next meeting, the committee decided to reserve the rink for an interracial roller skating party as a means of demonstrating to the management that such activities were possible. When the manager learned the party was to be interracial, he refused to rent the rink to the Y.W.C.A. In the meantime, interviewing of representatives of many community organizations took place. Because many of these groups were interested in the project, the special committee planned a community meeting on the subject, to which sixteen churches and social agencies sent representatives. There was lively discussion of possible action in the light of the manager's refusal to rent the rink. One subcommittee was appointed to proceed in gathering information and evidence for possible use in filing a suit against the skating rink, under the Civil Rights laws of the state. Another committee was to prepare petitions to be circulated, requesting that the rink be opened, and to arrange for visits to the manager by influential people. One member of the Hi-hos was appointed to the latter committee. After consideration of the results of many interviews with community leaders, it was decided to proceed with petitions to and interviews with the manager before attempting to enforce the Civil Rights law, since this might have more educational value and since the skating rink could probably circumvent the law on its claim of being a private skating rink rather than a public rink. Petitions were distributed to club members, committee members, and cooperating organizations for securing signatures. The Hi-hos circulated petitions among their friends and in groups to which they belonged. When the chairman of the special committee and two appointed members took the petitions to the rink manager, he reiterated his stand that opening the rink to Negroes would ruin his business and that he would not take the risk.

During the many months that passed while these events were taking place, the Hiland Community Council was becoming reactivated and sufficiently well established to begin to work on vital community projects. The newly elected chairman began to take an active role and went with the chairman of the special committee to interview again the managers of both the Wellington and Roxford rinks. The manager of the Roxford rink was somewhat conciliatory in his attitude, and agreed to permit at least one interracial roller skating party, under adequate sponsorship, providing the Wellington rink would act accordingly. This the Wellington refused to do.

Another milestone in community cooperation was reached when the Executive Committee of the Hiland Community Council, of which the director of the Y-Teen Department was a member, decided upon a program of education and action around the theme of Intercultural Relations for its first council meeting in the fall. The program included movies and discussion of the many facets of interracial tensions in the community. The Council formally voted to focus on the opening of recreational facilities on a non-discriminatory basis and to begin, specifically, with the interracial roller skating project. It mapped out a plan of bringing the problems and their possible solutions to all of the community groups who were a part of the council. It was agreed that the Y.W.C.A. would merge its efforts with those of the Council for most effective action. The chairman of the Y.W.C.A.'s special committee became a member of the Council Committee appointed to work on the project. After months of work, the chairman announced at a council meeting that the manager of the Roxford had agreed to open his rink to Negroes on a regular non-discriminatory basis. Many organizations expressed their willingness to support this rink in order to ease the manager's fears that this might result in loss of his "white business to the Wellington." This change in policy was to be publicized only among groups or agencies represented in the council, in order to avoid possible difficulties at the beginning.

As the over-all Y.W.C.A. and Community Council committees were working, the Hi-ho club continued its interest in the project and in other aspects of intercultural relations. A special youth sub-committee was set up, under the structure of the interclub council, on which two representatives from the Hi-hos served. It worked on the stimulation of program around the area of intercultural relations in all senior Y-Teen clubs in the department. Members offered to other groups such services as going to meetings to show films, using a quiz on interracial attitudes as a basis for discussion, and stimulating interest in the project.

The Hi-hos spent parts of many meetings discussing the progress of the project or problems related to discrimination. At one meeting, for example, the movie "Gentleman's Agreement" was used as a basis for discussion. This gave the girls some new knowledge about the problems of other minority groups in this country and helped them better to accept and understand similarities and differences between racial and religious groups. There were times when progress on the project seemed too slow, as in October, 1948, when:

"Julia asked, 'What ever happened about the Wellington?' Doris said, 'Oh, that—that never got anywhere.' The new adviser asked, 'Where were things concerning the Wellington when last you heard?' Julia started to explain the club's interest in the project last year. Marjorie chimed in, 'Oh, why get into all that again?' Adviser asked if they weren't interested any more. Marjorie said, 'It ain't that we aren't interested, but what's the use of being interested in something that doesn't get anywhere?' Doris agreed that it was hopeless. Adviser said she thought they had gotten somewhere, she recognized it might be hard for them to see this, but they had started the project, and did they know the Community Council was going to take it up this month? . . . Marjorie moaned, 'Yeah, but I sure would like to skate there just once before I die.' . . . By the end of the meeting, the girls had decided there was some hope, and something might yet be done."

All during the year, the Hi-ho representatives functioned on the various committees concerned, and brought in reports to the full club. The girls participated in a variety of interracial activities including the branch Christmas party, a skating party in the gym with a group of white Y-Teens, and Y-Teen fashion show. In the latter, one of the Hi-hos was a model and was later offered a permanent position as a teenage model at the department store which had sponsored the style show. This was the first such opportunity in the city for a Negro girl. These were some of the satisfying experiences which had made it possible for the club to maintain interest in and bear the frustration of the inevitably slow progress of the project itself.

At the meeting, when the new open door policy of the Roxford was announced to the Hi-hos by the adviser, there were many expressions of pleasure and satisfaction about their role in achieving this, combined with some hesitancy about being among the first Negroes to attend. At a subsequent meeting:

"Doris brought up the question, 'When are we going to the Roxford?' The following Wednesday was decided upon with the thought that a week-day would be less crowded and as Bernadine suggested, 'there might be some difficulty.' The adviser picked up on Bernadine's statement, said she hoped things would go smoothly —but they needed to be prepared for difficulties. Sara said, 'We're willing to risk it,' to which there was general agreement. Betty said that everyone in the area knows about the Roxford, but that no one wanted to be the first to go. Jane said she'd been talking with the kids at school about it and that was the way they felt—'and maybe if we started it, then kids would feel more like going.' "

So, the group went to the Roxford:

"The kids were rather nervous about going in and hung back, letting adviser go first. When inside, the group lined up against the wall and adviser approached the ticket window to be told that we could not enter because we didn't have membership cards in the skating club. The ticket seller averred that she had no knowledge of any different policy of admission and refused to let adviser see the manager."

This was a difficult experience for the Y-Teens. They reacted with expressions of anger toward the rink, adviser, Y.W., and Council for "letting them down." The adviser recognized with them that this was difficult, interpreted that there must have been some misunderstanding, and suggested they clear it with the Council either through letter or in person. Because they were too disappointed to act at this time, she let the matter drop. The next week, however, it was brought up by one of the girls, and the club appointed one member to report to the Council chairman its experience and to ask for clarification of the situation. When the adviser and representatives from the Council interviewed the manager again, he said the Roxford could not be open on an interracial basis during regular skating periods, but would be available one evening a week for use by organized groups, on a nondiscriminatory basis. The Council recommended that, because of its experience in interracial programming, the Y.W.C.A. sponsor the first such party as a demonstration to the community. The Y.W.C.A. explored with its groups the extent of interest in such an affair, and a decision was made to have a party for all members as soon as possible.

In enabling the Hi-hos to find some degree of satisfaction in pursuing their concerns, the role of leadership was significant. The advisers, through regular agency channels for individualized supervision, were given support and help in working directly with the club on this project and related program. The supervisor helped the advisers to relate the work of the club to other groups in the agency and community. She worked with other staff workers giving service to interclub councils and committees to help them use the Hi-hos and other Y-Teens effectively in the project. She co-operated with the professional worker and officers of the Community Council in relating club and agency to the larger whole.

The role of the adviser changed with the specific situation, but always involved skill in using understanding of these particular teen-agers' interests and needs and of the group work process in helping them to achieve their goals which coincided with those of the agency-as-a-whole. The adviser was a sensitive listener, who recognized and freed the members to express their feelings and concern about discrimination. She recognized when the members were ready to move from expressing feelings to taking action. Through the use of appropriately timed questions, she stimulated them to see that they might do something about their concerns and gave them concrete suggestions about the what and how of achieving their goals. She helped them use appropriate program resources within the agency and wider community. She shared her knowledge of agency philosophy, policy and administrative channels with them. She helped them to participate actively at their level—in getting information, planning program around this emphasis, circulating petitions, writing letters, participating on committees and attending the skating rink. She prepared them for certain difficulties which she foresaw, helped them to face the reality of conditions in the community, and at the same time gave them support and encouragement. She helped them to participate in other Y.W.C.A. program which would increasingly broaden their experiences in interracial groups, thus making it more possible for them to bear some of the frustrations inevitable to the situation. She helped them to select representatives wisely and these representatives to understand their functions in relating to and from club to committee or inter-group.

The role of the agency itself cannot be minimized. The "climate" of the agency was one of acceptance, so that the Hi-hos felt comfortable and identified with it, and hence could make good use of its resources and channels. The Association had accepted the national Public Affairs platform and Interracial Policies and was trying to move as rapidly as possible in all areas to implement these into practice. There was good experience in interracial groups and programming so that many people were ready to support and participate in the project. Administrative channels were clearly defined so that staff members and volunteers understood them and their use clearly. Staff and volunteers were active in many community groups so that relations between agency and community were relatively easy and effective.

The agency recognizes that the basic community problem of discrimination in recreational facilities is far from solved. It does believe, however, that a sound foundation in terms of agency and community education and support has been laid as a basis for continuous, appropriately timed action. Many groups in the Y.W. and larger community were made aware of the problem, learned to recognize and think through their own attitudes toward people of different backgrounds, and participated in action to bring about non-discrimination. The project served as a demonstration of how youth and adults, each in their appropriate role and according to interests and abilities, worked together to achieve the social goals of the agency.

Assignment in Social Action [1]
By Lucy P. Carner

When we received an assignment from the National AAGW to study the group worker's role in social action, we had the benefit of work recently done by Chapters in Boston, New York, Cleveland and Los Angeles. These reports, as well as policy statements of the AAGW, pertinent articles in

---

[1] Members of Committee: Lucy P. Carner, Chairman; Harry Frantz, Katherine Halsey, Helen Ray, Eunice Squires, Frances Edwards.

"The Group," and Kenneth Pray's presidential address at the 1946 National Conference were studied by our committee.

We began by asking ourselves two questions:

1) Is there a role the group worker should play aside from the role of the agency?

2) Is there a distinction between the role of the social worker in general and that of the social group worker?

Still licking our wounds from the battles in the Council Chambers of Chicago's City Hall over the proposed sites for housing projects for which federal money had been promised (provided Chicago presented a plan by August, 1950) we decided to examine the current struggle for public housing as a specific situation in which the following factors prevailed:

a) Social agencies (including group work agencies) were concerned.

b) The people with whom we work were directly affected.

c) There was a possibility of examining the tactics of a variety of organizations including neighborhood groups.

d) There was national as well as local significance.

e) The subject was included in the national program of the AAGW.

We first outlined our plan; we then invited two people from our own field who had given leadership to social and civic organizations working for a public housing program to meet with us. From them we wanted to find out what the group work agencies had done or had failed to do, and what could be learned from the tactics of the opposition. Finally, our committee met to pull together conclusions as to the role of the group worker and to outline our progress report.

General Observations:

Some of our observations are obviously not new, and are repeated here simply because they form the background for the concrete aspects of social action which we pulled out of our discussion on housing. We recognize the group worker as assuming responsibility for social action as a

1) *Citizen:*

As Benjamin Youngdahl stated in the March, 1947 issue of the Compass, "Social Workers: Stand Up and Be Counted": "A social worker is not only a professional person but a citizen of a local community, of a commonwealth or province, of a nation, and of the world." The committee recognized this responsibility but did not deal with it except to agree that it is healthy for a group worker to have relationships as a citizen outside the agency through which he can express himself on issues of personal concern to him. The issue of civil rights involved in this citizen function was recognized by us as an important issue of equal concern to all professional social workers, but we have not yet dealt with it.

This takes us to the next type of responsibility—that of

2) *Social Worker:*

Here we might have dealt with the special kinds of competence the professional worker brings to the task of social action, but we did not have time to do so except as our examination of functioning in the housing struggle implied certain types of competence arising out of our relationships to our constituency. We did, however, answer rather quickly one of our own questions as to whether there is a role for the professional worker aside from the role of the agency. We stated emphatically that the role of the worker is not passively waiting for the agency to act but constantly interpreting to the agency (to the Board, if the worker is the executive, or to the executive or committees if the worker is a program staff member) the situation of the agency's own constituency, the effect of social conditions upon them; and the connection, therefore, between the agency's services and efforts to change those conditions which so deeply and widely affect the lives of people served. Such efforts to change local conditions may take the agency all the way from the neighborhood to City Hall, to the State Capitol, to Washington, to the United Nations. We assume also that there is both a right and a responsibility for the professional social worker to engage in social action not only through the agency but through professional organizations.

Eveline Burns in the May, 1947 issue of The Compass, sets forth the types of knowledge and skill on which the social worker's claim to special competence in the field of social action should rest:

"In the first place, he has, or should have, an understanding of human beings and of how they behave as individuals and in groups, and a skill in dealing with them. Second, he has, or should have, a knowledge of the inter-actions of personal and environmental factors insofar as they influence a behavior and attitudes of the individual. Third, he has, or should have, a knowledge of the structure, functioning and potentialities of social institutions and in particular of those special measures, such as social security, child welfare institutions, and the like, whose direct objective is the enhancement of the welfare of the individual or family in contemporary society. Fourth, he has, or should have, an understanding of the relative contribution to human welfare which can be expected from the various social welfare approaches or techniques at different times in different places. In other words, he has a sense of priorities within the field of social welfare. . . .

It is the possession of this combination of knowledge and skill which gives the social worker the possibility of making a specific professional contribution and the specific areas in which he decides to operate must be those where these equalities have a direct bearing upon the issues raised. At the same time, if he is to be really effective in social action, he needs in addition a working knowledge of the kind of world in which he intends to operate."

3) Group Worker, per se

We come now to the heart of our questions: Has the group worker a specific function to perform in the field of social action, different from and complementary to the function of the social worker in general? Our answer is an emphatic "yes." For the group worker has the responsibility and the special opportunity of developing social awareness and skills in social action in a community.

We then examine our specific problem (the housing situation) to see what is involved in the group worker's efforts to perform this unique role in social action. And as we do this, we realize that the elements we considered are, in some instances, equally applicable to any well-directed attempt at social action.

The disconcerting fact about the civic and social work forces working for the housing sites (and the major social work agencies were the Chicago Federation of Settlements and the YWCA) is that these forces, well marshalled and impressive as they were on the city-wide level, were with only one or two exceptions, ineffective on the neighborhood level. But the strategy of the opposition was the strategy of enlisting neighborhood groups. One of the exceptions was the head of a settlement who, through the local neighborhood, and through church and civic groups in the neighborhood in which he lives, really affected the policies and the overt action of local neighborhood groups so that they withstood the pressures of the local improvement associations and stood up for the housing sites.

As the committee analyzed this situation, we compared it with others in which agencies and individual workers had been more effective in working with members of the constituency to effect social change. Settlements' action on recent relief cuts was one example. And we can cite instances in which a street light was achieved, or an alley cleaned or an interracial situation harmonized by club groups acting in terms of their "super-personal" interests. But we spent most of our time on the tougher problem.

This list is not a discovery but a reminder. It might have come out of an abstract discussion but in fact, it resulted from our discussion of successes and failures in social action in relation to the housing controversy.

1. The group worker should constantly cultivate first-hand intimate acquaintance with the experience of his constituency.

This sounds obvious but it is more difficult than it seems. One member of the committee, for example, confessed that rather than concentrate on the "gripes" of a group about neighborhood conditions, she ran off to make coffee. It is difficult but imperative that we be "good listeners."

2. The group worker should record that experience.

It was the story of a neighborhood family's inability to find a home that put the finishing touches on one board's hesitancy about coming out for public housing. It was a collection of firsthand stories of neighbors' experiences with relief cuts that drew a request from one congressman to a settlement for an interview on the relief situation. Records of the effects of social conditions upon people we know are useful not only with boards and congressmen but might be useful with our own groups as stories are written up in house organs, club papers, etc.

3. The group worker should recognize the clues to program in the casual reactions of members of groups toward the problems that press upon them.

A "gripe" can be a starting point for program if the group worker knows the art of making a connection between personal experience and wider social issues. It is obvious that it is the group worker's job to start where individuals and groups are in terms of concern that are real to them and their own degree of social development. This means that some form of social action is possible for a wide variety of age groups.

4. The group worker should use a variety of the recreation arts in helping groups to express their experiences and their attitudes.

The discussion group is by no means the only form of expression for social concern. Songs, living newspapers, posters, dramatics, the dance, all of these are forms of expression for social concern.

5. The group worker should keep clear for himself and others,

the principles underlying issues and should work for a wide area of agreement on principles.

On this basis a few battles were won in neighborhoods for public housing sites. The strategy used was not to imitate the tactics of demagogy, false information and appeals to prejudice of the opposition, but to remind people of the principles to which they were committed.

6. The appeal should be to motives of decency.

The committee was told that some of the groups that opposed housing were now ashamed. In a few cases, an appeal rather than an attack might have won them over.

7. The group worker needs to educate himself the hard way on some of the political realities of any situation.

He will do well to sit in Council Chambers or State Legislature or committee meetings and listen. Chicago group workers who are members of a housing committee were scheduled to attend hearings on housing sites in the City Council and to write up those hearings for the committee and found it an invaluable experience. He naturally then asks himself such questions as "Who is for a given proposal?" "Who is against it?" "Why?" "What is the relation of these forces to the board of the agency?" "To the constituency?" "Where were we when these representatives were elected?"

8. The group worker (in consultation, of course, with others concerned) should think out a strategy.

A strategy would have to take into account such factors as pressures in the agency's constituency, the most effective spokesman, the question of what and how, when do we do work with our membership? When do we act with them? When do we push them from behind? The sub-committee recognized that there are occasions when agencies and individual workers need to speak for people who cannot or dare not speak for themselves. We also recognize, however, the importance of seeking this as a temporary measure and striving always to help groups to speak for themselves. A practical dilemma is deciding to what extent we have a right to appeal to a group to do something because we ask it, knowing that once they have some experience, they can go forward on their own.

9. If representatives from the constituency are to play a part out in the front, the group worker needs to figure out ahead of time the kind of arrangements that will make this possible and effective.

For example, can the person afford to miss work, if not, can some compensation be arranged? Does a woman need to have her children cared for while she speaks at a hearing? Are carefare and lunch money needed? If a club representative is to come downtown to take part in a public function, all these details as well as help in organizing a speech or practicing so that one's voice can be heard, may be necessary arrangements if people are to speak for themselves.

10. Last, but not least, the group worker needs to begin far upstream.

The situation around which the sub-committee's thinking was organized was a crisis situation, but we recognize that where effective work had been done, it had begun long before the crisis rose. As has been said, it is the essence of group work to recognize stages of development and to expose people to situations and methods appropriate to their age and maturity. We should grasp at opportunities for groups to do small things. We should expand the areas of interest from the tight little group to the house council or community youth council or the inter-agency activity—thus broadening experience and exposing people to new ideas.

Beginning upstream also means keeping our boards informed of neighborhood conditions and working conditions, as well as agency activities. It may be as important for a board to know what wages girls make as to know what hour their club meets. It may be as important for a board to know what kinds of houses little children come from as what games they play. One executive, whom some of us know, includes in her monthly report to the board facts such as these as naturally as she includes reports of activities within the house.

Our Sense of Urgency

Members of our sub-committee feel a sense of personal urgency on this matter of social action which has been expressed for us in a statement by Kenneth Pray, in which he says that for a social worker to struggle to alleviate the social ills of society without working on the causes of these ills, so that there might be gradual progress toward a more just and democratic society, is to that extent practically living as a parasite on society. In addition to our sense of urgency on a personal basis, we wish again to remind ourselves that social action is of the very essence of our job—it is not a frill nor a fringe. It seems worthwhile to quote again from the definition of the function of the group worker in the words of Grace Coyle:

"The group worker enables various types of groups to function in such a way that both group inter-action and program activities contribute to the growth of the individual, and the achievement of desirable social goals. The objectives of the group worker include provision for personal growth according to individual capacity and need, the adjustment of the individual to other persons, to groups and to society, and the motivation of the individual toward the improvement of society; the recognition by the individual of his own rights, limitations and abilities as well as his acceptance of the rights, abilities, and differences of others. Through his participation the group worker aims to affect the group process so that decisions come about as a result of knowledge and a sharing and integration of ideas, experience and knowledge rather than as a result of domination from within or without the group. Through experience he aims to produce these relations with other groups and the wider community which contribute to responsible citizenship, mutual understanding between cultural, religious, economic or social groupings in the community and a participation in the constant improvement of our society toward democratic goals."

Recommendations

The sub-committee proposes that members of the AAGW record their experiences with groups (either constituencies or boards) in which social action is involved, that Chapters collect and discuss these records and that the National Social Action Committee attempt to have these records analyzed and widely distributed to the membership.

9

Group Work Services and the Community

GROUP WORK AND COMMUNITY SURVEYS
By Jean M. Maxwell

Honolulu, San Francisco, Los Angeles, Hot Springs, Columbus, Detroit, Syracuse, Greenwich, Hartford, Springfield, Worcester and Boston. Not the calling of a cross-country air flight this, but instead a geographic listing of some of the surveys of social health, welfare and recreation which have taken place in the past ten years.

In chronological review, one sees the marked beginning of community-wide surveys of social welfare services following the depression. With the war came interruption. In the post-war years, with increasing momentum, city after city has voted large sums of public and/or private monies, employed a staff, gathered facts, and the survey proceeded.

This increase would hardly seem to be happenstance. There have been at least four factors which have had influence in

257

moving local communities to review their needs, problems and services by the survey method.

One of these four factors is shifting, changing population make-up. Awareness of this change is seen in the constant anticipation of the 1950 Census by social workers everywhere wanting accurate up-to-date facts. Population changes in specific areas have come about in many ways. In one section of Indianapolis, rural groups came to an urban center during the war because of the call of industrial employment. Such changes as this have meant that as a country the United States has become in the last decade more than 50% urban. The housing shortage has meant that families have taken what they could find to live in, so that in some cases economic and social factors in an area are not so consistent as they were before. New housing projects have arisen to change the face of a section of a city. A visitor of ten years ago would be lost today on the east side of New York from 42nd Street to the Brooklyn Bridge. With these shifting populations have come many new problems in human relationships. To understand these new groups which bring different needs, surveys have been initiated.

A second factor which seems to have played a major role in the increasing desire for surveys is the new developments in understanding human relationships. The basic social sciences which contribute in major degree to the applied science of social work have taken many strides. Social work is not yet fully cognizant of the implications of the material found in such works as the Yankee City Series by Warner and Lunt, the work of Allison Davis and many others in sociology. The broad efforts of the mental hygiene movement to bring into the average citizen's realization the effects of his emotional state on his everyday life is shown by the articles appearing constantly in popular women's magazines today. The learnings of psychiatry from the programs in the armed services during the war years, from experimentation by such groups as the Menninger Clinic and the Cornelian Corner push social work practice to better understanding of individual motivation. The advancement of the technique of group therapy in the treatment of problems should have more careful understanding by those of us in the group work profession. Anyone who has heard Margaret Mead, the social anthropologist, analyze the position of women in our present-day society realizes the implications this has for understanding the modern woman in group life and community participation. While the extension of life through better medical care is an individual blessing society has not, in parallel fashion, extended opportunity for decent human relations for old people.

This list could be extended. The few citations are intended only as examples. Similarly we could review the new knowledge in the applied science of social work in techniques, understandings, and practice. The point in this second factor is that communities are being stimulated by a wide variety of sources toward increased understanding of human relationships. The marked lag between the available knowledge of human living and its problems and the practices being carried out by many of our existing agencies and organizations in our communities has called for investigation by survey. This would seem to be especially true of the education-recreation services.

A third factor would seem to result from the foregoing. The greater recognition of problems and the advancement of scientific knowledge has brought awareness of the need for more and better services. This means that more capable, well-informed people must be found to carry out these services. This has posed problems of finance to communities for the support of broadened services, and for the payment of adequate salaries to attract capable people. Is there a limit to voluntary contributions for either a single organization or federated financing? This financial problem has thrown us into great confusion which can be dispelled only by a clearer understanding of which services are accepted widely enough to be tax-supported and which are, peculiarly or temporarily, solely the responsibility of private agencies. Thus, we have in this third factor a two-fold problem, the securing of broader services and better equipped practitioners, and the pressures of community support. This will continue to plague us as we pass through the transition stage of understanding the division of public and private services, especially in recreation. Most surveys have had impetus because of the pressures of financing.

The fourth point which has been a factor in the need for community-wide surveys grows out of the newness of community planning for social welfare. The aims and goals of planning, the factors involved and the skills necessary are less well understood than those in other areas of social work. In some cities and towns, planning is still non-existent. Thus, communities come to a point of crisis which would have been avoided had the knowledge and skill been available. Pressure from influential groups for or against one particular form of service, pressure to cut down or hold down costs, misinterpretations of services—all of these can give rise to a crisis, the only solution to which seems to be a survey. A staff of experts drawn from without the community can be more bluntly articulate than can community residents. The Field Service Committee of the National Social Welfare Assembly has published an excellent statement which helps to clarify this question of the process of a study.

This list of factors is not exhaustive but does include four of the major reasons why a tremendous increase in money, time, and human effort is going into community-wide surveys city by city, month by month.

Because of several committee commitments, it has been our responsibility recently to read many of these survey reports, directing our concerns to the education-recreation sections. As one reads one after another, he becomes sensitive to the dilemma in which the study consultant finds himself. He faces, in fact, a series of dilemma which confront the total field, but which become intensified for him as he assumes responsibility for being the expert.

The consultant carries into a survey at this point little more than his own opinion, or the opinion of a small group with which he is affiliated. The criteria of measurement which he uses must of necessity stem from his own orientation, philosophy, and work experience, because the few agreements and understandings which we have in the field are so broad and philosophical that they are in essence non-measurable. The few principles which have broad acceptance get misinterpreted because there is no common agreement about the factors which relate to the principles, nor are there common criteria of measurement.

These several people who have done surveys have made a most creative contribution in written form by bringing together some of the best material available in this area. However, the best efforts to date are only milestones and the road ahead to good measurement is a long and rough one. It is in an effort to stimulate further examination and thought toward making principles more specific, to isolate measurable factors, to push for more scientific research on development of criteria against which to measure that this article has developed. It is a real case of rushing in where angels fear to tread.

One confusion in our thinking has arisen from considering need for recreation in terms of the existing services as they are popularly recognized. This has frequently resulted in studies of recreation actually being studies of the existing agencies which make recreation available. To avoid this error, it seems wise to start from a premise which each study used. That premise is that recreation should be available to everyone in the community, regardless of social or economic status, race or creed, age or sex.

This is a positive statement. But in several studies the positiveness was undercut by measuring need, not against the total population of the community, but against twelve social breakdown factors, primarily negative factors of infant mortality, tuberculosis rates, juvenile delinquency rates, etc. The Los Angeles Study [1] made a beginning in positive measurement by articulating certain categories of services and facilities which are necessary in a community recreation program. In that study, the total population's needs were analyzed by manageable geographic breakdowns by sex, age and ethnic background. However, the study was only able to go so far because at this time we do not have clearly articulated criteria against which to evaluate such findings.

We have said that recreation should be available to all. What kind? How much? Provided by whom? Please note that this discussion is on services, not facilities. Too often these two factors are completely confused. Do we believe that if only a limited sum of money is available it should go into facilities for children? This is a principle on which we have acted, even though at no point is it written. Do we see the need for physical activity in recreation as more basic than the need for group experience which will contribute to good human relationships? This again is a principle on which we have operated without articulating it.

Are we at the point in recreation where we can describe a positive maximum program of recreation services for a community? Can we articulate in specific form the recreation needs of individuals or groups by factors of age, sex, nationality and race, family unity and security, health, attitudes toward people, cultural interests, etc.? Unless this is done, we shall be bound by the past, with priorities given to physical activities for children, especially boys.

[1] A Community Plan for Recreation & Youth Services for Los Angeles, Roy Sorenson, Director, January 1, 1946.

Two examples of need for new thinking lie in recreation for the aged, and hospital recreation. In our present society, we are aware that the number of persons sixty years and older in the United States today has increased and will continue to increase markedly. Due to our present organization of society, these people as a group are no longer an economic asset, but rather a liability to the family. Due to our smaller and smaller housing units, their place in the home becomes ever more difficult. Recreation programs for the older citizen have passed beyond the demonstration stage. And yet in no study made to date has there been a good statement on the needs of this group, nor a high priority recommendation on providing services.

Similarly in hospital recreation, we saw a widespread program of recreation in hospitals for the armed services during the war. It was successful to the degree that a broader and broader program is being carried out in the Veterans Administration hospitals. From all the evidence now available, it is believed that a recreation program aids in speeding the recovery of a patient. In most local community hospitals the problem of shortage of bed space is a major one. The problem to the patient of paying for daily care is great. In recreation lies a potential for more rapid recovery of patients, freeing needed bed space. Yet in no study could one find reference to the needs for civilian hospital recreation or to services to meet these needs.

Can we shake off our pedestrain habits of thought and begin to view the needs more scientifically? It may well be that after this process our emphasis in priority of needs will remain somewhat the same, but the basis of measurement will be more realistic and less patterned on the past.

In measuring available services we have met confusion not unlike our confusion in measuring needs. Measurement of services available in recreation becomes confused with agencies which have been traditionally thought of as "recreation" agencies. This pattern of thought has limited review of services largely to study of those agencies known as "youth-serving agencies," to school programs, and to public recreation departments. This has led to some unfortunate judgments and recommendations. First, few studies have included in the community-wide surveys of recreation any real consideration of the programs of recreation available in churches, schools, nationality halls, lodges, unions, industries, or good commercial recreation centers. One would suspect that the content of existing studies of recreation is strongly influenced by the financial sponsorship of the survey, mainly federated finance institutions. If our concern is with the availability of recreational opportunities to all citizens, then our measurement of recreation must be broadened to include all the sources of such opportunities.

The second dilemma faced in measuring services of recreation is the lack of understanding of what should constitute a basic minimum program of opportunities that each community should provide.[2] Now without this, the study consultant falls back on existing figures of attendance as it presently exists combined with availability of facilities as the measurement of adequacy of services.

Few studies have attempted to do a qualitative measurement of services. This is the point at which group work has fared poorly in most community-wide studies. Because the measurement of services has tended to be mainly by attendance and by geographic spread of services and facilities, and because most surveys have allowed inadequate time for study, the survey expert has had to make rough assumptions about the adequacy of the group experience for individuals. There are, however,

---

[2] A basic minimum program of recreation is the guide for which most local communities are asking. The profession should provide minimum service requirements as a floor and maximum service outline as a blueprint for community guidance.

other more basic professional reasons which have curtailed real scientific examination of the quality of services. The main ones are the confusions which exist and the lack of criteria for measurement.

Are there degrees of qualitative experience in the field of recreation? Is group work the high quality service of recreation? Or is group work a method which *can* be used in a recreational setting, an industrial labor-management setting, a parent-education setting, an institutional setting? Is group work a method of helping people to relate to each other in groups, which the world needs as a professional service in all types of group association? Is it the hope that all recreation workers become group workers come the millenium? Can we not also conceive that all church workers become group workers?

Is this the time to step back and view dispassionately the perhaps accidental fact that group work grew up out of the recreational setting? Is this the point at which real distinction between recreation and group work should be made, and criteria for good recreation and good group work be developed, each measured separately as services to a community? Is it not recognized that group work as a method has as much to contribute to the growing field of intercultural relations as it has to recreation? Why then in community surveys is it combined with recreation, and not equally with intercultural relations.[3]

Group work has grown, and with its stages of growth have come new, changing concepts of its nature. A definite statement representing a concensus of A.A.G.W. members has recently been released in this journal. This represents in itself a stage of growth. Most of the work in the past in group work has wisely emphasized how it is done. Now we are stating what it is, as exemplified by the statement on definition. But the

---

[3] If group work is a part of recreation, then studies of recreation must provide for measurement of intensity of group experience, not just quantitative measurement.

momentum of community surveys now pushes us hard to state where this method and process can be applied, what makes this method different from others, and how one measures the effectiveness of this method.

Experimentation with the use of the group work method in intercultural relations, labor organizations, religious settings, institutions for mental patients, institutions for children without families—and many others, is helping to define the settings where this method can be applied. This experimentation should and will be broadened.

The point where the pressure is greatest is the measuring of the effectiveness of the group work method. We have sold communities on the need for good salaries to hire group workers to do group work. But the definition of a group worker varies tremendously. We have relied mainly on educational attainment and years of experience as the measure of the competency of a group worker. There is little consistency in the areas represented by educational attainment or in types of work represented in the years of experience. What factors, then, can be agreed upon as the measure of a professional group worker? Having agreed upon these factors, what criteria of performance can be established to distinguish good group work from poor group work?

This need for isolating measurable factors and establishing criteria holds for each aspect of the group work process and method. For example, we need criteria by which to measure our effectiveness in relation to:

1. Individual within the group. We state that one of our goals is to enable each individual to grow at his own rate of speed. Have we developed any organized set of factors by which we measure the growth of *each* individual in the group setting?

2. Group growth and development. What are the criteria of a "mature" group? We often speak of a group's "not being ready." What are the criteria we have in mind by which we

measure "group readiness"? Can we specify factors which distinguish stages of group development? Are there degrees of group unity? What are the factors involved and what are the characteristics of the various degrees?

3. Relation to society: What are the factors which show a group's relation to the wider community setting in which it is located? Can we isolate and define stages of responsible citizenship related to the interest and maturity of the group?

Similarly, we must work not only on getting wider use of supervision and recording as devices which must accompany the group work method, not only broaden our understanding of how supervision is done, and what constitutes good recording, but must also determine the elements of recording and determine degrees of adequacy, not to fit the time schedule of a job but to fit the real requirements for good group work.

So often one hears "this person has grown through supervision." What are the distinguishable characteristics which mark the growth of a professional group worker? Certain schools of social group work in their manuals of field work have isolated specific areas of knowledge and skill necessary to professional competence, and established criteria of what the student may reasonably be expected to know and do at specific time periods. This kind of analysis needs to be done for the professional worker. These are only simple questions posed as illustrations. Another way to state the problem is to ask what measurable factors do we consider essential in each part of the group work process, and what criteria do we use to measure these factors? The answers lie piece-meal in the minds and files of group workers, in printed material and staff discussion of agencies, local and national, using the group work method, in starts made in agency and community studies, in teaching materials of group work schools. We must now pull these pieces of work into an orderly arrangement, consciously recognizing that we are developing criteria of measurement for the use of the group work method that holds in any setting in which it might be used.

Here there are years of work ahead on clarifying purposes, isolating the affects of certain factors of need, and establishing types of services, before any sound basis for evaluating such a thing as group load per leader can be achieved. Are we any nearer to stating what is a good recreation leader? What a group load is for recreation leadership? [4]

Something should be done to clear the confusion around agency function and purposes as related to surveys of recreation. Most of the private agencies we know today as "national youth-serving" agencies grew up as movements prior to the widespread recognition of the need for recreation. Each grew up around a core of purpose directed toward a defined constituency, using recreational interests as one means to its end. Each group has consciously established its constituency feeling that an individual's personality and citizenship development is most effectively influenced by associations with this particular group of people. These divide themselves mainly into three groups, by age, and sex, culture and/or religion, and proximity, as of family, or working relationships.

These differences in purpose and function among private agencies must be considered in surveying recreation in a community. The definition of the function and purpose is the right of an agency in a democratic setting, even as it is the individual's right in a democracy to determine what he shall be. Any evaluation of the work of the agency must be in terms of that function and purpose, to determine whether or not it is doing what it says it set out to do. To measure the work of an agency only

---

[4] It is obvious that until we have answered some of the above mentioned questions about recreation and group work, nothing definitive can be said about group load. It is understandable that the attempts which have been made at establishing criteria of group load per leader for group workers have been questioned.

on recreation criteria, when recreation is only one means by which the agency works toward its purpose is unfair. As long as the agency has a group which believes sufficiently in its purposes and functions to support it, it has the right to exist, no matter what its state or being, in a free society. Through community planning, it is hoped that the relation between needs and available services can be more adequately seen by more people and especially by those who determine administrative policies of agencies. Agencies, national and local, must constantly be aware of the changing society in which they exist, testing whether their functions and purposes are valid in meeting needs. As new needs develop, some agencies must revise their existing raison d'etre to meet these needs, or bend every effort to create new ways or organizations to meet the new needs. This must always be viewed within the realistic control of finance, both private and public. Standards of democratic administration and efficiency must be articulated as criteria for agency functioning for good community service, but it must always be done within the framework of the statement of function and purpose of the agency, and not confused by power policies or professional prejudice.

Thus we face Herculean tasks before new studies arise:

1. The development of a good sound statement of principles of public-private responsibilities. This must take into consideration factors of local lag, local historical influences, and local politics. A constant forum of discussion must go on across the country to strive toward public education on the subject, and moulding of a statement of principles which can be applied in light of the different rates of speed with which communities develop.
2. The development of scientific study and scientific methods of measurement to create criteria for:
   a. Recreational facilities needed in towns, cities, suburban and rural communities.

b. Basic minimum recreational services for which a community could be held accountable.

c. The realistic correlation of recreational needs with social factors such as age, stability or instability of family life, intergroup attitudes, etc., and with new situations such as exist in hospital or insitutional settings.

d. All aspects of group work and its relationship to recreation as well as other functions.

e. Reconsideration of the present function and purposes of agencies in the light of the changed life of society today, along with recognition of the principle of self-determination in a free society.

The final need is one of the greatest. As the library of community studies grows, the importance of this tool of community planning and organization increases. How long will the field of social work, by default, permit itself to be studied by methods and processes inconsistent with the methods and processes of social work? Testimonies to the ineffectiveness of the "hit and run" methods of studies we have known in the past lie in the files of many communities, in the form of written reports about which nothing was ever done. They represent thousands of dollars and man-hours spent in learning the hard way. Communities will be as hard to educate on the need for sound methods and processes in surveys as they have been in any other form of good social work practice. This education cannot be left only to the study directors and experts, but must be a continuous process by all socially minded persons.

In group work, we believe that people thinking and working together produce new and better solutions to problems. This then is the Herculean source of strength from which will spring the solutions to the problems before us.

10

Group Work Supervision

"On-Lookers—An Investigation of the
Influence of an Observer's Presence
on Group Behavior" *By David F.
DeMarche and G. Michel Iskander*

Two schools of thought exist with regard to observation as part of the supervisory process. One states that observation visits to groups are very necessary, and that guidance of the leader solely on the basis of his reports is not really adequate.[1] The advocates of "observation" see this technique as part of teaching, yet they are aware that the supervisor's presence may alter the group situation and interfere with the group process. They are quite willing to concede this point, but hasten to add that frequent visits to the group will reduce this hazard and generally will result in the group's acceptance of the observer as an integral part of the agency.

The second school of thought holds such visitation to be

[1] Sidney J. Lindenberg, in his *Supervision in Social Group Work* presents this position quite clearly.

unnecessary—in fact, to be quite objectionable.[2] Its adherents believe that the presence of a visitor affects the interaction of the group and alters the role of the worker. The worker, or leader, becomes self-conscious and supervisor-conscious, and may tend to feel a lesser responsibility for the group because of the observer's presence.

Undoubtedly both groups can muster arguments to support their particular point of view. However, there is little evidence of scientifically gathered data to substantiate the opinion of either group. In order to determine the extent to which the presence of an observer actually does influence group interaction, the authors conducted the experiment presented in this article. This limitation of the experiment should be kept in mind.

The Experimental Design

In setting up the experiment it was necessary to meet certain conditions, to secure groups for observation which: 1) were fairly comparable as to age and socio-economic status, 2) met regularly, 3) were engaged in similar activities, 4) had leadership with comparable training and experience, and 5) had clubroom facilities permitting various types of observation.

Four groups were selected for observation. These were boys' clubs belonging to the Springfield College "campus clubs." These boys resided in the neighborhood and represented a similar socio-economic background. The ages of the members ranged from 9 to 16 years. Each club had an adult leader or worker. All the leaders were Springfield College students majoring in Group Work. Each club met once a week and in addition to its recreation activities held a club "meeting," lasting from 20 to 40 minutes. In such a meeting, the group usually engaged in accepting new members and collect-

[2] Gertrude Wilson and Gladys Ryland in *Social Group Work Practice* are spokesmen for this conception.

ing dues, in discussing problems facing the group, and in evaluating previous activities and planning new ones. These meetings were held in the special clubrooms provided by the College.

Over a period of eight weeks, each of the four groups was observed eight times, or once per week. Four of the meetings were observed from an observation room without the group's, or the leader's, knowledge. The other four meetings were observed while the observer was sitting with the group members in their clubroom, with their knowledge. The observation alternated each week between the first and second types of observation. To clarify: meetings 1, 3, 5, and 7 were observed from an observation room, without the group's knowledge. In meetings 2, 4, 6, and 8, the worker conducted the observation while sitting with the group.

The observation conducted without the group's knowledge required two sets of conditions: 1) Physical facilities which would make such observation possible. These facilities consisted of a regular clubroom adjacent to an observation room. The latter was provided with a "one way glass." Through this window the observer, sitting in a darkened room was able to watch without being seen. 2) The worker had to plan his observations in such a way as to eliminate the possibility of the leader and the group members knowing that they were being observed. This required his getting to the observation room prior to the meeting time and leaving it only after making certain that his exit would not be noticed.

In preparation for observation of the group with the group's knowledge, the worker asked permission from the leader to sit with the group in its meeting. The leader was told that the purpose of the observation was for the observer to learn something about the group.

At the meeting time the worker sat somewhat removed from

the group usually behind the group or on one side. He was introduced by the leader as a person who was interested in learning about the group. The observer recorded his observations on special observation schedules.

The Observation Instrument

For the purpose of the experiment, controlled observation was considered to be a requisite. Controlled observation may be defined as observation under standardized conditions to which the observer conforms, and, in addition, the use of certain mechanical aids to accuracy.[3]

Those persons believing that the "observer's" presence influences group behavior likely would agree that an observer using some kind of schedule and busily engaged in filling out such a schedule would increase the degree of disturbance. On the other hand, in order to stand the test of scientific accuracy, an observation schedule was necessary.

The next step was to select such a schedule. It was recognized that the early observation schedules had as their units of description, "microscopical ones such as social acts of individuals."[4] The more recent trend is to attempt description of intercorrelated data, such as group structure, group activity, group ideology, and group atmosphere. Using the old method of observation, depending on the subjective narrative reports, the observer was bound to misunderstand many of the events he described. "This is partly due to the fact that he is describing events in the group by retrospection, but is also due to the lack of explicitly pre-defined categories of observation."[5]

To avoid this tendency for different observers to put different interpretations upon the same observed activity according

[3] Pauline Z. Young, *Scientific Social Survey and Research*, p. 118.

[4] R. Lippit, "Techniques for Research in Group Living," *The Journal of Social Issues*, 2:55-61, Nov., 1946.

[5] Alvin Zander, "The W. P. Club: an Objective Case Study of a Group," *Human Relations* (Volume 7, No. 3, 1948), pp. 321-332.

to the interest and bias of the observer, an instrument was developed to yield more accurate reproduction of the phenomena and characteristics of the group.

The instrument used in both the observed and unobserved situations was the "Adult-Youth Participation Sheet," [6] a device for obtaining data about the conduct and interaction of adult-led youth groups.

Forty items are included in the instrument. They fall into five categories, as follows: Identifying Data, Adult-Child Interaction, Pattern of Group Transitions, Transmission of Ideology, and Group Activity.

Complete observations were made every five minutes. This permitted the observer a continuous picture of the trends in the activities and atmosphere of the group. It also made possible the tracing of certain elements in relation to time.

After the observation was completed, the separate items in the total observation were integrated to give a unified picture of the group. The second step was to bring together all of the information from any number of categories which seem related to one central idea. One of these ideas might come from three or four different places in the observation sheet. In the present study all the data were integrated under five items: 1) personal interactions; 2) leadership; 3) program or group activity; 4) ideology of the group; 5) group process and organization.

The Experimental Results

To measure the effects of the observer's presence on the behavior of the group, the following procedure was followed:

The recorded observations of a group, conducted from an observation room without the group's knowledge, were studied together, and from the integrated reports a behavior profile was drawn in descriptive form. Since there was no known in-

6 The Lippit-Zander Adult-Youth Participation Sheet.

terference with group reaction, this behavior profile represented general characteristics of the behavior of that group, as observed during the club meeting. This pattern of behavior was then compared to the behavior of the same group in the four alternating meetings, those observed while the worker was sitting with the group. Since the observer's presence is obvious to the group, and since no other variable factor could be found in the situation, any variations in the behavior of the group as compared to its behavior profile under ordinary conditions, were considered to be the effects of the observer's presence with the group.

All the recorded observations of the four groups were treated in the same manner. To illustrate this procedure, one group—group A—will be taken as an example.

BEHAVIOR PROFILE OF GROUP A

This profile was drawn from the four observations made without the group's knowledge.

1. Personality Interrelationships

The group members participated freely and actively in the group activities with the exception of a very few members. The relationship between the group members and the adult leader was warm, friendly, and spontaneous.

No traditions of any kind held this group to a special procedure in conducting the activity. Procedure followed only expediency as to what was better for the group to do at the moment. No special "etiquette" of communication was followed. Every member spoke when he felt moved to do so, but no serious disorder followed. Some members raised their hands when they wished to speak as a sign for the leader to give them the floor, but this procedure was not followed as a rule.

2. *Leadership*

The leader was accepted by the group as an advisor or counselor. They expected guidance from him. His predominant role was to reinforce the direction of the group, but rarely to initiate the direction for it. In other words, he encouraged the group's initiative. Occasionally, he changed the group direction.

His actions most of the time were directed toward the group as a whole and not toward the individual member. His behavior indicated that he expected autonomy of reaction on the part of the group members. On some occasions this was openly stated and invited.

The role of the leader in interaction varied. In some cases the group took the leading part in interaction, while the leader was more or less in a listening role. On other occasions, the leader took a more active part and his interactions became as frequent as those of the group members.

3. *Activity*

The group usually carried some administrative functions during its meeting, such as voting on new members, collecting dues, and issuing membership cards. The activities undertaken by the group and the way in which they were conducted, allowed considerable opportunity for creativity.

The intensity of interest of group activity ranged between mild lack of interest and attentive interest. The fluctuation in interest varied with the kind of activity conducted at the time, and with the length of time of the meeting.

4. *Ideology*

The predominant way in which the adult leader introduced ideology items to the group members was to appeal to the "right of others." Words like "should do" and "should not do" were usually used. On certain occasions, he appealed to the code of ethics accepted by that age group. Rarely did the leader appeal to his own authority.

5. Group Process and Organization

The group had two elected officers, a president and a secretary-treasurer. The president chaired the meetings. He carried his responsibility with a fair amount of success, but always was assisted by the adult leader.

The predominant method of arriving at decisions was by consensus, and by voting on the various issues presented. The group members displayed a great deal of initiative, but occasionally asked for direction from the leader.

The Effects of the Observer's Presence on the Behavior of Group A

The previous description of the general characteristics of Group "A" represent a behavior-profile of that group under ordinary conditions—that is, when no observer was sitting with the group. This was considered as the standard for comparison when the group was observed with its knowledge, while the observer was sitting with the group. The following description of group behavior under the latter condition will follow group A from one meeting to another, chronologically. It should be remembered that these observations occur two weeks apart.

The First Meeting

During the first time unit (first 5 minutes) there were definite signs of the group's consciousness of the presence of the observer. These signs took the following forms:

1. Restraint of interaction and sluggishness in starting the meeting. The members were hesitant in their interaction, many of them glancing at the observer, who was sitting in the back

of the room. This reaction was so frequent that the leader had to exert a special effort to distract the group's attention from the observer.

2. Overt action: two of the group members directed questions to the leader about the nature of the sheets on which the worker was recording his observation—questions like "Mr. Leader, what are those sheets he is writing on?", and "What is he doing that for?" These questions were asked in spite of the fact that the observer had been introduced to the group at the beginning of the meeting, and his job explained in simple terms.

3. The adult leader was over-anxious in his efforts to start the meeting in an orderly fashion, as if to impress the observer. This was accompanied by frequent glances toward the observer. Signs of that disappeared toward the end of the first observation unit.

4. A slight change in the predominant role of the leader was observed in all the groups. Compared to his role during the meetings observed without the group's knowledge, he tended more towards reinforcing the direction of the group and less toward initiating its direction.

5. No change in the nature of the activity, or in the method of transmitting ideologies resulting from the observer's presence, were observed.

During the second five minutes in the same meeting these signs were less prominent. The meeting was getting under way in a normal fashion, but still a few members kept glancing back at the observer. This reaction was less frequent in this time unit. On the whole, the group was interacting with favorable restraint. The adult leader assumed his normal role, and he seemed to lose all consciousness of the observer's presence.

In the third five minutes, no sign of the group's consciousness of the observer's presence were reflected at all, and the group proceeded with its activities as if the observer were not there. This continued until the meeting was over.

The Second Meeting

During the first five minutes, reactions to the observer's presence were prominent. Frequent glances toward the observer from the group members, but less frequent from the adult leader, were noted. Sluggishness in starting the meeting still existed, but lasted a shorter period than in the first meeting. The leader seemed less concerned with the observer's presence.

In the second five minutes of the second meeting very few reactions from the group toward the observer were noted. Except for a very few glances, the group members and the adult leader seemed to go on their way with their activities in a carefree manner, and undisturbed. The meeting continued in this manner until its end.

The Third Meeting

Signs of the observer's effect on the group existed only during the first five minutes and were expressed in a manner similar to that described in the previous meeting.

The Fourth Meeting

Again, the first five minutes were marked by signs of reaction toward the observer's presence. These signs were similar to those in previous meetings, except that the adult leader did not seemed to be affected.

Summary

During the first five minutes in all four meetings, reactions to the presence of the observer were noted. While these declined toward the fourth meeting, they still existed, and marked a period of adjustment on behalf of the group to the observer's presence.

The second five minutes were marked in the first and second meetings with moderate or little reaction to the observer's presence. Favorable reaction was shown in the third and fourth meeting. After the second five minutes—that is, after ten minutes from the beginning of the meeting—very little or no reaction to the observer was observed in any of the meetings.

The behavior of the group leader was found to have an effect on the group members' reactions to the observer's presence. The more quickly the leader adjusted to the observer's presence, the more quickly did the group members react in the same way. The contrary was observed to be true.

Conclusion

The following conclusions were evident:

1. The first five minutes of the observation in any group, regardless of the number of observations per group, were always marked by strong reaction to the presence of the observer. In the four groups studied, no exception was evident.

2. In the second five minutes, reactions were found to decrease gradually in any one group, from the first meeting to the fourth. It usually disappeared completely in the fourth meeting.

3. After ten minutes from the beginning of the first meeting, moderate reaction still existed, which diminished gradually during the second meeting and disappeared in the following meetings.

4. It was found that the behavior of the leader in response to the observer's presence determined to some extent the reactions of the group members toward the observer. When the leader was highly conscious of the observer's presence and reacted very obviously toward him, the group members were highly conscious of the observer's presence. When the leader's reactions became less obvious, a corresponding change in the members' reactions occurred.

5. The leaders in all the groups tended more toward reinforcing the group direction and encouraging its initiative, rather than initiating the direction for the group.

6. The observation of any group once only did not give a true picture of the group, since the first ten to fifteen minutes were marked by adjustments to the observer's presence and as a result the group did not behave normally.[7] This was especially true if the meeting was a short one, and did not exceed twenty minutes.

7. A second observation of the same group recorded a truer picture of group behavior, since only from five to ten minutes were spent in adjusting to the observer's presence. This could be explained by the assumption that the group became more accustomed to the observer in the second meeting.

8. The third and fourth observations of the same group presented a more realistic picture of the group behavior, since only the first five minute periods were marked by reactions to the presence of the observer.

Practical Implications

These findings, though not definitive, seem to call for: a) a more careful study of the effects of the observer's presence upon group reaction, and b) a re-examination of the values of observation before discarding this tool in supervision.

The present study has merely raised the question of the advisability of throwing out observation as a part of the supervisory process, solely on the argument that such observation distorts group reaction and alters the leader's role. It is evident that the presence of the observer does influence group behavior to some extent and for varying periods of time. However, it has also shown that the distracting influence can be reduced to a minimum. This is true even when the observer is using an

---

[7] By "normal" here is meant the group behavior recorded from the observation made without the group's knowledge.

instrument and is engaged in recording during the period of the meeting, though it is reasoned that such an observer is probably more disturbing than one who sits passively by.

The question remains whether there are enough values inherent in observation as a tool in the supervisory process to warrant its retention, especially if the observer is cognizant of his influence on the group and takes this into account in analyzing group interaction and the leader's role.

On the other hand, the findings do not, nor are they intended to, compare the value of what the supervisor learns from observation and what he gleans from reading the group record. This should be the subject of a separate investigation.

A First Conference with an Inexperienced Group Leader
By George Brager

The inexperienced leader, in many agencies an undergraduate student, approaches the supervisor's office for his first conference. He has been interviewed, the program of the agency has been outlined, and specific assignments may have been explored. He may have participated in a two or three session orientation period as well, and the agency is no longer completely strange to him.

Now, however, the assignment has been made, and he is to meet his group. He approaches the first conference with his supervisor with considerable uneasiness, for at last he is really to begin. He may have learned that he must show confidence, must seem in control, the uneasiness is thus disguised. It is safe to assume, however, that it will be there, somewhere— the doubts, the fears of beginning which are inherent in a new situation.

Perhaps he is afraid of the impression he will make. What will the supervisor think? It's hard to know when he doesn't have a real idea of the necessary qualifications. What is the supervisor like anyway? Friendly? Remote? Suspicious? Or if the leader has a real stake in learning, he may worry about what the supervisor has to offer. Will he be able to teach him?

The fears are different for each leader, different in their intensity, different in the way they are acted out. One leader is frozen, and can barely talk. Another is "uncomfortable." He is sweating, or talking incessantly, or nervously moving his fingers. A third leader may be able to face the new experience with considerable equanimity. No matter what the supervisor does, the leader will still have fear. It cannot be taken away, and the tendency must be controlled to reach across the desk, pat the leader reassuringly, and say, "Really, now, there's nothing to be afraid of." Telling the inexperienced leader not to worry demonstrates only that the supervisor does not understand. How can he help but worry? Nevertheless, the fear can be shaken up, broken into, and the leader can be helped to begin, to function past the fear. The job of the supervisor is to free the leader, despite the fear, to function at maximum potential.

It is recognized that this is only a first conference, that everything cannot be handled in the initial one-half to one hour meeting of the supervisor and leader. The leader can be helped to feel more ready, however, if a relationship is really started with his supervisor, if supervisor and agency take sufficient responsibility so that the leader does not feel that he is in this alone, if he can get some idea of what is expected of him, and if appropriate content for use at the first group meeting is discussed. It is the purpose of this presentation to explore more fully the above-mentioned factors.

Beginning the Relationship

Supervisors, in their desire to make a contribution, because of their eagerness that the leader accept them as knowing people, or because of their own resistance to involvement in a supervisory relationship, oftentimes focus upon concepts, rather than relate to the person to whom they are talking. A supervisor began his first conference with: "I said that I thought it would be helpful if he gave me information about his past experience, since it would help me to understand him better, and possibly to know what he wanted to use from supervision." The supervisor's tone was distant. He was removed, bloodless, so involved with his own self, his own concerns, that he could not catch the leader's feeling or relate to them. The leader reacted in a burst of feeling at the second conference.

". . . He explained that he'd come out of our first conference very tense and ill at ease. He said that maybe he was wrong, but that it seemed to him that we really hadn't started much of a relationship, and I was off telling him what to do. He said that what I said sounded good, but it was so much. It was hard to take anything from me, since he really didn't know much about me. He ended by saying that he was sure that some of this feeling was due to his insecurity in the relationship."

The supervisor may have difficulty giving full attention to the conference. There may be tremendous time pressures in the agency, activities to get started, people to see, telephone calls to return, and he may want to get through the conference as quickly as possible. Perhaps he is more focused upon demonstrating to the leader, with subtlety of course, that the leader is fortunate to have been hired by the agency, that he will develop immeasurably from the contact.

Whatever the pressures, however, it is important that a friendly, unhurried tone be set at the first conference. The leader should know that there is a certain amount of time set aside for him, that it is his time, and that it will not be broken into with interruptions or telephone calls.

In setting the tone, the supervisor might evidence interest in something as inconsequential as whether or not the leader had difficulty in travelling to the agency. He might discuss the career focus of the leader, not simply as it pertains to his work in the agency, although this is most important, but as it pertains to the leader's life as well. The content here is not significant. What is important is that the supervisor be really interested in what the leader brings, and evidence that interest.

An understanding of the leader's feelings, and a willingness to share the understanding, are vital factors in beginning the relationship. It will be helpful to the leader, for example, if he knows that the supervisor is aware of his insecurity in beginning, even though the leader may be too fearful to tell this to the supervisor. A burden is lifted when a secret fear no longer remains a secret. Certainly too, this sharing sets at the very beginning something of the contents of future conferences.

It can be done lightly, unthreateningly, however. The supervisor might say, "Most leaders are fearful of meeting their groups, and you may feel that way too." Where the discussion would go from there, if anywhere, would then depend upon the particular leader. If it went no further, however, the purpose would be served that the leader heard from the supervisor (although, realistically, many leaders do not actually believe this), that the fear is natural, and that it is accepted.

Caution must be exercised here. Our preconceived notion of how the leader *should* feel may blind us to how this particular leader does feel, and it is necessary to explore feeling with the leader, rather than proceed from assumptions. This means really seeing the leader, and what he brings, rather than demonstrating our own sensitivity. We should also remember that this is a first conference, and that intense examination might be more threatening than helpful. (Somehow, we must control our inclination to try to do everything at once; and we must be humble about the limits of what we know.) Further it is important that we do not toss the entire problem into the lap of the leader with a question such as: "How do you feel about beginning with your group?"

Taking Responsibility

In order that the leader feel that he is not in this alone, to sink or swim, it must be transmitted to him that there is an agency, and a supervisor, who are prepared to share responsibility with him for what happens in the group. Saying this is not enough. There must be a belief on the part of the supervisor that it is really so, and a demonstration in practice that agency and supervisor do share responsibility.

For example, if there are distinct procedures in the agency which are imparted to the leader, such as where he signs in, where he hangs his hat, where he will pick up room keys, and how he goes about requisitioning material, he will be more likely to feel that the agency is prepared for him, well-organized, able to help. Whether this is handled in the first conference, or in orientation sessions previous to the first conference, is not important. What is important is that it does get handled—that the leader feels that some thought has gone into the setting up of the program before he has arrived, and that agency people care about his comfort, about facilitating his work. Too often in our agencies, we open the doors, and handle problems on a crisis basis, without anticipating what the needs of leaders and groups will be. An agency takes responsibility when it is structured to facilitate the meeting of a leader with his group. Thus, whether the supervisor is available to introduce members to the leader, how the children come into the agency, where they go, will have bearing on the smoothness, or lack of it, with which the group begins. Factors such as the facilities which are available, program material, etc., also contribute. A leader's sense of aloneness is lessened when an agency has planned thoughtfully.

Another way in which it may be demonstrated that the agency and supervisor share responsibility is by the supervisor's taking responsibility for the first conference, or beginning conferences, until the leader is able to assume more of the load. Unfortunately, supervisors avoid this under the guise of wanting material to "come from the leader," or because of a too great fear of imposing. We should be aware that experientially, the leader is unprepared for material to come from him, or that his feelings may be such in the beginning, that he cannot afford risking the wrong answers, and is thus increasingly uncomfortable that the supervisor has burdened him with the necessity of knowing.

Specific examples of the above may be seen in excerpts from this first conference record:

"... X asked what I wanted in records. I asked what he thought should go into records. He went into some general statements about who did what...."

"... I had asked X to bring in some ideas for his first meeting. He came in with some plans, and we started to discuss them. He immediately gave the paper to me, and said that I would have trouble reading the plan. I tried to read it, and said that he was right. Would he please write or type it so that it could be read...."

"... I asked him to start reading his ideas for the first group meeting. He said that he wanted to find out what the kids are like. I asked how he was going to do this. He said he wouldn't want to go into the meeting with fixed ideas...."

In the above instance, the leader felt more uncertain about beginning after the conference than he had before. In questioning the leader regarding what ought to go into records, and in suggesting that he bring in a plan for the first meeting, the supervisor actually abrogated his own responsibility. Most helpful would have been the supervisor's initiating what he thought ought to be planned for the first meeting. How the supervisor can take responsibility for the latter will be discussed in the section of this paper dealing with specific ideas for the first meeting.

Outlining What Is Expected

Considerable comfort may be forthcoming for the leader if the supervisor is able to outline, in a specific way, what is expected of him. It is recognized that this is difficult in social work. We do not have any one, two, three lists of expectations. What we are looking for in leadership is ordinarily so general as to be meaningless when applied to a particular person. Also, many leaders are not satisfied, for themselves, with limited expectations; aspirations are often boundless.

Nevertheless, it is possible to outline some specific demands, such as arriving at the agency at a certain time, taking attendance, cleaning up, etc. Often, these provide the possibility for support in a second conference which, if not originally discussed, would otherwise be unavailable. Further, we ought to assure the leader (even if this is something he does not completely believe, or which is not particularly satisfying to him), that we do not expect a quality of work for which he is not prepared. Recognizing with him that his experience is limited, that it places him at a certain level of development, takes away, in some measure, the necessity of the student seeming something he is not.

Helping to Get Started with the Group

The major concern of most leaders is what will happen when the group first meets. "How do I get started?" and "What am I going to do?" are the most frequent questions. It is here that the supervisor must take responsibility for providing specific help.

There is information about the group which the leader will

need to know. There are the obvious things, such as the number of members, age, previous experience in the agency. If the agency does individual and/or group intake, or if the group has functioned in previous seasons, there will be further information to share with the leader. Their program interests, readiness for specific activities, the behavior of individual members, or of the group as a whole, may be pertinent. It is not necessary, however, that the leader know *everything* about the group. It is less confusing if he is not burdened with information he cannot use at the beginning, and it is important that he be permitted the freedom to make his own discoveries, to form his own relationship with the members. Sharing information about the group will, therefore, be determined by the need of the particular leader at the particular moment. Leaders with more experience will use information differently, and thus, our knowledge about the leader becomes a factor in deciding what we share.

It is nevertheless true, however, that if we anticipate particular behavior from membership in a first group meeting, this should be discussed with the leader. When the behavior has been anticipated, the leader will know, while in the midst of the maelstrom, that he is not totally responsible, that this is the group. In our uncertainty, our limited understanding about the behavior of people, we prepare a leader for a group with generalities about the members. Thus, we may say that so-and-so is "hostile"; X and Y are "aggressive"; Z is "repressed"; or the group is "immature." With the words serving as a shield, we are comfortable that our task is finished. The rest is up to the leader.

In actuality, of course, we have contributed little. Social work terms and psychological language mean different things to different people, and often tend to confuse and frighten the inexperienced leader. While the leader may be impressed by the supervisor's erudition, he will "take hold," learn, only from experience with concrete situations, rather than from verbalized concepts.

What we really need to describe to the leader is what the group has done (or might do), and further, discuss ways in which this behavior can be handled most effectively. It is not enough to pose the problem; answers must be explored as well. For example, if we expect that the group will be extremely active, we might discuss use of the gym, and games which can be played there. If we expect that a different situation will arise, the leader might be informed that it is agency policy for the supervisor to be called in such situations. (We do not, of course, raise the spectre of problem behavior unless it is strongly anticipated.) Whatever it is that we anticipate, however, it is as important, or more important, that "What do I do?" be discussed, as well as "What will I find?"

Specific program ideas, specific games, crafts, should be explored with the leader. They should be discussed in sufficient detail so that he will feel minimally comfortable in introducing them to the group. Initiative for this should come from the supervisor, rather than asking the leader what program he thinks ought to be planned. Connection can be made between the leader's past experience and his present assignment, and if this has been limited to counselorship at a camp, program which is transferrable to the agency setting might be examined with him.

Program ideas should include material for discussion with the club. Leaders wonder what they will talk to group members about, and with specific content, will feel considerably more ready to begin. Thus, it can be suggested that the leader ask the members about their interests, their previous club experience, what they'd like to do this year, and even tell something about himself. In instances where the group has had previous agency experience, the leader should be prepared for possible discussion of previous club leaders.

The supervisor might take as considerable responsibility as saying to the leader that "here are one, two, three things it is possible to do in a first meeting with a group such as yours." It is recognized, of course, that when this is done, opportunity should be provided for the leader to reject the suggestions. He should also be encouraged to make his own contribution to the suggested content, although, as has been pointed out, pressure should not be exerted in this direction.

Supervision

Finally, supervision should be discussed. The time for the leader's regular conference, and its duration, should be told to him. Something of the content for conferences, and what his role in them can be, should be suggested. We should let him know that we will be discussing some of the things he does not do well, but that this is anticipated and usual.

It is suggested that this discussion come at the end of the conference. For the inexperienced leader, there is the danger that "supervision" will become a professional concept with little real meaning, or with frightening mystery. It is more specific, and meaningful, to relate supervision to what has gone before in the present discussion.

The first conference might, thus, be concluded with "This conference is what supervision is about."

11

Refining the Group Work Process

THE RESEARCH PROCESS—AN AID IN DAILY
PRACTICE *By Ralph L. Kolodny*

OUT of her experience as director of the research program at New York's Educational Alliance, Gertrude
Wilson has written, "The significance of this program lies less
in its findings and conclusions than in its process." [1] During the
past several months group workers in the Department of Neighborhood Clubs of the Children's Aid Association of Boston
have come to understand more fully the implications of Miss
Wilson's statement. They have done so despite the fact that
the department has not yet formally organized a research program. Only the preliminary exploration of the possibilities of
such a program has been completed. This is precisely why the
department's experience in this regard should be shared with
other group workers; for it indicates the concrete effect which

[1] Gertrude Wilson, "Measurement and Evaluation of Group Work Practice,"
Proceedings, National Conference of Social Work, 1952, p. 218. For a similar
point of view see David French, *An Approach to Measuring Results in Social
Work,* p. 105.

even the procedure of simply "thinking in research terms" can have upon the day-to-day practice of a group work agency.

The Department of Neighborhood Clubs is a specialized group work service functioning as part of a child welfare agency. Its practice has a number of distinguishing features. The combination of case work with group work is the most prominent of these. Groups carried on by the department, for the most part, meet in members' homes. These groups are usually composed of friends or acquaintances of the child referred to the department for help, rather than of children with similar problems. The main effort of the department is directed toward helping, through a carefully planned group experience, children who are faced with difficulties in their social relationships, arising out of chronic illness, physical handicap, or personality problems. These children live in all parts of Metropolitan Boston. The department is given such referrals because the agencies involved feel that its services can provide a necessary and valuable supplement to their own.[2]

As the department has grown staff members have entered into professional relationships with agencies of many different types and on many different levels. The functioning of the department has had to keep pace with the involved procedures entailed in this process. In sum, the uniqueness of the service has resulted for the department in an increased complexity of operation. This being the case, in the spring of 1952 the agency and department executives decided that a rigorous self-study for the purpose of sharpening up the department's work was called for. Such a self-study, they felt, would have as its basic aim the answering of the question, "Who can best be helped by the type of service the department offers?" The process since set in motion by the decision of the executives and

---

[2] A more detailed discussion of the work of the Department can be found in Marjory Warren's article "One Agency's Approach to Specialized Group Work Services," *The Group*, Vol. 12, No. 2, March 1950, pp. 3-6.

its effect on daily practice is the major concern of this article.

From the beginning, planning for the proposed research has gone ahead on both the committee and staff levels. From members of the department's advisory committee, made up of professionals from allied fields as well as laymen, came two members of a sub-committee on research. Two other members were secured from the fields of psychological research and medical social work.

Several meetings were first held in which both staff and committee members participated for the purpose of delimiting the area to be covered by the proposed project. At these meetings, also, suggestions as to possible approaches to the study were considered. In any evaluation of this sort the perennial question of "success" must be taken into account. The place of criteria for "success" and the types of criteria most applicable to the work of the department were therefore discussed. Like other social workers confronted with the necessity of studying this problem of criteria for evaluating results, department staff members had to begin to wrestle with the question of the extent to which changes in a youngster's behavior are the result of the department's work. Although only the barest beginning has been made in dealing with this question, the very fact of its having been raised has caused staff members to look more closely at the specific part played by their work in a child's life and to understand it better as one of many forces operating in his environment. Such a closer look can help a department or agency to understand better in general terms what it can reasonably expect from its efforts in working with children.

The problem of financing the proposed project necessitated the formulation of a formal request for funds to be submitted to various foundations. The request, it was felt, should include a detailed, though not necessarily exhaustive, description of the department, its history and its present operation. It also involved the compiling of a list of general approaches to problem situations commonly faced by staff. Some nine situations were considered:

1. Working with the parents of the referred child.
2. Group formation.
3. Exploring the referred child's interests.
4. Aggressive behavior by the referred child.
5. Helping other group members to accept the referred child's handicap.
6. Absences or lateness on the part of the referred child or other club members.
7. Meeting in club members' homes.
8. Meeting in other institutions or agencies.
9. Terminating a group.

After analyzing these situations the staff then together spelled out the approaches commonly used and most likely to be successful in these situations.

One should not be disarmed by the apparent simplicity of this list and, therefore, neglect its implications. The process of cataloging, classifying, and systematizing lies at the heart of research. Beyond this, when fed back into the day-to-day work of the department, it has a great deal of practical meaning. Such classification of techniques enables the group leader to draw with greater facility upon the experience of other group leaders. For the new worker especially, but also for the old, it provides, when completed, a body of knowledge to which he can refer for concrete help. In the process of organization of experience, workers assume at once the roles of "learner from" and "teachers to" each other. The experience becomes, thereby, both a supplement to and an extension of the normal process of supervision.

In addition to this list of problem situations and approaches, the "outline for the request for funds" consisted of sections describing various phases of the department's operation, summaries of work done with specific children, and information as to the necessity and potential productivity of research into the department's functioning at the present time. The necessity for accurate and usable accounts of operation, both statistical and otherwise, was re-emphasized through the department's engaging in this procedure.

When completed, copies of the outline were submitted to members of the advisory committee who expressed their views on the outline, and made suggestions for its improvement. The committee decided that, because of the complexity of the research problem, the department worker who would be assigned to the project should be afforded further help. One of the research committee's members experienced in this area was appointed as a regular part-time consultant on research. Together the consultant and department worker began to examine further the department's operation. The purpose of this examination, which is still in process, is to discover those areas of the department's work which are most important and adaptable to study, and to develop that research approach, either clinical-descriptive or experimental or combining the two, to which departmental data and practice best lend themselves, and which will be most productive in terms of answering crucial questions about our practice.

Under this plan the research consultant is to develop the research design and set the direction of the project. The department research worker is to implement the project within the framework of this design.

However, the two persons primarily concerned with the research have not been separated off to carry on their activities independent of the rest of the staff. On the contrary, their work has involved the cooperation and active participation of staff workers at every turn.

As part of their exploratory work, for example, the research consultant and worker turned again to the question of "criteria for success." Workers were first asked to select that group in their experience in which they had been most successful in terms of the improvement shown by the referred child, and that in which they had been least successful. They then were requested to describe in narrative form their reasons for considering the results of their work as good or poor. The research personnel's immediate aim in this connection was to piece out the criteria of success held in common by department workers, and to obtain some idea of those areas in which workers' standards for assessing positive or negative change in the referred child are at variance. The effects of the procedure on the thinking of staff members should be noted. By looking back on their own work, workers were enabled to make their goals more concrete and to set them down in more specific fashion. In their own minds, for example, they could no longer accept a goal such as "socialization" without delineating for themselves in a more clear cut way the behavior manifestations and changes which indicate that a child may be becoming "socialized."

Careful consideration of the goals of practice has led to more precise thinking about departmental function. With this clearer definition of function have come some changes in intake policy. Intake is now being geared more adequately to the goals of the department, and to the services it is equipped to provide.

The importance of recording has also been given further impetus by the research process. In order to bring to light the crucial questions in the minds of staff concerning their own work, the research personnel examined the records on specific individuals and groups. Conferences followed this examination in which, in response to questioning, workers described in some detail the problems met and approaches used to overcome them in the groups being considered. This process involved expansion and supplementation of record material. Through it workers were helped to see some of the gaps which existed in their own recording, and the steps which need to be taken if these gaps are to be filled in the future. In one sense, perhaps the most important of all, this process has re-emphasized to workers the fact that their records are being systematically and concretely used. Nothing is more conducive to a worker's morale around this matter of recording than the realization that his records are really useful.

Some of the effects of our agency's research effort are of a more subtle nature and not easily defined. The research process, for one thing, has introduced a climate of reflectiveness into the department. Group workers are constantly encountering behavior phenomena about which they have questions. Occupied with the on-going demands of program planning and group meetings, they often are unable to give more than passing notice and are unable to think through the implications of that which they have experienced. The research process, by raising the problem of what are the important questions about our practice which must be studied, turns the attention of workers back to these questions and increases staff's awareness of their importance. It helps to move workers from a point where, confronted by a particular development in the group process, they think "Isn't this interesting. I wonder what it means?" to one where they ask themselves, "How important is this development? Have other workers seen it in their groups? When is it likely to occur? Are there any changes in practice that should be made in order to deal with it? How can it be studied?" Research thinking gives rise to more purposeful staff discussions, to wider professional study and reading and, in general, to more thoughtful practice.

A final by-product of the research process deserves mention. It is inevitable that even in the early stages of research there will be a good deal of compilation of facts about numerous areas of a department or agency's operation. Material previously deposited under widely scattered headings, and sometimes not even written, is assembled into some kind of coherent whole. In interpreting the work of the department or agency to committees, board, and other agencies, workers are thus provided with an organized fund of information to which they have easy access. Research can provide a vital link in the interpretation of group work practice.

Although the Department of Neighborhood Clubs has not yet developed a full-blown research program, it has shown how research-oriented thinking and the process of exploring the possible construction of a research design have been of aid to departmental practice. We have found that the research process, even in its early stages, has the following effects:

1. It makes for clearer thinking and greater accuracy concerning the goals of practice.

2. It leads to a better understanding by workers of the place of their work among the many environmental forces influencing a child's behavior.

3. It stimulates increased idea-sharing among staff members.

4. It provides workers with more practical knowledge of how to deal with problem situations.

5. It supplements and extends supervision through placing workers in the positions of both "learners from" and "teachers to" each other.

6. It helps to bring intake into line with department goals and function.

7. It heightens staff interest in and morale around recording.

8. It introduces a climate of reflectiveness leading to more purposeful staff discussions, and to wider professional study and reading.

9. It provides a coherent body of facts from which fuller and clearer interpretation of practice can be made by staff.

Although our agency's experience with the research process has not given us a neatly packaged statistical picture of various

hases of the department's operation nor provided us with any
arge amount of new information, it has done something that
s more important. It has led us to a more careful analysis of
ur procedures and to harder thinking about the planning of
ur activities. The research process even in this quite early, and
n many ways uncertain, phase has begun to identify for us the
lements of our art. This will make more possible the transmis-
ion and teaching of these elements to workers and students as
hey come into the department. It is only through the continued accumulation and transmission of such knowledge that
an agency, and indeed the field as a whole, can begin to improve its day-by-day service to the community.

WHAT IS GROUP WORK SKILL?
By Helen U. Phillips

IN this brief article I have not attempted to
describe group work skill comprehensively. As a matter of fact,
one of the reasons that our particular field of practice is so dynamic and exciting to be engaged in, is that its practitioners are
constantly in the process of testing and refining the group work
method of helping people. This has been going on for approximately the last twenty-five years, ever since group workers
started to give attention to their methodology—building on their
past tested experience, and seeking new ways of making their
work more effective. I believe this constant examination of
practice to be an important function of our professional association of group workers and certainly of every worker in a group
work agency, as well as of the educational centers for professional training in group work.

The intent of this paper is to state and examine some of the
fundamental principles or concepts that I believe to be essential
to social group work skill. But we will have to start a little behind the skill to consider briefly what has brought about the

need for its development and, therefore, our concern with i
Group workers are committed to a professional purpose. Ou
group work literature is full of definitions of the professiona
group work purpose including the provocative statements o
national committees of our own professional association. I
essence, all of these definitions affirm the dual aim of the de
velopment of individuals and development of the group as
whole toward social usefulness. In more specific terms, the pro
fessional purpose of group work is:

(1) to help the members of a group to become and to value
their real selves and to discover, use and develop their strengths
through their group associations so that they may find a more
responsible and satisfying relation to other group members, the
worker, agency and community;

(2) to help the group as a whole to develop social interests
and activities that will contribute to movement toward a more
democratic society.

Most group work agencies subscribe in general to the professional purpose of group work and, in additon, have formulated unique objectives for which the agencies are organized.
Specific purposes grow out of the particular community and
clientele which the agency serves, combined with the aims of
the national agencies with which it may be affiliated and the
unique interests of the original or present leadership of the
agency.

Every worker in every group work agency must focus his
efforts on contributing to the fulfillment of the professional
and agency purpose. In the last analysis, the effectiveness of
the help given by group work agencies to people of the community rests on the skill of the workers who meet directly with
groups or who supervise those who carry the direct responsibility of group leadership. This is our reason for considering

vhat is meant by group work skill and for examining concepts hat underlie helpful group work practice.

One word on the relation of professional skill to dedication— he professional commitment, implicit in professional purpose, that demands more of the worker's concern for the people whom he serves than for himself: dedication exclusive of skill results in questionable service; but skill without dedication is practically useless. Indeed, I would go as far as to say that professional commitment to the service of others is a basic quality, essential to the group work skill I will be describing.

The Agency Function

Let us start out with the group work agency itself since it is the agency that gives the worker his reason for being. The very fact that the worker is part of an agency means that he has a professional rather than a personal relationship to offer to his group members. Quite naturally, I think, groups will often try to separate their worker from the agency—especially when he is holding them to some requirement that they do not like. Older teen-agers will say, for example, "But why do we have to report the *full* amount of money we made at our dance? Nobody except you will know about it!"

Or, in the usual turnover of leadership, the group will test out each new worker to find out if he is really part of the agency or if he will just "be a good fellow." When the worker is clear about an agency policy and can interpret it in reasonable terms, he removes the issue from the area of personal battle and puts it into the agency frame-work. Certainly this is supporting for the worker but, more important, it provides something stable for the group members in that they know what they can count on, along with the sense that the agency is there for other groups as well as themselves. Those of you who meet with groups outside of an agency building—in homes, schools or on street-corners—have to be especially conscious

of the agency connection since there is no visible reminder in
the form of a physical building, of the auspices under which the
group is meeting. You approach your groups, not just as the
friendly, interested person that you are, but as the representative of your agency which provides services to community
groups.

The function of the group work agency is to give help to people through group experiences. If one can be clear about that,
he finds direction for his answer to the somewhat controversial
question of what kind of help to individuals is a legitimate part
of the group worker's responsibility. (I am aware that some
agencies that offer group work services do not call themselves
group work agencies. A recent statement from the National
Federation of Settlements made it quite clear that most social
settlements and neighborhood houses are multi-functional and
include group work as only one of their important functions.
This may be true of other agencies as well as settlements but
I am addressing myself here to the group work part of the
agency function and to you as group workers.)

If a worker knows that his focus is to be on helping people
to use their group experiences as fully as possible, he will find
that every contact that he has with individual members of the
group will be related to that end. Individual interviews or just
informal conversations with group members are a familiar part
of every group worker's activity. Many of the individual problems that group members feel free enough to discuss with their
worker may be directed back to possible program development
in the group. Vocational questions, impending draft for the
young men, relations with the opposite sex—these are examples
of this. Problems that have to do with relationships with other
group members or with the worker, stem directly from the
group situation and clearly must be dealt with by the group
worker to help the member to participate in the group with
more satisfaction to himself and with greater benefit to the

group. But when the group member brings problems of personal relationships, with members of his family, for example, the worker is faced with a question: what is my responsibility here? Can I help this person with something that is very important to him but that has nothing to do directly with the group experience that I share with him? One unsatisfactory answer to these questions is that the group worker does not have time for intensive, individualized work; another, that he is not trained in giving individualized help. Either of these answers would leave the worker filled with guilt for what he cannot do—and, furthermore, begs the question. Doesn't the answer lie in the function of the agency? If the function of the group work agency or of the group worker's part of the agency service is to help people to use group experience, the worker has his direction for the kinds of problems on which he can truly help his group members. This does not exclude the necessity of helping members to move toward casework services in the process of referrals. But, I believe that it is very supporting to the group member to discover that his group worker will be there every minute for him as his *group* worker to help him on every conceivable aspect of his group experience but that he will not try to be all things to him.

The point of view I have been expressing could be stated as the following concept: *The worker who clearly represents his agency and holds to its function in all of his relationships with his group members provides stability for them.*

The Dynamic of Present Reality

Lest this principle of holding to the agency function appear to be too limiting or to cut off the worker from the group members' needs, I hasten to state a second group work concept, namely, that *there are dynamic possibilities for helping through the group work process.* When the group worker believes this to be so, he does not feel guilty or frustrated for what he *cannot* do, because he knows the rich potentialities of group participation to which he contributes—not confining in nature, but expansive and positive, with unknown depths of experience and development there to be plumbed. He knows that he can help and he considers the *reality* of the group meeting as the framework where his help can be effective.

Perhaps a word is pertinent here as to what the worker needs to know about his group members if he is to help them. It is my conviction, as I have often said publicly, that it is not necessary for a worker to know about his members' family, work or school relationships in order to be able to help them; that indeed, possession of such information may block the worker's freedom to feel and know what the members are like right in the current group situation. Certainly, the worker's richest source of understanding of members' needs is the group meeting itself where he not only sees each member in relation to the others and to himself but is in direct interaction with him. The worker's real connection with the group member, as well as his competence, is in the group experience which he shares. The engagement between group members and worker, right in the present group situation can have profound significance for the members in bringing about change in their way of relating to others. The worker attempts to meet the needs as he senses them, as he actively relates to the members in the ever-changing facets of their use of program activities, their relations with each other, with him, and with the agency.

Every one of you from your rich experience in leading groups could readily give illustrations of what I am asserting—where you have seen clear indication that group members have changed in their attitudes and in their relations to others in the course of a group meeting. Here is one such example, recorded by the worker with a gang of older teen-agers who had sought the leadership services of a settlement house although they lived too far from the agency building to avail themselves of its

cilities. They were looking for a meeting-place in their local
neighborhood since the police were objecting to their habitual
se of street-corners.

". . . Angelo said, 'Man, we can't stand here any more! It's getting
o hot around here. We can't even have our old corner.' Vic asked
ow we were doing about places to meet. I said that neither the
oys who were working on it nor I had any success to date but that
e had applied to Humboldt School. This brought up a whole
urry of feeling—'Man, if we go over there, we sure are going to
ght with those niggers!' I questioned this and said that they
eemed to do a whole lot of talking about fighting everybody. I
ouldn't help thinking that guys who fought absolutely everybody
must be pretty much in the wrong themselves and I was getting a
ittle tired of hearing them down everybody else and say they were
oing to fight wherever they went. There really wasn't much sense
n our trying to find a meeting-place because wherever they went,
hey would find somebody to fight. This sobered them down. . . .

"Chris said, 'Look, you guys, how about going up to St. Vincent's?
They have a gym there and everything. Man, that would be a
errific place if we could get in.' Rocky said, 'We sure are going to
angle with those guys up there!' I turned to the group and said,
There you go again! Before you even get to a building you're
getting into a fight. You'll never get a place to meet if you figure
on fighting. If we go up there figuring we're going to mind our
own business and have our own fun, then we won't have any trouble. If we go there the way you are talking now, we'll be out of
there in a week—out in the cold again.' Stan and Ted told Rocky
to shut up and Chris said, 'Look, you guys, if we get our own place
and time, we can get along with those guys up there. They're not
so bad anyway. They never bothered me too much.' The boys
began to simmer down and talk in a more positive way about the
opportunities at the church. . . ."

Now here was a real problem these boys were facing—one
very important to them. They wanted and needed a place to
meet but they wouldn't be able to find one until they began

to take some responsibility for their behavior. And what di
the worker do in this meeting? He helped them to face one (
the reasons for their dilemma and the boys seemed to take i
what he was saying and to move a little, in response to him.]
would be ridiculous to assume that with this slight beginning
this club of boys would never get into another fight! But th
worker did start them looking at their own responsibility. Afte
all, it does take two to start a fight! He knew that they ha
chosen to be belligerent and he knew that there was anothe
choice they could make that no one else could make for them
I am convinced that in such an incident that lasts for only a fev
minutes of time, right in the reality of the present, a group car
be helped to discover something new and useful in themselves

Developing Strengths

We have been looking briefly at the concept that there are
dynamic possibilities for individual and group growth in the
group work process. The very word "process" connotes in the
world of nature, movement between two or more substances
in which organic change can occur in reaction to an external
force. In the area of human society, the word denotes dynamic
movement or interaction between one or more persons or
groups. In group work terms, process requires that both worker
and group are actively involved in reaction to each other—each
in a different way since the worker carries the professional responsibility of the helping person—and the group members, as
individual participants in the group. I believe that the strong-
est factor that keeps the group worker from being controlling
and manipulative is his conviction that *all people have
strengths*. This I submit as a third concept essential to group
work skill although, if I were pressed to say which concept of
the several we are examining today I hold to be the most significant, I would put this one *first* at the head of my list.

Some of the clearest statements and elaborations of this concept of belief in the strength of the person who comes to the social agency for service are to be found in the writings of Kenneth L. M. Pray. The final paper of Mr. Pray's productive life was "A Restatement of the Generic Principles of Social Casework Practice." In describing functional casework, he wrote: "This approach clings steadily to the conception that the client, whatever his strengths and weaknesses, carries responsibility for his own life as a whole and must continue to carry it. At least he has not asked us and we cannot consent, to take that responsibility from him. He has asked us, rather, to help him to carry that responsibility by helping him to overcome some obstacle he has faced in carrying it, and in the very act of seeking this help he has disclosed at least some elements of strength for dealing with this responsibility. The worker's task is to enable him to build on this latent strength, to face whatever realities are decisive in determining his own use of himself and of available resources in relation to the problem he faces and upon which he wants to work. The problem remains his own; the responsibility for dealing with it remains with him. Furthermore, this approach . . . also starts with the assumption—indeed, the profound conviction—that the helping dynamic, the source of healing power, is also in the client himself as he reaches out for help. It is not primarily in the worker." [1]

Mr. Pray was addressing himself to social casework but he was expressing a philosophy, universal in its meaning and fully applicable to social group work.

In the excerpted record of the meeting with teen-age boys previously referred to, it would seem that the worker was acting from this principle. He could help them with external arrangements such as finding a meeting-place but the deeper problem of their behavior was their responsibility alone and his greatest

[1] Kenneth L. M. Pray, "A Restatement of the Generic Principles of Social Casework," *Social Work in a Revolutionary Age*, University of Pennsylvania Press, 1949, p. 249.

help to them lay in enabling them to face their attitudes and the reality of the consequences of their behavior, with the *expectation,* not expressed in words, that they were quite capable of responsible behavior if they chose it for themselves.

The Significance of Feelings

If the group worker is to be engaged in a process with his group members, it is essential that he be sensitive to their feelings. I find it difficult to describe this important area of group work skill in the limited words of a concept. It might be expressed in this way: *The acknowledgement of one's own feeling is important to inner movement, and the expression of it produces something real for another person to respond to.* This applies both to worker and to group members. Sensitivity to feelings is not enough but the feelings must be responded to if the worker is to have relatedness to his group members—and relatedness is the essence of group work skill.

Could we look first at the worker's own feelings? Perhaps one of the most difficult things for a beginning social worker to get hold of is the willingness and freedom to face his own feelings—both sides of them, the negative as well as the positive —and then, as well as acknowledging them to himself, to be willing to share them with someone else. And yet, I am convinced that not until a group worker has claimed and shared his real feelings, can he be sensitive to and respond to the feelings of his group members. Think of what happens, for example, when a worker realizes and admits to himself that what he had fondly thought was his deep desire to help his group to have a good experience was actually his own need to have a "successful" group, stemming from his own feeling of insecurity. With that sudden revelation, he is free to permit and to help the group members take their rightful part of the responsibility for their group life. Or, the worker who has always felt hostile toward a particular economic class of society—and this could be upper, middle or lower economic group—who has to examine his feelings before he can let himself know, accept and welcome the feelings of his group comprised of that class and begin to help them.

I have mentioned the matter of sharing feelings with another and this applies to letting the group members know how one feels. The members have the right to know the worker as *real* —a person with both positive and negative feelings but in this, the worker has the responsibility of disciplining his feelings so that they do not damage the group members. And how is feeling communicated? Not only by spoken words but by facial expressions and gestures and an intangible sort of air. The workers' concern with his own feeling, acknowledgment and expression of it, is legitimate and indeed, essential, only as it frees the worker to "take in" the feelings of his group members, to let them have their feelings and to hear what they really are saying.

Much of the worker's effort must be directed to sensing and meeting the positive and negative feelings of his group members and helping them to claim, break up into parts and express their feelings as they move into new relationships—but more important, to take responsibility for their feelings and the expression of them. There is so much concern over helping members to express their negative feelings—perhaps because when unexpressed they produce hostile behavior that is disruptive to the group—that it is necessary to emphasize the need for help in acknowledging and expressing positive feelings as well. These may emerge as identification with the group, worker or agency or positive acceptance of one's self or just a general sense of well-being. At any rate, whether the feelings are positive or negative, the worker must be free to be sensitive to them and actively respond to them.

A recorded incident in a club of eleven- and twelve-year-old boys will serve to illuminate the concept we are discussing.

The group had been driven by the worker in the agency's station-wagon to a playground for a game of baseball. The worker records:

"After the ball-game as they piled into the station-wagon, Earl accidentally stepped on Sam and Sam shoved him. At that, Earl completely lost his temper and started after Sam with a rock that he picked up from the road, shouting, 'I'll kill that guy!' I got between them and Earl hollered, 'Get out of the road, Mr. Mac! I'm going to split his head open.' I said that was exactly why I wouldn't get out of the way. I wasn't protecting Sam so much as I was protecting him. Cliff said, 'Cut it out, Earl. You do that and you'll end up in jail sure. Mr. Mac's only seeing you take care of yourself.' Earl said, 'I ain't fighting Mr. Mac. I want that Sam!' I said that as long as he wanted to kill somebody, I guessed he'd be fighting me because I certainly wouldn't let him do that if I could help it. When Earl began to quiet down, I told Sam to get out of the station-wagon and re-arranged the seating. I told Earl to get in and cool off and that we could talk about this after the meeting.

"When we got back to the agency and the other boys had left, Earl and I talked about what had happened out on the road by the playground. Earl said: 'Mr. Mac, I get so mad I can't see straight.' I said I knew that and could understand that sometimes he had a right to get mad but I was worried about what would happen to him. Earl leaned over and sort of put his arms around me and said, 'We're friends, aren't we, Mr. Mac?' I replied, 'You know we are, Earl. Even when you do something I don't like, you know I'm still your friend.' He smiled a little wistfully and said, 'You just tell that Sam to stay away from me, that's all!' I said I couldn't tell everybody in the world that he got mad at to stay away from him. Maybe he just had to learn to be with people and maybe be angry without getting so angry that he would let himself go and mess up his own life. . . ."

This conversation was centered right on the boy's feeling—the angry, mad, hostile feeling that must have felt "bad" to the boy. At the same time this boy could express the warm, scared, little-boy side of himself that reached out for the security of the worker's acceptance of him. And the worker responded to both sides of the feeling, assuring him that he was his friend and letting him know his understanding of the "mad" feelings and his concern for the boy's welfare if he let his feelings control him. But he was putting the responsibility on to the boy and he helped him to move toward that responsibility by responding to the feelings that he was encouraging the boy to express. There was relatedness between these two that encompassed the reality of both the positive and negative kinds of feeling, with no pretense between them. And relatedness comes only when the worker has separated his own feelings sufficiently that he can let himself know what feeling the other person is conveying to him.

I have touched briefly on four of the major concepts whose use is essential to group work skill: the use of the agency function; the dynamic possibilities for helping in the reality of a present group situation; the strength in people; the significance of feelings in relationships. The use of one of these concepts without the others does not result in group work skill. To hold to the agency function, for example, without taking in the feelings of the members, would be more damaging than helpful. It is the use of these concepts *combined* that creates skill in group work.

I have had a real problem of selection as I faced the limits of a short paper and I have omitted several concepts that carry significance equal to those I have discussed. Some may be puzzled by my failure to include the concepts that relate to the constructive use of limits; the worker's responsibility for introducing and sustaining a focus; the dynamic of difference. There may be other concepts that many have found give direction to their work. It will be noticed, too, that I have not been using the word "techniques." It is many years since I have thought that techniques as such were essential to group work practice.

I am a little fearful that a technique may be like something in a bag of tricks that a worker opens up now and then to select from and use *on* a group. I believe that a worker's sureness in his work with people comes from a steady base of underlying principles—or concepts as we have been calling them today—and that when a worker has made those principles his own by his use of them, he finds a way to help people use the services of his agency.

Knowledge about group work principles is not enough to produce skillful group work. Anyone who has the interest can become familiar with these concepts if he takes the time to do so—but skill comes from using them in practice. In the early forties, Virginia Robinson discussed the meaning of skill in a volume called, *Training for Skill in Social Casework*. She wrote, "Skill implies first of all an activity, an ability to perform, and while it rests on knowledge it is clearly distinguishable from knowledge. . . . The skillful way of working . . . develops out of some relationship between the workman and the material in which he works. . . . His understanding of his material and his capacity to work *with* it, instead of *against* it, to utilize and not do violence to its essential nature, determine his ability to develop skill in his handling of the process. Skill might be defined, then, as the capacity to set in motion and control a process of change in specific material in such a way that the change that takes place in the material is effected with the greatest degree of consideration for and utilization of the quality and capacity of the material." [2]

Translating this general definition of skill into social work—specifically group work—terms, I would say that group work skill rests on the worker's sensitive relatedness to group members, his firm connection with the agency and its function, his clarity of focus—all of which enable him to develop a process

[2] Virginia P. Robinson, "The Meaning of Skill," *Training for Skill in Social Casework*, University of Pennsylvania Press, 1942, pp. 11-12.

with his groups which he consciously accelerates, trusting them
to take their part in it and helping them to do so.

Skill is developed only as one turns concepts to convictions
as he tests them in his work with people, integrating his knowledge with real, living experience. As a group worker gets hold
of these basic concepts—has them "in his muscles," as Gertrude
Wilson would say—he finds a steady and sure way to help the
members of his groups and thereby to make his contribution to
the fulfillment of the professional purpose of social group work.

ACCEPTANCE AND REJECTION IN
MEMBERSHIP *By Godfrey Frankel*

FORMATION of a group just doesn't happen spontaneously. Individuals with common needs are not attracted
and integrated toward a goal like nails toward a magnet. Considerable stress and struggle, thinking and plotting will go on
before individuals become part of the group, if they do. For a
variety of reasons, avowed and unavowed, some may be rejected before entering the club; others may be superficially accepted through pressure of the group worker or by the group's
or agency's faulty procedure and then rejected once they are
members of the club.

Bertha Reynolds has pointed out that while every group at
some time or other has membership difficulties and other frustrations, the group will survive as long as these problems are
incidental to the need to be together.

Common goals are woven out of the needs of a particular
group of individuals. A dynamic process takes place as each
member both brings to and takes from the group his notion of
what is expected from a new member. And this includes
everything that has been impressed upon the club member
from the sum total of his life's experiences. His idea of personality and class may be even more important (consciously or

unconsciously) than what the prospective member can contribute to the group's goals or program.

Who comes in and who doesn't, the reasons given and not given, at what times and places this important decision takes place and what can the worker do are major aspects of this problem which will be taken up in this article.

What are the pressures of this process of selection? Given certain types of individuals, what can we expect if they are exposed to certain groups? If the individual is ready for group experience, is the channel of membership open? As workers, can we facilitate admission if we think this is the step called for?

This excerpt from a record is typical of the experience re-enacted countless times in hundreds of groups each year.

Elaine, the prospective member, entered the room. She nervously looked around to see if she was acquainted with anyone. They were all strangers and I felt her aloneness. The other members looked at her, her clothes, her face, her shoes. I wondered if they would accept her, if she would fit their ideal of a sister club member. I also wondered if they did decide to take her in, would she be happy in the club and would this be a good experience for her.

There was a dead crucial silence, brief but meaningful because in that split second period the new member was on trial. Though nothing was said, I knew by their eyes the other members were beginning to make up their minds—if they liked her, if they wanted her. At that moment as I held Elaine's perspiring hand, I introduced her and spoke about the club's favorite activities. I also mentioned some of the things that Elaine enjoyed doing.

Will the group accept Elaine? Can she become a happy part of the group? What is the role of the group worker?

Dr. Horace Miller in his article "Psychic Trauma of Becoming Part of a Group" [1] states, "Anyone who comes into an unfamiliar group of people with their strange rules, customs, and personal

---

[1] Sullivan, Dorothea, *Readings in Group Work*, Association Press, 1952, p. 270.

relationships will tend to feel insecure. Some degree of psychic trauma appears unavoidable as the newcomer has to lose some of his more immature pattern so that he can accept his new relationship without too much conflict. Whatever one has become dependent upon will hamper this new adjustment and the willingness to accept very early in life the feeling of respect for something bigger than one can ever hope to understand seems to be the only attitude which will not constrict future growth and one's acceptance of the world of reality."

First we have to start with agency purpose and program. If its purpose is to work with all individuals and groups in the community, then its program, policy, and staff must demonstrate this.

But as soon as membership walks through the front door, we are reminded that our test begins. Our open policy may run counter to what Margaret Berry calls "the need of individuals to seek support of those who are like themselves and who find that desire reinforced by important institutions such as family and church."[2]

That individual may be aware of the agency ruling to accept members regardless of race or class, as long as individually they are suited to the group. But because of personal prejudices, that individual prefers to keep out anyone to whom he thinks he may have difficulty relating. And here the worker clearly has an interpretive job to perform so that barriers are lifted and biased members get an opportunity to know the new member and at least see what he is like.

At the same time, we have to be sensitive to community patterns and membership's state of readiness so that we will have more preparation in dealing with these matters which might have contradiction for some members.

One of the unavowed reasons people come to the center is

[2] Agency Initiated Groups, Social Work in the Current Scene, National Conference of Social Work, 1950.

because other people like themselves are members. This happens to most agencies and in a more specific manner happens to the groups operating within the agency. Even if an agency has an open policy with a program of wide community appeal, members will tend to join because of the culture and class of people already members.

Rejection from a group can be a disturbing experience whether the reasons are valid or not. The non-admitted individual receives others rebuffs in life, understood and not understood. But when he receives them from a community sanctioned agency operated by professionally trained workers whose purpose is quite the opposite, it may have a double-barrelled effect.

Ann's family had recently moved to the new suburb. Ann is 13, beginning to have occasional dates, is quite presentable, and seems to get along rather well with her peers and adults. It wasn't long before she made friends with Jane, one of the members of the Dreamers Club, whom she met at school. Ann was overjoyed when Jane invited her to join the club which is a neighborhood friendship group of 11- and 12-year-olds and must accept all members after proper clearance through the worker. But without any knowledge of the worker or the other members except Jane, her friend Ann came to the next club meeting.

This was bad preparation for Ann and for the group and even though she got along well in the meeting, feelings were mixed as to her admission to the group. The worker sensed this and staved off any kind of vote or expressed negative feelings toward Ann during the meeting. Her plan was to call each member on the phone before the next meeting after discussing the club experience fully with Ann and her mother. But on the way home from the meeting, two of the girls walking with Ann indicated that the club was not taking in any more members.

Ann's mother called the agency that night after learning about the club and her daughter's experience. The mother seemed to be interested in her daughter joining a club, but stated that Ann felt she wasn't wanted. The mother said, "I'm not blaming you, but as professionals you should know what to do in a situation like this."

After conferences with Ann and her mother and discussing the situation fully over the phone with the other members, Ann was admitted and after that seemed to get along with the other members of the group.

Friendship clubs for 8- to 11-year-olds are established at my agency on a neighborhood basis. A mother calls the agency and states she has spoken to nine other mothers who would like to have an extension club in their neighborhood. A meeting is called at which the ten mothers are present and the service of the agency is explained by the worker. If all goes well, memberships are taken out, a meeting day is selected, and the club is launched. Marie is in one of these clubs. Her difficulty did not show up until several meetings with the group had been held.

Marie had never really been accepted by a small friendship group of 10-year-old girls, but she still came to meetings. The members complained at various times about her being "loud, hard to get along with, too young, and a creep." She seemed to go out of her way to do things which she knew put her in a bad light. The club leader indicated that she was quiet, a poor dresser, unsophisticated, and could not attract boys like the other girls. The girls are not particularly glamorous, but they are looking for glamor to identify with.

Marie has had a difficult time relating to the girls and after talking with her mother a few times, referral to a case work agency was suggested. Case work was begun, but not continued. After conferring with the case worker, it was felt that perhaps Marie was not able to use this group as there were enough masochistic tendencies indicated to consider discontinuing her membership.

This club met in the neighborhood and there was no other club in this area for Marie to be transferred to. Nor does she live close enough to the community center to join an activity group which might offer a better approach.

At this point the club leader and supervisor of the program are observing Marie closely and attempting to effect a better relationship for her in the group, although the outlook is not too bright.

The question of what is best to do with Marie is a moot point. It is not easy to make a decision on whether it is better to stay in the group, especially if one can't observe any overt changes in her. Yet with no other group for her to try out, and we have found out that she does not belong to any synagogue or school clubs, there is a hesitation on the part of the worker to expect Marie to progress more if she were not a member of the group.

The overdependent child may be submerged and lost in his difficulty to relate to a group, the never-cared-for child may have too many and too great aggressions for the average group. One of the problems that many agencies have serving more-or-less normal groups is the integrating of marginal personalities who have not yet learned how to use the group. In many cases of this kind, it is safer to try an activity or day camp group where membership requirements are relaxed or non-existent. Only a few children can be absorbed—one agency indicates it can take only one individual per group of twelve who may be referred from a treatment agency or have enough problems to be given special attention. And this can only be done with competent staff. Every effort should be made to give these children a beginning group experience. The extra aggression, poor motor coordination or introverted attitude may serve as real life experience in testing the elasticity of a group. But this cannot be overdone. The group should gain and we should be sure the individual is not being hurt and is deriving, or at least learning how to derive some satisfactions out of the experience.

I think it can be readily seen that as group life becomes more intimate and personal, the criteria for membership tend to be based more on the personal identifications of the members. What looks like a capricious reason for rejecting a popular individual might actually be a feeling of class difference in a homogeneous intimate group.

College fraternities and sororities often represent this kind of intimate narcissistic group and because of the almost total living pattern with members residing at the houses, there is more emphasis on personality and class than other factors.

Country clubs, exclusive social clubs and children's friendship clubs are inclined to attach a precious, highly personalized quality to their groups. As goals become less self-centered, groups tend to be more fluid and the basis for acceptance and rejection of membership not as personal and crucial as in the fraternity picture.

As groups become less avowedly social in goals, there is probably less emphasis upon the personality or class structure and more upon the individual interest and contribution to the common goal. This is true of political parties, large civic and service groups such as the Lions, and Kiwanis clubs. But as an individual moves closer to the top echelon of almost any group, more elements of his background and associations will be scrutinized either intuitively or consciously.

We find in children's activity groups such as athletics, arts and crafts, and canteens, etc., that acceptance and rejection of new members is not as crucial as in social clubs. Groups whose program and goals are clearly designed to attract certain abilities and interests such as a basketball group, camera club, stamp club or swimming club are more likely to appraise the new member on the basis of interest and ability than on personality or other life associations.

All house activity groups at the center I am associated with are formed by the staff and this is on the basis of age, sex, and interest. Only in special cases is there any question of an individual joining a particular group and that is generally a referral from a treatment agency. These groups run from 3½ years through 18 and a few adult groups. We seldom hear of any membership problems with these groups. Pre-teen extension clubs organized on a neighborhood basis, and described earlier, can discuss and are encouraged to discuss prospective members, but they do not vote and cannot refuse to accept a child once she has cleared intake.

Teen age social clubs may be formed before coming to the agency or agency organized. In the former case it is generally more difficult for new members (other than friends of present members) to be accepted. In agency organized groups membership barriers are apt to be less rigid. At the adolescent age, individuals become more selective about their friends. They voice their opinions or secretly decide whom they want in and whom they don't. Sometimes the club resorts to the majority vote. This can be a strangler under a democratic façade and if the worker can't avoid this, he should guide the discussion on a firm basis of selection of members. Actually, the worker does everything possible to avoid a vote. The staff worker is aware enough of the situation and attempts to work out the problem if he spots it soon enough. Even before an individual is presented to a group, the feelings and attitudes of the group and of the individual presented should be known. The relationship of a worker to a group should be so well established that membership requirements and procedure be known and clearly understood by everyone so that there is little chance for stress situations.

In many cases the child who is a member of either a social or activity group sees most group work agencies as permissive play schools where there are no artificial barriers in membership restrictions. But as the child grows into pre-teens and teen-age, he is apt to show more interest in selecting certain individuals for his closest friends. It is in the social groups for pre-teens and teens that the solidarity and feeling of group consciousness becomes stronger than with younger children, according to Goodenough. This means that inter-personal relationships become keener and the individual brings his life's influences to bear in making the decision on a prospective member.

One of the areas of confusion in the membership requirement question is how far youth should be permitted to select membership on the basis of personal identification. Shouldn't children and youth have the free choice to select whom they want for new members? After all, their parents do in their clubs, and the patterns of class differences are integrally woven into our social fabric. Are we telling our youth that they can't dislike some individuals? This question hits groups with strong social motivations more than others. The other side of the picture is that many never realized friendships do not get a chance to develop because the individual did not possess an expected poise or social skills necessary for initial impressions, and a hasty negative decision was made.

The whole discussion is a fertile field in which the group worker can take a strong role.

We must work closely with our club members informing them that they do not have to like all the prospective members on the same basis as their best friends; that they should respect difference in personality and background as long as they feel the new members are suited to the group and that everyone interviewed beforehand (intake) deserves a fair chance. This statement may be easy to say and hard to implement especially with those social groups built strongly on personal identifications.

One thing we have to decide for ourselves and that is that we cannot serve the fraternity-sorority concept of group life in our agencies. And as groups come closer to that precious concept, we have more difficulty working with them within our agency ranks.

We certainly do not want to deemphasize the values of warm relationships in group life. It is known that some of the most satisfying interpersonal experiences are derived from intimate friendship groups or what Helen Jennings calls the "Psyche-Group." Our aim rather is to stimulate intimate friendships within the framework of our policies and functions.

Summation

Most of the bases for choice of accepting or rejecting a new member are:

(1) personality—emotional self, ability to relate, physical appearance;
(2) culture and class associations, family, economic and status position;
(3) interest or ability in program;
(4) support goal;
(5) personal identification;
(6) friends of members;
(7) impersonal—new members to change balance of power, activity or goals;
(8) pressure or pattern by parents, staff workers or custom of the agency or community;
(9) capricious reasons without any apparent basis.

Decisions to accept or reject new members are often made in the following situations:

1. When the group is unofficially assembled and the club leader and prospective member are not present and they can talk freely outside of the agency and make their decision. Procedure is repeated at official meeting. Worker may have difficult time here because of the full rehearsal and subterfuge and perhaps ineffective relationship with group.

2. When one or more members outside of official club meeting make the decision and hand it to the rejected individual. Worker may never get to see or even hear of this individual. Also it may indicate poor relationship with group.

3. When club members seek the aid of influential adults and staff workers in a membership problem. This is often an effective approach in resolving a question of membership because it means that the members feel free to discuss this with others (adults) outside of their club and ask for assistance on making a decision.

4. When agency forms group on neighborhood or activity basis or on basis of age, emotional level, social development and background.

5. When members think separately in an official meeting yet act together without discussion on a membership they know is a foregone conclusion. The club members may attempt to forestall any action from the worker, hence the lack of discussion. Naturally this approach is to be avoided at all cost. This indicates an ineffective relationship between worker and group.

6. Postponing, tabling, or otherwise stalling a membership problem because the group does not want to face the problem or because the group is using this means to keep the new member out. These maneuvers are sometimes perpetuated on the new worker or the worker with an ineffective relationship with the group. As the worker's relationship with the group improves, the group will feel too guilty to create underhanded tactics. More clear information about the applying member might air views and give the worker a better chance to enable the group to make up its mind on the basis of concrete information.

7. When the group, using criteria, discusses the prospective member and acceptance is on a majority vote. This is a ticklish situation, but if it looks like rejection from the discussion, perhaps an interview by the worker will help direct the prospective member to a more suitable club if this is indicated, and this should be suggested before a vote is taken.

Emphasis should be on criteria and a vote avoided if possible. It may be found in holding close to criteria for membership that the individual's attributes will be seen more clearly. It may be that a rejection occurs because of inadequate intake; for example, an individual is not ready to enter into hetero-sexual contacts yet the group he wishes to enter is quite advanced in dating. This kind of detailed knowledge about individuals must be known so that the most appropriate group placement can be made.

Some concrete steps a group worker can take to minimize difficulties in the membership process are:

1. Agency rules for membership in social clubs and other groups should be clear and open so that group members know what is expected and set up more standard membership procedures.

2. Social groups should have written or accepted criteria. This should comprise a set of reasonable requirements related to the purposes and aims of the group within the framework of agency policy. The criteria should be formulated jointly by the worker and the group. In the case of a worker or group that inherits criteria which are clearly unworkable and restrictive, careful inventory is called for.

3. There should be careful intake so that most membership problems are avoided before they start. Before referral to a club a worked out system of "feelers" might be tried to see if a prospective member will be accepted.

4. Interview between representative of club and prospective member introduced by worker. This is where point No. 3 ends.

5. Interview between worker and club representative to hear reactions to prospective member. Prospective member may not be able to present himself well at first meeting, but would be suitable to club. This needs worker's interpretation and support.

6. Worker or club representative presents prospective member to club for membership.

7. This step is only taken if the others break down. Worker

should attempt to meet with any individuals who were rejected in activities or club to try to fit them into other activities. They should also be given an opportunity to discuss any problems they may have.

The above steps not only facilitate the membership process, but also aid in integrating the new member into the group.

Our general approach to the role of the group worker in this paper does not attempt to create an antiseptic atmosphere where negative attitudes do not exist in group life. It is at the initial stage where social barriers can be drawn without reason or knowledge before a relationship even begins that the worker can help the group give the individual a fair chance. We must make it possible for children and youth to move in and out of groups if they think they can profit by the association and particularly if we as group workers think so too.

The group worker must be in on the membership process at all times, following an individual until he either becomes a member of a club or joins another worthwhile activity or if neither, at least tells him he cannot be served at present.

The needs, drives, and aspirations of the individuals applying for membership and the intricate structure of each group the worker is responsible for must be studied and understood before referrals to groups can be made. The worker must have some idea how certain individuals will be able to use group experience, how a few may not be able to do so, and how others may be permitted a trial period.

We have a professional responsibility to see that the members in our groups understand the framework of the agency practices and limitations under which the group is operating, that new and old members understand clearly the membership requirements and goals of the group, that they have the full facts on prospective members, that they use criteria, that they try to think straight, and that the entire process is handled with sensitivity and skill for the best interests of the individual and for the enrichment of the group.

12

Professional Developments in Group Work

ON BECOMING PROFESSIONAL
By Grace Coyle

Within the ten years since the American Association for the Study of Group Work was born, there has been increasing evidence that group workers were coming to regard themselves as professional and that other groups were demanding of us the assumption of such responsibilities. As the founders of the organization will, I am sure, all agree, this was not our intention in the beginning. The method of group work was still too new; its foundations were still too fragile; and the body of practitioners was not only small, but it was uncertain as to its place in the field of the social services. While not all this has changed in ten years, no one can view the developments that have occurred without recognizing within them the evidences of a process familiar in many allied occupations.

Professional Criteria

The growth of occupations into professions is a social phenomenon that is characteristic of our society. The ancient learned professions—medicine, law, teaching and the priesthood—obviously were the first to acquire the characteristics that we now call "professional." With the advance of modern knowledge, a crop of new professions based on the application of scientific knowledge to various social needs has sprung up. One has only to mention the nurse, the public accountant, the engineer, the pharmacist, the librarian, the social case worker, to illustrate this tendency. It is as significant for our time as the medieval guilds of skilled craftsmen were in that period, and grows as they did out of the social conditions of the present. As Carr-Saunders has pointed out, there are certain common characteristics in all the professions, of which the most significant are: [1]

1. The development of the body of knowledge upon which the skill rests.
2. The "reservation of function to the qualified" by means of licensing or the restrictions of the professional bodies.
3. The development of professional consciousness among practitioners.
4. The contribution of the specialized skill and viewpoint to appropriate problems in the surrounding society.

Let us consider what has been happening to and among group workers in the light of these criteria. Obviously, no group becomes professional by making claims; true professional status must be achieved. It can only be achieved by solid intellectual effort related to the body of knowledge, by self-discipline among practitioners and devotion to high standards of practice, and by competent and responsible organization.

[1] Carr-Saunders, "Professions," in *Encyclopedia of the Social Sciences*, Vol. VI, pp. 476-480.

If we consider our ten years' progress along these lines, we see a persistent but spotty trend, with real achievements here and there, with exaggerated and unfounded claims at certain points, and with considerable steady growth in the members and competence of the organization. If we are to go forward effectively into the next period, it is perhaps valuable to take stock of our achievements.

Toward a Tested Body of Knowledge

The first and basic essential in the process by which an occupation turns into a profession is its development of a tested body of related knowledge upon which the skill of its practitioners rests. Where are we in this regard? Some of us veterans remember the first struggles to get a group-work section into the National Conference of Social Work, where we could have a place to explore our common problems and to present what experience existed. To us it seems that some progress has been made in this regard, since the group-work section was started in 1935. The accumulation of articles in *The Group* and the slow addition of a few books—still too few—are other evidences. Through these and other efforts we can, I think, see certain accomplishments. I would list them as three:

1. The skeleton of what will become our body of knowledge is now visible. It was formulated in the recent A.A.S.G.W. document on the *Body of Knowledge and Skills*. It appears again in the report of the Curriculum Committee on Group Work of the American Association of Schools of Social Work. It is largely a framework of topics, but it gives shape and relation to what we see is involved in the practice of group work. It contains in each of its expressions the same elements: the understanding of individual behavior, of group process, of community relations, of program content and activities, and of supervision in group-work practice.

2. Beyond this framework another advance is evident: we have achieved a common collection of concepts with which to think and to communicate our experience. Skilled practitioners now know and use certain common tools of thought that did not exist twenty years ago, when we began. They include such concepts as group acceptance and rejection, integration, group control, group climate, problem-solving discussion, and a growing number of others that our channels of expression at conferences and in periodicals now help to define and clarify for those in contact with this stream of thought.

3. A third and most significant development we are only beginning: the study of the dynamics of group behavior, the penetration into the process itself. All other developments are preliminary to this which, if we can achieve it, will be our real contribution to knowledge and so to practice.

To do this we need two levels of activity. First, we must have competent and adequately supported research. So far we have had practically none accept that done by Kurt Lewin and his associates, which may now be expanded in the new exploration of group dynamics at M.I.T. The research of Moreno and Jennings, and of Newstetter is of this kind. A great deal more of it is needed than is now in prospect. Some research by social scientists—not related consciously to group work—will contribute something to it, but we will have to make the adaptations to our field. Such borrowings from the "pure" scientists and from related fields will help in some ways, but they are not as pertinent as the research directly on group behavior and on group leadership, which we so badly need.

A second source of knowledge should come, I think, from practitioners in the field, and from faculty and students in professional schools. This can come by a greatly expanded use of process recording of groups and the constant analysis of those records in supervision, in discussion groups of practitioners, and in classes in the schools. This is our present chief source of improved skill and heightened insight, and it is within the range of all of us—or should be. Upon these two—research and close examination of our own practice—we must rely if we are to develop an adequate body of knowledge.

One trend within recent years should be examined here. Anyone who knows the Association well will know that we have developed within it schools of thought. This is, I believe, a healthy sign of growth. It came about with the beginning of our attempt to understand *why* groups behave as they do. In doing this, we dug below the level of practice to underlying theory. Some people went for the answers to social psychology, especially the Gestalt school, some turned to the explanations rooted in psychiatry and psycho-analysis. When we emerged again after this plunge into theory, we brought up from the depths somewhat different explanations. But at least we had dug below the surface! Similar differences among case workers are familiar to us in the differences between the Freudians and the Rankians, among educators in the controversies over progressive education, and earlier among psychiatrists among the Freudians and the followers of Jung and Adler. This tendency to form schools of thought is a normal sign of growth in theoretical development. It is harmful only if it turns into sectarianism with the usual accompaniments of mutual recrimination. Of all people group workers, with their familiarity with subgroups and their conscious and subconscious bases, should be able to deal with this tendency in themselves. The mature answer, I believe, lies in the practice of eclecticism—that is, the reasoned choice of the best we can get from each stream of thought. If we know the meaning of integration, let us use it on ourselves.

We must, as I am sure we do, recognize that to date we have only begun to explore the real bases of group behavior. If the science of human relations, of which this a part, ever develops, we shall see that this period was embryonic. We have at present about as much understanding as that represented in medieval medicine by the belief that all diseases arose from the four humors. All science is a slow growth, and we were born into the generation when social science is in its infancy—perhaps its late infancy, but certainly not its maturity. We have our chance, however, to contribute our part to that essential body of knowledge.

The Reservation of Function

The second mark of a profession is the process described by Carr-Saunders as the "reservation of the function to the qualified" and known to us as the setting of standards. In every occupation, it consists of the same steps:

1. The analysis of the functions and the classification of jobs to carry out specific functions.

2. The establishing of qualifications for each type of job.

3. The determining of the professional education required for such jobs.

4. The determination of fees and salaries appropriate to the jobs included in the professional group.

I think we have to admit that we, as an Association, have so far done little in this area. The fields of recreation and informal education in which most group workers are employed have been moving in this direction, but with little assistance from the A.A.S.G.W. This is one of the points in which outside demands upon us have pushed the A.A.S.G.W into performing some of the functions of a professional organization—perhaps before it was ready internally to do so adequately.

I should like to mention a few evidences of this trend. The most significant in the long run is the spread of job-analysis and job-classification studies through Councils of Social Agencies. We now have at least seven cities in which such studies have covered group-work positions. The recent pamphlet published by the A.Y.S.O., *Positions in Youth-serving Organizations,* serves the same purpose in classifying and setting qualifications.

The demands made during the war by the setting up of the National Roster of Scientific and Specialized Personnel, the development of the *Occupational Dictionary,* the organization by the A.A.S.W. of the wartime Committee on Personnel, the joint Army and Navy Committee on Welfare and Recreation—all of these made demands upon individuals or upon the A.A.S.G.W. which said plainly: "The time has come for you to tell us what are the requirements for competent practitioners." In the fall of 1946, the American Red Cross, in a three-day conference on the training of hospital recreation workers, came forth again with a similar request to the A.A.S.G.W.—namely, that it and the Society of Recreation Workers get together to work out standards in professional education. All of these are significant straws in the wind. They show that the field is ready for the formulation of standards and the development of training to meet such standards. They indicate to most of us that, as a group of practitioners, we have been backward in getting into this. I believe this is one of the major reasons for the rising demand that A.A.S.G.W. take on the character of a professional organization.

If we are to do this, however, we must deal with certain doubts and confusions that beset us. I should like to mention briefly the impediments which I believe stand in the way:

1. I think one fear often expressed during these ten years still haunts us: the fear of professionalization in a rigid and mechanical sense. There is some apprehension lest the "spirit" be lost and a hard or rigid technique be substituted, or sometimes that nothing but lingo will result. There is always this

danger. Not all doctors are as human as we could wish, not all teachers as inspired. The answer lies, I believe, not in trusting to intuition or hunch, which seems to be the real alternative, but in the eternal vigilance upon which excellence in any line must ultimately depend. "Consecrated ignorance," however consecrated, is not the answer. Consecrated knowledge is our only safety in the practice of all the professions.

We need, however, at this stage of our development as an occupation, to recognize especially the contribution of those pioneers in our field out of whose experience we have gathered what knowledge we have. We are just now in a transitional period in which many of us grew our own body of knowledge unaided or learned it in apprenticeship to those just before us. But that is no reason why a new generation should not start farther along and so go further. That is the simple basis of the progress we have made in training, and it is the same process as that which has gone on in other budding professions.

2. Another objection to the formulation of experience into requirements and the accompanying education is that we are crystallizing too soon. That is a matter of judgment. It is approximately twenty years since group work began to be formulated. That is a considerable period, and I think one real answer to this objection here lies in the demands already mentioned that we do formulate what is needed for effective practitioners. If we cannot do it after twenty years, we are certainly on the wrong track.

3. A third fear is that this setting of standards and then using membership requirements in this Association to strengthen them will make us an exclusive body. Group workers have a tendency to feel guilty about excluding anyone. I believe, however, that any standard setting is necessarily exclusive in one sense. It is, however, not discriminatory. The Association is open to all who are able and willing to meet the requirements. Furthermore, the requirements exist, not for the pleasure of

creating an exclusive fraternity, but in order to see that better service is rendered to the people with whom we work. This is the characteristic of all professional organization and is an inevitable part of standard setting, where membership in the professional organization will be taken as evidence of having met certain requirements.

As I have said, I think the Association needs to put a great deal more of its time and effort into the careful analysis of qualifications for various jobs requiring group-work skill and the professional education needed to prepare people for such jobs. When it has done that, I hope it can also do something about the protective function common to most professional groups—namely, the setting of personnel standards of work, including salaries.

A Professional Consciousness

A third mark of a developing profession is the growth of a professional consciousness, the sense of belonging. The growth of a common bond among group workers seems to me an astonishing phenomenon, perhaps because I remember that little conference on group work in New York in the 1920's, which had about twenty members. The rise in membership of the A.A.S.G.W. from zero in 1936 to twenty-three hundred in 1946 is itself the prime evidence that a bond exists. However, this sense of identification is only one element in it. If we are to become professional, it will require more than this. The rise of this consciousness and the growth of the Association has already created a certain new alignment of loyalties which is a symptom of professional consciousness.

The first step we have had to take is to clarify our relation with organizational employers and our relation to other group workers. Most of the organizations that employ group workers are twenty-five to seventy-five years old, and many of them have long and strong traditions. There has been in the past some tendency to regard employment by a certain organization as evidence of a profession. As we know, there are organizations of workers in most of our large agencies that have called themselves professional and that have fulfilled certain professional functions. An accurate use of the word "professional" in its true sense, as defined by Carr-Saunders, and a careful scrutiny of our agencies will reveal that organizations employ many types of professional workers. Just as a hospital employs doctors, nurses, dietitians, and laboratory technicians, so a recreation agency employs physical directors, group workers, sometimes case workers or counselors, sometimes dietitians or institutional managers, sometimes teachers of art, music, or dramatics. Each of these specialists has in fact his own tie to his professional group. The group worker, in creating his, is meeting for himself a need that has already created similar organizations for the physical directors, case workers, or dietitians who work for him. It has taken some time, however, to establish the relation between loyalty to the employing agency and loyalty to the profession.

It is only when this loyalty is clearly established that any professional worker is ready to carry out one of the essential responsibilities of being professional—namely, the insistence upon high standards of work. The major contribution that saves professions from becoming exclusive monopolies run for the benefit of the practitioners is the fact that society relies upon them to develop high quality of performance and to uphold each other in practicing at that level. No group is ready to do this until it has found out what high quality of work is. It was this need that made us organize to study group work ten years ago. We have now some, but nowhere near enough, idea of what constitutes good group work. We will only develop that out of a disciplined, persistent struggle to study what we do, select the best, teach it to beginners, and hold everyone to as high levels as we can. We have only to mention this to make it clear how far we have to go. But I am sure we are making progress here and that local groups of the new A.A.G.W. can serve by exchange of experience and continuous evaluation of practice to establish better levels.

One other aspect of the professional consciousness that I should like to mention briefly is our understanding of the professional relationships involved. These include professional relations to those we work with, to other staff members, and to the community where we function as professional workers. This is the area of professional ethics. We have, I believe, some development of professional ethics in our relations to members of groups. This is in essence not very different from the similar responsibility of all the professions that deal with people—whether doctor, case worker, or teacher. We need, however, to sharpen and define the particular requirements of group leadership in its responsibility and the self-imposed limitations that our basic philosophy in group work will determine. Ethics must grow out of a philosophy, a sense of direction and of values. Group work as a method has, I believe, such a philosophy, even if it is still not wholly defined. The turning of that philosophy into guiding principles which will control and direct our skill is the process of developing professional ethics. This too we are only beginning to do.

One baffling problem has plagued the development of professional consciousness among group workers over this decade. It is usually phrased in terms of alignment, and a dilemma is presented. We must, it seems, be either educators or social workers. When a problem persists so long among intelligent people, as of course we are, it is usually a proof that we are trying to solve it by a wrong set of assumptions. It is not an either-or proposition, and we shall never solve it by organizing teams and instituting a tug of war. Like all persistent problems, it has in it accretions of the irrational—old loyalties and prejudices, an occasional vested interest, and a considerable admixture of misinformation or once good information now out of date.

If I may insert my own proposal for a solution to this problem, I should like to do so for discussion purposes and in the interest of contributing to a clarification, even if I cannot produce it. Such a solution involves, in the first place, accepting group work as a method that developed chiefly in the field of recreation and informal education. The functions in the community that are fulfilled by recreation and informal-education agencies run parallel to other community services, including child welfare, family welfare, health, religious services, public compulsory education, and the cultural services of museums and libraries. While group work as a method developed in the recreation and informal-education agencies, it should be used in and in fact is spreading into agencies with other functions, such as children's institutions, hospitals, or churches. Many of these community services, though not all, are grouped locally into Councils of Social Agencies and nationally into the National Conference of Social Work. Most group workers, therefore, are fulfilling recreation and education functions in agencies often called a part of "social work" or sometimes more accurately and more recently called "community services" or "health-and-welfare services."

A large part of our difficulty in knowing what we are has come out of the words "social work." To many people, they connote relief, or dealing with the poor, or uplift, or some other unpleasant facet of life. We need to realize that not only we but other people are changing. The A.A.S.W. is in process of defining social work, and Kenneth Pray's presidential speech at the National Conference of Social Work in 1946 is an indication of where such exploration may lead. My own hope is that the emerging definition of social work may define it as involving the conscious use of social relations in performing certain community functions, such as child welfare, family welfare or health services, recreation, and informal education. Case work, group work, and community organization have this common factor, that they are all based on understanding human relations. While the specific relations used in each are different, the underlying philosophy and approach are the same: a respect for personality and a belief in democracy. This we share with case workers and expert community organization people. It is for this reason that I believe group work as a method falls within the larger scope of social work *as a method* and as defined above.

Another link that group work has to the field of education and upon which alignment is often based, besides the fact that the group worker is fulfilling an educational function, is the fact that the basic philosophy of group work drew so heavily upon the philosophy and methods of Dewey and Kilpatrick, especially in the beginning. Progressive education, however, like group work, is a method of approach used to carry on educational functions; and when it is understood as such, our relation to it further clarifies the proposed solution to our dilemma. Until we can clarify this question of alignment, we will, I am afraid, be bedevilled by it. As I have said, I present this merely as one person's solution to our most persistent problem. Certainly before we can go ahead to develop our professional consciousness without confusion or dissension, some solution to the question of alignment must be found.

Group-work Skills and Social Action

Finally, I wish to consider the fourth test of professional behavior which Carr-Saunders suggests—namely, the contribution of special skill to the formulation of public policy. This tendency for professional organizations to play a part through social action on matters relevant to their special skill is, as Carr-Saunders believes, "one of the most hopeful means of bringing the expert into the service of democracy."

We are perhaps still too immature as an organization and too undeveloped in our body of knowledge to have much to offer to society. I have been considerably disturbed in recent years by a tendency to make pronouncements on the war and post-war world, as if any special expertness qualified us to speak. If we are not to get lost in a bog of diffused and futile good intentions, we need to make a few distinctions. The first is the difference between what any of us believe personally on political and social questions and what we have come to as group workers. In the first instance, we need to find outlets for our social impulses in all the variety of "good societies" available to us. But if we try to bring all those causes into the A.A.G.W., it will obviously merely ride off in all directions.

There are, however, a number of areas in which our professional competence gives us a right to speak with a special weight. It is well to get clear that group work is not synonymous with recreation, nor with youth, nor with general democratic advance. At the same time, since so many of us work in recreation agencies or with youth, it seems reasonable to me that the A.A.G.W. should be qualified as an organization to have an expert opinion on legislation in those fields. This certainly is a large part of our expert knowledge, and I hope it can be used as needed to bring intelligent pressure on appropriate bodies. This has its parallels in the case workers' concern with public-assistance legislation, or adequate care for the mentally ill, or the teachers' opinion on Federal subsidy for education. Here we can and should work with other groups like the Society of Recreation Workers and the A.A.S.W.

There is also another area in which it is conceivable that in time we might make a public contribution. It is possible that our understanding of group relations itself might lead us into appropriate social action of a broader sort. This, I realize, is speculative at present. However, I should like to suggest a line of thought that might lead in this direction. Stuart Chase, in a recent review of Dr. Elton Mayo's new book, draws this conclusion as to our present needs: [2]

Unless we develop social skills to help us adjust to change, the adaptive society, failing to adapt well enough itself, is doomed. In the past social skills were handed down from father to son in the family, in the guild, the shop, the church, the village green. Now, if they are to be developed at all, the social sciences will have to lead the way.

Actually, Dr. Mayo shows, informal organizations are the heart and the reality of human communities. If they are functioning well, they will adjust the individual effectively to society and make a great state apparatus redundant. When they are functioning badly and the state tries to provide a pulmotor, the relief cannot be for long. The most efficient politician can hardly hope to keep a community going which has lost its internal organs. It is not statism we should fear so much as the destruction of our social skills. The real constructive task lies in replacing them.

It may seem like making the undue claims to which I objected above to point to this as our contribution. I believe this expresses the real significance of our search into group behavior and our developing of a practice in group leadership. I do not think we can claim much achievement as yet. But I believe we, along with other professional workers also dealing with personal relations, are among those who can help in the replacing of the social skills necessary in the present distracted state of our world.

[2] Stuart Chase, "Calling All Social Scientists," in *The Nation* (May 4, 1946), pp. 539-540.

GROUP WORKERS AND PROFESSIONAL
ETHICS *By L. K. Hall*

PROFESSIONAL workers moving into the group work field often get into situations where ethical questions arise. This article will point out what some of them are and attempt to provide some general principles for determining the basis for good professional conduct.

What Ethics Means

Ethics refers to what a conscientious person is obliged to do or not to do in a given situation or set of relationships. The ethical person does not spread slanderous gossip, short-change a customer, avoid payment of properly assessed taxes, expose others to infection, make a promise and not fulfill it, or engage to do what he knows he is not equipped to do. The ethical person will stop his car and remove a loose piece of nail-studded board from the road. He is loyal to his family and to his country. He is a good neighbor. He has what Gelett Burgess calls an "educated heart" that makes him sensitive to the obligations of his relationships and responsibilities, that imposes restraint, and at the same time prompts him to go the second mile.

In familiar situations and relationships the ethics of conduct has entered our mores and we tend to behave ethically without thinking much about it. In new situations, or in situations involving conflicts of values and interests, even a very sensitive person may sometimes have trouble finding his way. The primary ethical obligation for any person is that he shall seek always to base his attitudes and actions on more reliable considerations than impulse, prejudice, personal preference and convenience, or a partial view of the situation.

Every specialized occupation produces its particular kinds of situations and relationships in which the rules of good professional conduct have to be discovered and defined. Thus "codes" of professional ethics appear. In some cases the rules have almost the force of law—and in fact are often written into the legal code—and the professional worker disregards them at his peril. There are no fewer than 5,000 codes of professional conduct in American business and professional groups. Group workers do not yet have a formal code, though the principles of right professional conduct are now quite generally understood.

Group Work Situations Involving Ethical Questions

This is an "arm-chair" list. It is not complete and the classification, for convenience only, has no special significance other than to illustrate the scope of the problems. Less experienced workers may not have encountered all the kinds of problems suggested by the questions. More experienced workers will think of many problems not included.

1. *Situations involving the aims, methods, and responsibilities of the employing agency:*

   a. What is the group worker's responsibility in respect to the general and specific objectives of his employing agency (e.g., a religious organization)?

   b. If a group worker is not wholly in sympathy with the agency's aims and methods what should he do? (e.g., the agency has a policy of cultural segregation.)

   c. If the board of the agency objects to any aspect of his work with groups, whether of aim or method, what should he do? (Suppose, for instance, that the board should object to the showing of a good film on sex education.)

   d. What is the group worker's responsibility when the board feels that a position he has conscientiously taken on a public question threatens the good public relations of the agency?

(Illustration: A pacifist group worker whose agency is under pressure to discharge him.)

    e. If the worker disagrees with the agency's labor policies what is his duty?

2. *Situations involving the group worker's relationships to the group:*

    a. What is his general obligation in respect to group procedures?

    b. What is his obligation in respect to relating the group's objectives and methods to the objectives and methods of the agency (e.g., a scout troop identified with a church)?

    c. What is his obligation in case of conflict between group and agency on such matters as program content, use of property (damage), participation in public affairs, and the like?

    d. What is his obligation when the internal workings of the group threaten harm to one or more of its members (ridicule, ostracism, scape-goating, snobbery, etc.)?

    e. What is his obligation when the group comes into conflict with other groups because of cultural, or other, differences?

    f. What is his obligation in respect to possible or actual emergencies and danger, the group's attempt to deal with matters beyond its competence, or the group's decision to do something that is wrong or unwise?

3. *Situations involving relationship to individual group members:*

    a. How does he deal with confidences?

    b. What is his responsibility when faced by a personal problem with which he is not professionally competent to deal (deep emotional disturbance, serious antisocial conduct, and the like)?

    c. What is his obligation when he knows a member is engaged in anti-social or illegal conduct (dope-peddling, for instance)?

    d. What is his responsibility when he learns that a group member is planning to do something to which his parents would seriously object (an elopement between two under-age youngsters)?

4. *Situations involving "third parties" (parents, teachers, employers, agencies making referrals):*

    a. What obligations to parents are assumed when group work is done with children?

    b. What is his responsibility when he finds himself "in between" (as when a group makes plans he knows are not acceptable to parents)?

    c. What is his obligation when parents use ingratiating behavior (money gifts or special favors to the worker)?

    d. What is his responsibility for example as a H-Y Club advisor, when asked by the school management for co-operation by the club on a school discipline problem?

5. *Situations involving relationships with fellow workers and with the profession as a whole:*

    a. How does a group worker deal ethically with real or imagined injustice done to him by a fellow-worker, superior, or employer?

    b. What is a group worker's ethical responsibility if he believes that an associate's attitude or behavior is unethical (homosexuality, disloyal political activity, etc.)?

    c. What ethical responsibility does he have toward an associate, volunteer or employed, who is in difficulty because of conscience or because of poor judgment?

    d. What is the ethical responsibility of a group worker with respect to his own professional growth?

e. What is the ethical responsibility of a group worker with respect to the organized labor movement?

Some General Principles and Assumptions That Should Help Determine the Basis for Good Professional Conduct

How does a group worker decide what is right in cases like the foregoing? It is not possible to reduce conduct in all situations to simple rules. Strict conformity to a rule is a good thing if its applicability is clear. (Stop at red lights. Never use ridicule when dealing with an insecure person.) But to add rule to rule does not produce a complete code of ethical behavior. To obey all the rules does not make one an ethical person. Immanuel Kant gave us his "categorical imperative" in an attempt to provide one universal ethical rule: "Act in such a way that I can wish that the maximum for my conduct might become a universal law." This can be paraphrased to read: "Act on the basis of what is best for the most persons in the long run," which is another way of describing how a person with an "educated heart" tries to think and act.

A truly ethical person does not mind having to keep on thinking things through, turning the general principle into concrete behavior in given situations. A genuinely ethical person knows that very few absolute rules can be laid down. Readers are doubtless familiar with the problem placed before army trainees of the truck out of control dashing down a hill toward a child playing in the roadway. Should the driver turn the truck into the ditch at the risk of his own life to save that of the child? But suppose the truck was loaded with soldiers, many of whom might be killed? Suppose the truck was racing to an engagement where there were men badly needed to turn the tide of battle? The answers to the questions showed that the trainees quite properly recognized the fact that an absolute answer did not suffice. Almost always there are values to be weighed, and a choice to be made between alternatives. Absolute rules help only in the simplest of circumstances.

There are, however, some important principles that take us beyond the too-vague and too-general basic ethical attitude. Let us look at several of them:

1. The group worker is obliged at all times and in every way to respect the personality of each individual with whom he works. Negatively this means that he will not use any means that destroys the self-respect and security of any member, nor will he, within the limits of his ability to prevent it, permit others to do so, whether they are inside or outside the group. He will use every means possible to help each group member become a well-adjusted, growing person.

A corollary of this principle is that confidences are respected. In absolute terms it has been stated that "a group worker could never talk to a parent (about a confidential matter) without the knowledge and consent of the group member."[1] Like most absolute statements this one is debatable, but the principle abides. A group worker must be worthy of the confidences he receives.

2. An extension of the first principle gives the second: that at all times and in every way the group worker *will respect the group process*. Except under special circumstances, he will not trespass upon the group's activity in setting its own goals, making and carrying out its own plans, and evaluating its own experiences as a group. It is his responsibility to enter into the group's activity in ways appropriate to the age and competence of its members, to evoke it, to help create and maintain the conditions for its expression.

3. A third general principle is that group work is done in the context of a democratic society. In a sense this imposes obligations, as well as privileges, upon the group, and the ethics of

[1] Helen U. Phillips, "Group Work in 1950," *The Group*, mid-summer issue, 1950, p. 11.

group work requires that the leader be mindful at all times of these larger societal obligations. It is unethical, for instance, to encourage a group to take an irresponsible attitude toward its community or toward property. His goals for individual members derive their sanction not alone from the inner needs of individual members but from his sense of their roles in a democratic society and how they can be fitted for them.

A point of possible difficulty arises here. If objectives from *outside* the group and its members are involved, is not this indoctrination, and is not indoctrination a violation of the principle of respect for personality? Does it not imply imposing something on one's loyalties, on one's actions? One can get into a dialectical jam in trying to answer these questions unless he remembers that group work does not exist in a vacuum. Its context is our total way of life. An individual's adjustment, adequately conceived, is to our total way of life. Our way of life places the values of individual personality above all, but to make this achievement possible for each individual requires each individual to accept the philosophy of it and to learn to live on the basis of it. Of course indoctrination is involved. The person who is not articulate in work and act in respect to democratic *doctrine* is the one most likely to fall victim to its competitors—communism, for instance, or laissez-faire, or just plain hedonism.

The moral obligation, then, on the group worker is to accept democratic goals *and to use democratic methods in developing in groups the attitudes and skills of democratic living.* Just at this point some one asks how democratic one can be with a group of children blundering into a patch of poison ivy, or cruelly tormenting a cabin mate at camp? Suppose we skip this question here and assign it as homework!

4. Another ethical principle that is similar to the one just considered derives from the fact that most group work is sponsored by some agency that has general and specific objectives

of its own. The extent to which agencies will require group workers under their direction to give expression to the agency's overall objectives may vary. Perhaps a worker in an independent social settlement will feel somewhat less obligated by the agency's philosophy than would a worker, say, in a Catholic Youth Organization, or in a Y.M.C.A., or in a camp conducted by a religious agency. I am not sure that this is so; but I am sure that the group worker makes a mistake when he tries to divorce himself entirely from the agency context. Of course there are times when it may seem to him that the agency is denying its own genius; it would then be his ethical obligation to assert the values which he believes are being denied. When the agency is found by the worker not to believe in the values implicit for individuals or groups in a democracy the group worker may have no alternative but to resign.

When conflict arises as it sometimes does, between leader and agency, or between group and agency, it is the group worker's obligation to help clarify the issues, to get the values involved fully understood by all and, if possible, to work things out in a spirit of good will, without recrimination, with mutual appreciation, with values defined, recognized and affirmed. A chip-on-the-shoulder attitude is not professional. It is not ethical.

5. These considerations may help to identify principles of ethical relationship with parents. In the early days of group work it sometimes happened that group workers found themselves actually in competition with parents. At other times parents are simply ignored. Few group workers now make the mistake of brushing the parents aside. There is sincere desire for their cooperation. Many have shifted over to a desire to cooperate *with the parents,* recognizing the primary role of the family relationship. Awareness of this keeps the group worker sensitive to the delicate matter of member-parent relations.

Whatever weakens or ignores them is ethically *out*. Whatever strengthens and improves them is ethically right.

6. The group worker is obliged to exercise every reasonable means to get and keep a mastery of the knowledge and skills of group work. This may not be easy. It calls for paying a price in effort, time, and money. If my little girl were sick I would not take her to a doctor who doesn't keep himself up to the growing edge of his profession. The persons in our groups and those who are responsible for their being there should feel the same way about us.

This professional knowledge extends to self-knowledge on the part of the group worker. Nowhere is this better discussed than in Wittenberg's *So You Want to Help People*. The point he so effectively makes is that a group worker's motives are almost always mixed, and that the better he understands and accepts himself, the fewer mistakes he will make in his relations with group members and fellow workers.

The obligation to maintain his own growth is a corollary of the group worker's obligation to do all in his power to maintain and advance the theory and practice of group work everywhere.

7. And finally the group worker's own set of values for himself gives him his own basis for independent judgment. For many this will involve a view of life that transcends the here and now and invests every individual with eternal values. Something like this is what John Dewey called the religious mood. To him who has it, every group member is a child of God, and all human relations are as among children of God.

These paragraphs by no means exhaust the principles that help to define right professional conduct. I have tried to show that they derive from several sets of ethical considerations—those involving the worker's relations to individuals; those involving his relations to groups; those involving his relations to his agency; those involving his relations to the larger social context; those involving his relations to persons *outside* the groups who have stakes in what goes on in them; those involving his relations to his fellow workers and his profession; and those involving his own highly personal, highly private, and highly important system of values. When these considerations all point to *one* answer to a problem, the worker is indeed fortunate. Typically, however, they must be weighed against each other, and the ethical decision is some sort of compromise, or integration. Perhaps it is fair to say that the finest mark of an ethical person is the courage with which he supports his own final decision, and at the same time admits that he may be wrong.

Toward a Code of Ethics for Group Workers

Subject to the limitations of which we have spoken, a code is a good thing, a set of rules that gives us a square and compass with which to regulate our conduct, and to maintain professional relations with employers, clients, sponsors, fellow workers, and public, and which tells us what we must and must not do.

Group workers do not have such a code written down, though the proposed "Personnel Practices Code" includes some points of ethical practice. How may we get it? There are two ways, one of which I think is better than the other.

The first is to appoint a committee of experienced persons to write it. If they are wise and have the gift of quotable expression, what they say may be duly approved and become widely influential. This is the "arm-chair" approach. The American Association of Marriage Counselors has a committee at work developing a code in this way.

A second method is being demonstrated by the American Psychological Association—a down-to-earth, grass-roots approach. It began with 1,000 descriptions of actual incidents of tough ethical problems reported by psychologists all over the country. "We wanted a Code which, through the very process of developing it, would help psychologists to be more ethical. Any psychologist might suddenly face some issue, or problem new to him. The code will be a hand-book to guide him in making decisions more wisely." Out of a thousand such cases the rules that emerge are likely to be earthy and good and flexible. The Committee on Professional Ethics of the National Education Association is revising its code of ethics that has been in effect for thirty-one years. The revision is being based on 1,309 reports from teachers of what they considered to be ethical problems.

I hope the American Association of Group Workers will use a similar method in developing a code of ethical practice for group workers. It is needed. Maybe the Ford Foundation, or some other Fund, would be interested in helping to finance a three-year study of the problem.

GROUP WORK EDUCATION IN THE LAST DECADE *By Clara A. Kaiser*

Historical Perspectives

IT is appropriate for *The Group* as the official organ of the American Association of Group Workers to review the developments and trends in professional education for group work since one of the major concerns of the Association has been the defining and furthering of programs preparing persons for professional practice in this ever-expanding field. One of the major components which identifies a field of activity as a profession is a body of transmissible knowledge and skills and systematic methods and facilities for teaching it. It is therefore no coincidence that the establishment and growth of education for group work was closely interwoven with the initiation and development of an association of practitioners which, starting as the "Association for the Study of Group Work," became the "American Association of Group Workers."

Space allotted to this article does not permit detailed review of the historical development of education for group work but, in order to examine its current status, it seems important to point out certain major problems which affected the early stages of instituting professional education programs. To a considerable extent, these problems still pertain although marked progress has been made especially in the last decade toward resolving them.

The term group work as a defined method did not come into usage until the late twenties. Even then its acceptance as a basic process for furthering educational and social goals was limited to a relatively small group of practitioners and educators in fields of informal and adult education and in social work. On the other hand, many agencies providing leisure-time programs for youth and adults had long recognized the need for training workers to carry out their programs which, to a large extent, were directed toward meeting group interests and needs. They met these training needs through the establishment of in-service training programs both on a national and local scale. In her article on "Social Group Work" in the 1951 *Social Work Year Book,* Grace Coyle has summarized the process which characterized the gradual emergence of a common conceptual base essential to the development of a core of professional disciplines pertinent to practice not in one agency but in all having similar objectives.

"Following World War I centralized financing of community services and central planning began to bring agencies into closer contact. Members of the various staffs became acquainted, and a cross fertilization of experience began to create the realization that, although agency functions differed somewhat, a large area of common ground existed. Although not all the agencies participated in this cooperative concern in examining their existing methods, a sufficient number did start a new ferment in several centers in the country.

"Simultaneously with this movement, great intellectual stimulus began to play upon those concerned through the evolvement of new concepts of human growth and the use of new educational methods. The relation of learning to interest, the place of creative rather than conforming behavior, the emphasis on democratic handling of authority, and most of all the awareness of group relations as such—these and related ideas were in a wide circulation, especially in the fields of education and personnel management, and began to affect those employed in youth-serving agencies, adult education, and other activities in the field." [1]

The first major problem, therefore, confronting those responsible for formulating professional education for group work was that of finding the common denominator in terms of a basic body of knowledge and skills relevant to practice in a variety of agencies differing with respect to auspices, philosophy and program. This problem has by no means been resolved and has in some ways been further complicated by the extension of the use of group work concepts and methods in other areas of community social services such as children's institutions, hospitals, etc.

A second problem which has to be considered in developing education for group work was that of determining its orientation within a wider professional discipline. Group work as a purposive method of furthering the social and emotional growth of individuals through productive and meaningful group experience had roots in the fields of both education and social work. The formulation of some basic concepts of group work as a method was undertaken by various groups of educators and practitioners in the early twenties. The persons participating in these efforts were concerned with the training of workers

[1] Coyle, Grace, "Social Group Work," *Social Work Year Book*, 1951, p. 467.

engaged in the fields of recreation, adult education and in youth serving programs in which character education and citizenship training were stressed. The common denominator in these otherwise diversified activities was that they all made use of groups as a means for furthering the growth of the individual physically, mentally and emotionally and for the achievement of socially desirable group goals. The philosophical and methodological concepts of education of John Dewey, the new focus of the dynamics of the group process in modern society contained in the work of Mary Follett, and the application of Freudian psychology to the understanding of human behavior all contributed to the evolution of group work as one of the disciplines directed toward furthering the socialization of individuals and for improving the quality of social relationships.

Since many of the agencies offering informal education and recreation programs were integrally a part of the social services of the community, it was natural that they turned to schools of social work to develop professional training programs for this field of practice. The first school of social work to incorporate group work as an area of social work practice into its curriculum was the School of Applied Social Sciences at Western Reserve University. This program was initiated in 1923 and was originally termed as training for "Group Service Work." In Chicago, under the leadership of Neva Boyd, a training program for recreation workers was at first an integral part of the Chicago School of Civics and Philanthropy and later transferred to Northwestern University.

The process of introducing a professional curriculum in group work into schools of social work was a slow and difficult one. The majority of the existing schools tended to identify professional education for social work with education for social case work. Because the body of knowledge and skill of case work had been defined more clearly and because standards of professional practice in agencies making use of case work methods were more firmly established, there was a tendency for those responsible for formulating curricula for group work to become imitative rather than creative in carving out the subject matter and experiential learning pertinent to professional practice and group work. This by no means implies that there is not a core of knowledge and skill generic to all social work practice but there are also some specifics, theoretical and pragmatic, essential to developing insights and skills in any one of the major processes in social work. This problem is gradually being resolved as more schools have introduced programs in group work and as the field of practice has developed.

Organizations Contributing to Development of Group Work Education

Although fifteen schools of social work were offering a special curriculum for group work in 1943, the number of graduates was still relatively small as compared to the growing demand for trained workers in the field. A Committee on Professional Education had been established in 1939 by the American Association for the Study of Group Work to study the courses offered on both a graduate and undergraduate level in schools of social work and in other divisions of colleges and universities. This committee was responsible for bringing together and coordinating the interests of the various groups concerned with professional education. It was clearly recognized by the committee that the formulation of sound and realistic educational programs for group work must be a cooperative process involving representatives from the employing agencies in the field, professional practitioners and educators from the institutions offering training programs. To implement this objective, the Conference of Professional Schools of Recreation and Group Work was formed in January 1943 at a meeting held in Detroit at which the representatives of ten schools were in attendance.

Although the majority of the ten schools were member schools of the American Association of Schools of Social Work, there were several whose programs were oriented to informal education and recreation. Membership in the Conference was limited to schools offering an integrated graduate curriculum including courses and field work.

The explicit purposes and proposed program of the Conference are indicated in the following excerpt quoted from the minutes of the first meeting of the Conference held in June 1943.

"The formation of this Conference resulted from previous meetings of schools offering professional education in recreation and group work which had been called by the Professional Education Committee of the American Association for the Study of Group Work. It was felt that a more permanent form of organization should be established for the purpose of providing a medium by which schools training for this field could work together among themselves and in cooperation with the agencies in the field in meeting the pressing needs of the field for trained workers during the war period and in the post-war period. It was felt by the people responsible for establishing this Conference that there were three groups concerned with problems of personnel for group work and recreation which should work more effectively together in developing standards for the field and in dealing with the problem necessary for securing competent and adequately equipped professional workers. These three are (1) the employing agencies; (2) the professional workers; (3) the professional schools. The Conference of Schools is attempting at this time to serve primarily as a means for consultation and for joint action when such action could best further the development of better professional education programs most fully adapted to meet the needs of the field. The stated purpose of the Conference included a plan for setting up an

Advisory Group composed of national agencies, public and private, to serve as a consultant body to the Conference."[2]

From 1943 to 1947, at least one conference a year of representatives of schools belonging to the Conference and of representatives of national agencies was held, usually in New York City. These conferences contributed greatly to the identification of common elements in professional knowledge and skill necessary for workers responsible for carrying out the purposes and programs of the various agencies. Marked progress was made in clarifying the relationship of in-service training programs of agencies to basic professional education afforded by the schools.

In 1947, the Executive Committee of the Conference reviewed the work of the Conference both for the purpose of evaluating the extent to which it had attained its original goals and to recommend its future course. The report of the committee listed the following specific areas in which substantial or limited contributions had been made through the activities of the Conference:

1. Methods of recruiting workers for the field.

2. Clarifying the relationship of in-service training to professional education.

3. Initiating cooperation between agencies and schools in short-term in-service training programs.

4. Exchange of information between agencies and schools regarding greatest areas of need for trained personnel and availability of graduates of schools.

5. Consideration of desirable content of curriculum for professional education in group work from point of view of the needs of the field.

6. Consideration of ways in which agencies could be encour-

[2] Minutes of the Meeting of the Advisory Group and the Executive Committee of Professional Schools of Recreation and Group Work, held on June 10, 1943.

aged to establish educational leave and scholarship programs for experienced workers and for college graduates.

7. The development of a group record pool to be used for teaching purposes.

8. Development of the principle of joint responsibility of agencies and schools in effecting qualitative field work teaching.

In the light of these significant achievements, the committee recommended that the Conference should be continued but that its structure should be modified because of the emergence of other organized channels for the furthering of professional education for group work.

The American Association of Schools of Social Work established a sub-committee of its Curriculum Committee to consider content for the teaching of group work "as one of the four basic methods of social work" in the member schools of the association. This subcommittee made its report in 1943 and it was incorporated into the total report of the Curriculum Committee which had been charged with the formulation of a basic first year curriculum. The recommendations contained in this document were adopted by the AASSW as constituting the basic curriculum content for its member schools and they included social group work as one of the areas of subject matter basic to the practice of social work and therefore to be required of all students. This represented the first formal recognition that group work was a primary method in social work practice. The specific recommendations of the subcommittee on social group work content will be referred to later in the article. The above development is described here to indicate the increasing integration of education for group work into the field of professional education for social work.

In 1946, the American Association for the Study of Group Work became the American Association of Group Workers. This change necessitated the establishment of requirements for membership based on education and experience. Although eligibility for membership could be met on the basis of several alternative combinations of education and experience, only those who had "graduated from a school of social work with a group work specialization or other graduate schools which are members of the Conference of National Agencies and Schools of Group Work and Recreation"[3] were eligible for membership without experience in the field. This emphasis on graduate professional education by the new professional association gave added impetus to the expansion of special curricula in group work particularly in schools of social work and accelerated the demand by many agencies for professionally trained workers.

In view of these developments, the Executive Committee of the Conference of Schools of Group Work and Recreation recommended that this organization should be reconstituted as the Conference of National Agencies and Schools of Group Work and Recreation with the stated purpose "to provide the schools and national agencies with a medium for joint consideration and recommendations for action on professional education and related problems."[4] It was further recommended that the National Social Welfare Assembly be requested to take over the sponsorship of the Conference. The Conference has been functioning since 1947 as an affiliated group in the National Social Welfare Assembly and has continued to serve as a vital link between national agencies in the field and schools offering professional education. It is true that only a few of the national agencies in the education-recreation field have consistently participated in the activities and meetings of the Conference, but those who have done so are convinced of its value in advancing standards of practice in their constituent local agencies. In the last year, the Conference has undertaken two study projects.

[3] By-laws, American Association of Group Workers.
[4] Report of Executive Committee, Conference of National Agencies and Schools of Group Work and Recreation, January 1947.

One of them sought to ascertain the actual enrollment of group work students in schools of social work and the potential capacity of these schools to afford group work training. The second project involves securing information from graduates of schools during the last three-year period regarding the positions they have held since completing their period of study. The results of the first study have been tabulated and those of the second one will be available in the near future.

Since the establishment of the Council on Social Work Education, the question has arisen as to whether the function of the Conference of National Agencies and Schools of Group Work and Recreation should be taken over by the Council. There is abundant evidence that the work of the Conference should be continued regardless of the auspices under which it functions.

Content of Curriculum in Group Work

As mentioned earlier, the first school of social work to establish a curriculum for group work on a two-year graduate level was the School of Applied Social Sciences of Western Reserve University. Since the writer joined the faculty of this school a few years after its inception in 1923, she has a vivid recollection of the early struggles of the persons engaged in the development of this program to formulate the body of knowledge and skills to be taught. There was no tested experience in education for this field and professional literature directly bearing on group work as a method was non-existent. Although the objectives and methods for field teaching had been formulated and applied for professional education for case work, there were no such standards formulated for group work training. The establishment in 1926 of a teaching and research agency known as the University Neighborhood Centers provided the school with an invaluable resource for experimentation in the formulation and integration of the knowledge and skills basic to group work as a method in social work practice. It also made possible the conduct of research in the area of group process recording which was so essential for teaching purposes both in the classroom and in field work. The first publications of group records made available to the field resulted from this project.

The 1943 report of the Sub-Committee on Group Work of the Curriculum Committee of the AASSW was the first documented statement of content for a curriculum in group work to be formulated. The committee worked over a period of two years in the preparation of this report and had secured through questionnaires detailed information from most of the forty-two member schools with respect to their curriculum offerings in group work. The recommendations contained in the report dealt both with the content of a basic course in group work for all students in a school of social work and with the content of a specialized curriculum in group work. The three major areas of knowledge and skill recommended by the committee for inclusion in an integrated sequence of courses and field work were (1) Theory and Methods in Group Work Practice, (2) Program Content and Skills for Group Work, (3) Supervisory and Administrative Processes and Methods in Group Work.[5] The report emphasized the need for the integration of the group work curriculum into the total curriculum of a school of social work. It also stressed the importance of close interrelation of field instruction with classroom teaching. The formulation of content for group work within the framework of a social work curriculum served a valuable purpose in that it pooled the experience of individual schools and also made use of the opinions of many individuals and groups representing the field of practice.

The Professional Education Committee for the AAGW car-

[5] Report of the Sub-Committee on Group Work of the Curriculum Committee of the AASSW, December 1943.

ried on the work of the early committee of the AASGW. After several years of careful study, this committee produced a statement on "Professional Education for Group Work Practice" which was adopted in 1947 by the AAGW and published in the June 1947 issue of *The Group*. This statement of needed areas of knowledge and skill for group work practice has been used as a guide both by schools and by the field.

In 1948 the Accreditation Committee of the AASSW in response to a request from the AAGW undertook the responsibility for the accrediting of special curricula in group work in member schools. A sub-committee composed of persons representing both professional practice and social work educators in group work was appointed to establish criteria and to review material submitted by schools applying for approval of their group work curricula.

The chairman of the Professional Education Committee of the AAGW, responsible for the formulation of the aforementioned statement, served as a member of this sub-committee and played a major role in the drafting of the criteria used in approving schools' programs. In 1950 the sub-committee on group work had recommended to the Accreditation Committee the approval of the group work programs in 21 schools of social work. Since that time the group work curricula of four additional schools have been approved. The criteria for the approval of group work programs deal with the content of courses and field work, the qualifications of faculty and field work supervisors, and the integration of the group work curriculum into the total curriculum as outlined in the "General Curriculum Policy Statement" of the Council on Social Work Education.

One of the most difficult problems confronting schools offering programs in group work was the development of qualitative field work for students. Even though agencies were cooperative in their willingness to provide field work for students, the supply of qualified supervisors was inadequate. The uneven distribution of professionally trained group workers in various sections of the country made this problem more acute for some schools especially those establishing new programs. The criteria for the approval of programs in group work states that supervisors should have a degree from an accredited school of social work with special training in social group work. However, recognition is given to the impossibility for some schools to meet this standard. Substantial progress has been made by all schools in attaining this goal.

The educational goals and content in field work learning have been much more clearly defined as have the methods of teaching through field supervision. Schools are developing more effective methods for training supervisors for this important aspect of professional education. The types of agencies affording field work to students are constantly expanding. Although social settlements, community centers, youth serving agencies are still in the majority as centers for field work, many schools are increasingly placing students in such settings as hospitals, children's institutions, child guidance clinics, correctional institutions and other agencies providing treatment to persons with physical, social and emotional disabilities. Camps, both resident and day camps, are affording field work to students to an increasing extent. This trend is indicative of the expanding field of services for which trained group workers are in demand.

Teaching Personnel

It is said that teachers are born, not made. This was almost literally true when schools of social work first undertook the development of group work programs. The first teachers of group work were drawn from many fields of professional practice and had a variety of educational backgrounds. This was not wholly a disadvantage, for it necessitated a close working together of those persons confronted with the carving out of a new era of subject matter and methods for teaching it. The description given previously of the various organizations and conferences of group work teachers and practitioners bear witness to the extent to which the group process was used to formulate some common concepts and methods for the teaching of group work. There is now a substantial body of persons with considerable experience in the field of group work education and their ranks are constantly being augmented by professionally trained and experienced workers from the field of practice. The availability of advanced curricula and doctoral programs in a number of schools of social work will enrich the opportunity for persons already in the teaching field and for those interested in entering it to secure more adequate professional preparation. In any professional education, but especially in social work education, the faculty member must bring to his teaching the qualities of a trained and disciplined mind, a commitment to the ideals and objectives of his profession, a capacity to inspire and develop the potentialities of students and a continuous understanding of the needs of the field for which he is training.

Group Work Literature and Teaching Materials

The almost complete dearth of literature related to group work methodology in the early period of group work education presented a serious handicap in developing curriculum and teaching tools. Since recording of group process was not done to any extent in agencies, little case material was available to use for teaching purposes. The resources now available through the rapidly expanding literature on group work and related fields of the social sciences and other professional disciplines are immeasurably greater today. Not only have selected and edited teaching records of groups been made available through a committee of the AASSW (Council on Social Work Education), but a number of the recently published textbooks contain case material that can enrich teaching tools. It is not possible within the space of this article to enumerate the specific books and periodicals which have added greatly to the body of theoretical and scientific knowledge basic to group work practice. The development of audio-visual aids for teaching the understanding of individual behavior and of group processes is also contributing much to enriching education for group work.

Quantitative Facts About Group Work Education

In spite of the rapidity with which education for group work has developed over the past ten years, the ratio between supply and demand of group workers has not been substantially affected. Even though there are now twenty-five schools of social work with special curricula for group work, the number of graduates each year is pitifully small. *Social Work Education in the U.S.*, by Ernest V. Hollis and Alice L. Taylor, sets forth vividly the great discrepancy between the demand for trained social workers and the supply provided by graduates of the schools of social work. This picture is even more true in group work than in some other fields. In the study of enrollment of group work students undertaken by the Conference of National Agencies and Schools of Group Work and Recreation, it was revealed that actual enrollment was considerably below the capacity of the schools presently offering group work training. The trend of decreasing enrollment in most of the schools is continuing. The explanations for the trend are multiple. The general drop in the number of students entering graduate schools of all types, the drafting of men for military service, the ending of the G.I. educational benefits, the increasing cost of graduate education are all cited. To be added to this list is the failure of the field of social work in general and group work in particular to initiate a vigorous recruitment program. Employing agencies, professional associations and the schools must work together to attack this problem. It is also necessary to analyze much more fully the types of positions in the field of practice which require professionally trained workers. This would aid greatly in clarifying the relationship between undergraduate training, in-service training, and graduate professional education, as they all have a role to play in supplying needed personnel for the field. The raising of standards of personnel practices, particularly salary levels, must also be accomplished if more able young people are to be attracted to the field.

In Summary

In this review of the developments in group work education, I have refrained from mentioning individual persons who have played a major role in this process. Needless to say there were many both from the field of practice and from the field of professional education. It has seemed more significant for purposes of this article to indicate the trends and developments as they were affected by changing conditions in the field and by organized efforts of various groups concerned with establishing the standards and facilities for group work education than to enumerate the contributions of individuals.

To summarize, I am listing some of the major trends and problems which must be reckoned with in the continued effort to improve the quantity and quality of education for group work practice.

1. Group work has become increasingly integrated into the wider professional field of social work as one of the primary processes in meeting individual and group needs.

2. Social work education is becoming more generic in its orientation with more emphasis on the training of professional social workers than on training skilled technicians for specialized fields of practice.

3. The necessity for a greater integration of the social sciences with social work as an applied discipline is apparent.

This has been especially true in relation to group work practice with the development of new areas of research in the field of group dynamics and other scientific methods for examining the phenomena of inter-personal and inter-group relations as well as in the field of psychotherapy.

4. The application of group work concepts and methods is spreading to many new areas in which group interaction is involved. This is true not only in the area of therapeutic programs but also in the group processes related to administration, supervision, and community organization.

5. There is an increasing need to develop more effective inter-disciplinary collaboration with case work, psychotherapy, with education and medicine, etc.

6. There is the continuing and urgent need to deepen not only the scientific basis on which professional practice rests but the ethical and philosophical values which must serve as the motivation for the fulfillment of the goals of our profession.

The Council on Social Work Education provides a new channel for collaborative efforts of agencies, professional organizations and schools to tackle these and other problems. A revitalized Committee on Professional Education of the AAGW is currently engaged in reviewing and revising the statement on professional education for group work practice in order to relate it to the changing needs of the field and to new areas of theoretical and practical knowledge coming from the fields of the social sciences, practice and research in social work and other related disciplines.

Part Two

THE FRONTIERS OF
GROUP WORK

Introduction

Iɴ the period which lies ahead, group workers have a unique opportunity to push forward the frontiers of professional practice. As we relate our energies more intimately to the total profession of social work, it can be assumed that once again we are on the threshold of another of our periods of accelerated forward progress.

In 1936 we began the systematic study of group work. In 1946 we took the next step of becoming a professional association. By early 1956 we should be deeply engaged in our new and wider professional fellowship in the National Association of Social Workers.

Roughly two decades of positive professional progress lie behind us. During these two decades, firm foundations have been established. What lies ahead for us? What will we achieve in the next 20 years? One can only speculate, but of this we are sure: namely, we need to put down clearly and definitively our "Agenda for the Future." What we are to become depends largely upon the choices we make as to where and how we will invest our energies.

The material which follows is a summary of the best thinking of over 40 group workers in various parts of the country. In addition to the author, the following persons have contributed their ideas:

373

HOMER C. BISHOP, *George Warren Brown School of Social Work, Washington University,* St. Louis, Missouri; LOUIS H. BLUMENTHAL, *Jewish Community Center,* San Francisco, California; ROBERT L. BOND, *Goodrich House,* Cleveland, Ohio; IRVING BRODSKY, *Jewish Association for Neighborhood Centers,* New York, N. Y.; R. PAUL BROTSMAN, *Department of Social Work, University of Kansas,* Kansas City, Missouri; WILLIAM BRUECKNER, *Chicago Commons Association,* Chicago, Illinois; LUCY CARNER, Philadelphia, Pennsylvania; LOIS CORKE, *National Federation of Settlements,* New York, N. Y.; FRANK FIERMAN, YMHA-YWHA, Philadelphia, Pennsylvania, Chairman, Editorial Committee, *The Group;* HOWARD GIBBS, *Boys Clubs of America,* New York; IRWIN H. GOLD, *Jewish Community Center,* Chicago, Illinois; MARY HAIGHT, Portland, Oregon; MARGARET E. HARTFORD, *School of Applied Social Sciences, Western Reserve University,* Cleveland, Ohio; JOSEPHINE HARRIS, *LaRue Carter Hospital,* Indianapolis, Indiana; GORDON HEARN, *School of Social Welfare, University of California,* Berkeley, California; SISTER MARY IMMACULATE, *Girls' Club of San Antonio,* San Antonio, Texas; RAY JOHNS, *Boston YMCA,* Boston, Massachusetts; MARJORIE JOHNSON, *Atlanta University School of Social Work,* Atlanta, Georgia; KENNETH KINDELSPERGER, *University College, Adult Education Division, Syracuse University,* Syracuse, New York; WALTER KINDELSPERGER, *School of Social Work, Tulane University,* New Orleans, Louisiana; ALAN KLEIN, *University of Toronto, School of Social Work,* Toronto, Canada; MRS. GISELA KONOPKA, *University of Minnesota, School of Social Work,* Minneapolis, Minnesota; FRED LIFF, *Jewish Community Center,* Chattanooga, Tennessee; ANNE W. LINDSAY, YWCA, Chicago, Illinois; HOWARD MC-CLARY, *Five Towns Community House,* Lawrence, Long Island; JOHN McDOWELL, *National Federation of Settlements,* New York, N. Y.; HERBERT J. MILLMAN, *National Jewish Welfare Board,* New York, N. Y.; RUTH H. MORGAN, *School of*

Social Welfare, University of California, Berkeley, California; MARGARET MUDGETT, *Neighborhood Settlement Association,* Los Angeles, California; HAZEL OSBORN, *School of Social Work, University of Pittsburgh,* Pittsburgh, Pennsylvania; BEATRIX A. PARK, *Boston University, School of Social Work,* Boston, Massachusetts; JOHN H. RAMEY, *Hyde Park Neighborhood Center,* Chicago, Illinois; FLORENCE E. RAY, *Welfare Federation of Cleveland,* Cleveland, Ohio; CATHERINE V. RICHARDS, *Girl Scouts of the United States of America,* New York, N. Y.; ETTA SALOSHIN, *School of Social Work, University of Minnesota,* Minneapolis, Minnesota; WILLIAM SCHWARTZ, *School of Social Administration, Ohio State University,* Columbus, Ohio; MRS. SHEILA SKLAR, *former Executive Secretary, American Association of Group Workers,* Pittsfield, Massachusetts; HOLLIS VICK, *Welfare Council,* Chicago, Illinois; ROBERT VINTER, *University of Michigan School of Social Work,* Ann Arbor, Michigan; MARJORIE C. WARREN, *Children's Aid Association,* Boston, Massachusetts.

Thus group workers from many points of vantage offered their ideas and suggestions as to our priorities for the future. These then are the frontiers which beckon to them. Here are the rewarding tasks of tomorrow. This is the unfinished business of group work. It is our hope that we will work upon these jobs as individual group workers, as members of chapters in the new association, as members of the group work section locally and nationally, as students and as teachers, as researchers, all with firm belief in the importance of high quality professional service.

To be sure, much of that which follows cannot be termed "new" in a strict sense. Readers will recognize familiar areas of concern, hardy "perennial problems" which have long been with us. Furthermore, in many cases, the area suggested is a matter of emphasis or re-emphasis. This is to be expected and accepted because we know there is a continuity about our growth and we know that there are seldom, if ever, sharp periods of sudden change. Rare it is when any professional assignment is completed once and for all. Hence much of what we are suggesting has been worked on, but more intensive work is needed. In addition, we will now work under different circumstances; namely, in purposeful association with the other social work disciplines. As social work itself becomes stronger, we can expect group work to become stronger too, and as group workers deepen their knowledge about, and skill in their own specialty, it can be supposed that all of social work will gain.

Fundamentally, however, the reason which motivates our quest for greater professional competence, is that in so doing we will learn to serve people better and add more meaning to life and to democracy. A professional service has value only when it meets the needs of people. In our judgment the needs of people will be better met if group workers utilize their professional association to work on these tasks. True it is not likely that all of us will work on all of these things or in any particular order, but perhaps from the broad array of items we will select those which have greatest application in our situation.

In the free and "conversational" response we received from our participants in this inquiry, many items came up again and again. Perhaps the wording was a little different in various cases and maybe the emphasis was shaded in one way or another, but on the whole it is reasonable to suggest that there was wide-spread general agreement on what follows. In essence we have here a rough map of the directions group work should follow in the period ahead. We have blocked out the areas for purposes of discussion and refinement. Such refinement will come when the profession as a whole, through its various formal and informal associations of workers, spells out in greater detail the specific steps to be taken. As put by one of our respondents, "In the past 20 years we have consolidated much of the meaning that led to the identification of the group work method. Now the task is to re-examine and clarify and deepen the effectiveness of our practice, relinquishing if necessary some of our familiar past, adding and incorporating the new learnings and the gains that have been made." In the same vein another participant writes, "The clarification of our own professional problems will progress soundly, only if we hold on to what has been the healthy core of our learning in the last 20 years, and see to it that it will be enriched. This enrichment cannot come only from the other specializations in social work, we will have to carry the full burden of responsibility of the development of the group worker's knowledge and skill."

The Social Scene—Backdrop for Our Efforts

One of the questions we asked was, "What do you see as being the most significant social, economic and political trends today which group workers need to study and to understand because of their likely influence in the future?" We received numerous thoughtful and penetrating answers to this question. The discussion was rich in meaning as professional workers endeavored to present their thinking regarding current national developments. It is possible to summarize the responses under six headings. They are:

1. The problem of world insecurity and tension.
2. The rise of fear and the struggle to control the minds of citizens.
3. The growth of population.
4. The mobility of population.
5. Technological changes and their impact on modern life.
6. The Supreme Court decision outlawing segregation in the public schools and its meaning for intercultural group work.

We will look briefly at these six areas and present to our readers some of the thinking of group workers from various points of vantage in different parts of the country.

World Insecurity and Tension

The over-riding consideration in the current social scene is naturally the problem of world insecurity and tension. Many of our respondents referred to the impact of the cold war and to the awesome implications of the thermo-nuclear age and the hydrogen bomb. While in some respects tension may have been eased, there was widespread belief that we should be prepared to live in a world of struggle and revolution for many years to come. Highlighted again and again was the supreme objective of leadership for peace. Unless ways can be found for the peoples of the world to live together in harmony, it is impossible to foresee anything but dire destruction for all. Education for peace and education for international understanding and cooperation loomed large in the minds of everyone. In fact a central objective of group work in a world of insecurity and tension is to help people to learn to understand one another and learn how to work together in harmony.

Fear and the Struggle to Control the Minds of Citizens

While the words were different, again and again, the participants in our study expressed their concern about the prevailing psychology of fear and the never-ceasing struggle to control the minds of men. Let us look at some of the replies using the words of our participants. As put by one such person, "The most significant political trend affecting all of us today is the struggle to control the minds and actions of our citizenry. More than ever before the contribution of group work in educating for intelligent participation in a democracy is needed. Ours is a profession that can exist only in a free society and it bears a responsibility for helping to perpetuate and preserve this freedom."

In the words of another writer, "The most important trend of our time is the shocking increase in reactionary thinking, fear, distrust and anti-intellectualism. As Professor Commager pointed out at the 1954 National Conference of Social Work, the most serious aspect of this as far as group workers are concerned is the threat that is developing in regard to the right to free association. People, as we know, are afraid to join groups for fear that this association may prove embarrassing or dangerous at some future date. Since group work is based upon the premise that people grow as they associate freely with one another in groups of their own choosing, the threat to this right is a very serious matter and one which must be fought on every occasion and in every possible way that is consistent with social work philosophy."

Another writer used these words, "Today there is a fear psychology which affects free speech in politics, education and life in general at a time in the world's history when we need to be compatible in a setting of great differences with divergent opinions. This presents a particularly great threat to our democracy."

Along the same lines with slightly different emphasis, one of our participants said, "I consider of particularly pressing and immediate concern the current trend and pressure towards conformity. This conformity, I am afraid, may pervade all areas of thought and may influence attitudes with regard to most issues. I am not overly optimistic with regard to the significant contribution which group work can make at this time to counterbalance this force. I do think however, that we can at least try to protect to some degree those people who are members of our groups. This means that we not only have to remember and use some of group work's basic principles and tenets, but that we have to work hard on realizing them. I am referring specifically to such concepts as the right to be different and the acceptance of and respect for differences and the various levels of the solution of conflict."

As related by another participant, "I believe the most crucial political and social trend which should challenge the group worker is the current social disapproval of dissent. Non-conformity is equated with treason by certain individuals and groups in our society. This attack must be met by constantly encouraging free and responsible inquiry into and discussion of all aspects of our community life. This is not disloyalty, but a call to a more intelligent and critical, therefore better, loyalty."

Or in the words of still another writer, "In these days a profession has a task to perform for society in keeping alive respect for intellectual achievement, safeguarding freedom of thought, research and speech, and holding up human values as paramount."

These are but a few of the remarks received from many persons. There is no question but what a big job for group work is to work diligently to set in motion positive programs which will strengthen freedom of thought and expression.

The Growth of Population

Almost everyone who responded to our inquiry discussed the growth of population. It has been predicted by some authorities that our population will reach 200,000,000 by the year 1970. In view of the fact that group work services have never been provided for more than a small percentage of the people who need them, we are faced with a tremendous challenge and a tremendous responsibility. If people are to be served, we will need thousands of workers and hundreds of additional facilities.

In the population category, considerable mention was made of the shift in age groupings. It was pointed out that during the period ahead we must expect to work with a greatly expanded older population and a rapidly growing younger population. In other words, the number of children and youth we will be called upon to serve in the next ten years will increase markedly. Likewise, the number of persons in the later years will increase. Thus far no one has projected a long-range plan of personnel and facilities to serve these groups. One of the top priority assignments would seem to be the drawing up of a definitive statement indicating how many group workers are needed and what is needed in the way of new facilities.

Mobility of Population

In addition to the growth of population, our respondents indicated that this is an age of movement and rapid mobility. People are shifting from rural areas to cities and from city to city. They move about as industries change their locations. In some situations whole new communities are being built. One writer refers to a new community of 15,000 families which will be in existence before these pages are printed. The phenomenon of the industrialization of the south was mentioned several times. Many of the same problems which have long plagued the northern industrial areas are beginning to appear in the south. As industry becomes more decentralized, and as defense requires increasing industrial dispersion, we can anticipate the growth of scores of new communities. Along this same line attention was placed upon the phenomenon of suburban living. As indicated by one respondent, "Another trend is the trend toward suburban living. Group work services for the most part have been developed for city dwellers. We are really only beginning to explore the best ways to serve the suburbanite. This would seem to suggest an important task for our agencies operating at the local level."

As viewed by another participant, "The most significant social trend that seems to have great influence on group work practice is the development of suburban community living. More than ever before community centers must conduct decentralized programs, establishing extensive extension-type programs in new suburban developments. Programs from the nursery school age group to the senior citizen should be conducted in the community in which people live. Together with recreation and education programs, such as the playgrounds and new schools in these housing developments, should come extended group work services. The need is to work closely together with planning groups to provide the best service possible, without duplication or any feeling of need to compete with each other. In the broad field of technology our respondents called attention to the continuous increase in the amount of leisure time. There is evidence that the shorter work week and the shorter work year are both important factors to consider. The need for recreational services continues to grow.

Many of our correspondents pointed out the fact that military service is an important factor in the life of young people. This seems to be giving rise to early marriages and the need for much counseling in this realm. Attention was focused on the new educational and economic levels that have emerged in the last half century. As one writer put it, "Our agencies tend to lag behind the new educational level of the population and the new economic level of industrial workers. One of our executives mentioned that they had a depression-rigged program for atomic day youth."

Another writer raised this question, "Are we supposing that the teen-ager of today in urban society is the same as he or she was in 1925?" Another writer quoted Dr. Margaret Mead who has said, "The rapidity of social change in contemporary society is so great that the younger generation lives almost literally in a different social world than that which nurtured their parents." In view of these remarks it seems obvious that we need to assess very closely the changes in community life which have a bearing upon the kinds of programs we should be offering in group work.

Supreme Court Decision Banning Segregation in the Public Schools

A good many of our respondents commented upon the 1954 Supreme Court decision making segregation in the nation's public schools unconstitutional. They pointed out that this act would have powerful implications in the entire field of community services. There will be a great need to move ahead rapidly in inter-cultural programming and in developing ways and means of facilitating the inevitable changes which will come about.

In the material which follows, we have selected 15 areas for the work of group workers in the new professional association. These have been arranged in a simple order, based largely upon the extent of the response we received from our participants.

AREA 1. GROUP WORK AND SOCIAL WORK

Many of the our participants said that the number one task in the early years of the new association will be for group workers to rethink and re-evaluate their relation to social work. There was a strong plea for stepping up the identification of group workers with social work as a whole. Many suggested that we should spell out the contribution that we may make as group workers to generic social work. There were several indications of a need for us to re-examine the meaning of working together and to rethink the teamwork approach involving referrals and joint service.

It was pointed out that the group worker will continue to carry many roles. In some instances he will function as a practitioner giving direct service to groups. He may also function as a supervisor of untrained workers or of volunteer workers. He may function as a cooperative member of a team, working with other social workers, educators and the like. He will be called upon to serve as a consultant and as an advisor to community organizations of various kinds. His relationships will be manifold and multiple. In maintaining his relationship with social work, with trained group workers, with untrained group workers, with volunteers, with other professionals in education, recreation, health and so forth, he must develop his skills and define more closely the role that he has to play.

In examining the replies, we have selected and excerpted a number of quotations from people who discussed this whole question of group work's relation to social work. For example, one of our respondents said, "On the national level and on the local level, I feel that the most vital single job for group workers is that of identifying themselves more closely with social work. This encompasses many areas which need studying, a few of which are: What is the unique contribution of the group worker in all settings, whether in formal education and recreation, institutions, hospitals, clinics, playgrounds, schools and so forth? How is the role of the group worker similar and different from the recreation leader, the occupational therapist, the psychotherapist, and the case worker doing group counseling? The immediate affiliation with the new organization will only be on paper unless all group workers seriously believe and follow a course of action that assures their colleagues and the public that they are social workers first and group workers second. The further ramifications of this have bearing on public relations, legal aspects of regulation of social work practice, recruitment for social work and social work education."

Another writer said, "We should do our share, nationally and locally, to consolidate the profession, and to retain within it the gains in methods made by the specializations. I hope that there may be also some cross-fertilization in method. If only we can create time to share experiences and points of view."

Another writer suggested that, "We must make a more vigorous contribution to the process of defining generic social work. In some ways we have been content just to be counted in and to establish cooperative relationships, rather than vigorously injecting and infiltrating what we have learned about the process of social work as carried out in group situations into the more traditional concept of the process with its extensive dependence upon the case work situation."

One of our other participants mentioned the same point in these words, "I hope that tomorrow will see new developments in the relationships between group work and other social work areas. I look forward to multi-functional social work where case work is not the be-all of family work, for example. Group work has a place in family work as it does in child welfare. How do they relate and what new inventions can be devised to use our separate skills together? Is there a generic base, can we regroup our social work entities?"

In a very penetrating way, one of our participants discussed the question in these words, "On the national level and in local communities, it would seem to me that the most important task for group workers is to clarify and define the relationship of group work to the profession of social work. Professional group work as such has its roots in several different fields of work and the agencies out of which it has grown themselves fall into different categories.

"We know that the decision to relate group work to social work was a somewhat arbitrary one in the minds of some people and very logical in the minds of others. Group work is work with people leading toward the better adjustment of the individual in his relationships with others and towards strengthening democracy through building up the skills of persons in democratic participation. It is logical that the tie should be to social work. Any of the disciplines in social work deal with persons in relative stages varying from unhealthy to healthy, or from maladjusted to adjusted. The problem has been that the accomplishment of group work objectives depends partially upon a program or program-content which is similar to that of educational and religious institutions which have other major purposes as well. To identify, therefore, the profession as social work and group work as a specialization has, I believe, put the major focus on the adjustment of the individual through groups leaving to the worker and the agencies the responsibility for the content. It is my belief that group workers through the professional association need to represent this point of view with clarity and confidence and not be absorbed by the other parts of the profession which deal primarily with maladjustment. I think that this means, then, that the task is a two-way one. Group workers to other social workers and group workers to other allied professions such as education."

Another interesting response came from a worker in still a different part of the country. He said, "During the past decade group work has become more and more recognized along with case work, community organization, administration and research as a basic service area in social work. In a sense, social work has at last developed a well rounded set of tools. One problem therefore will be to integrate more fully these tools and determine conditions under which they will jointly and severally make the solution to the given problem. In this area we will need to work on how the group worker may be used as a consultant with reference to other services. We will need to examine how group work itself may have wider application in the community, industry, commerce and other voluntary associations. We will need to study both on a national and local basis various applications that are now being made of the group work method in clinical settings, in community organization settings, and in many other situations where group work is provided in a 'host' setting. These areas include children's institutions, school systems, religious organizations and many other new areas. The problem here would appear to be one of legitimately specializing without losing the generic focus."

Still another comment in this general area came from one of our respondents. In his words, "One of the most important tasks for group workers to give attention to through the new single association of social workers is that of assuming that group workers make their proper contribution to the total practice of social work. This means continued striving to have group work included in any consideration of social work practice, whether in the planning of new projects or in the reordering of past efforts. It is also important for the relation of group work to social work practice in medical, psychiatric, school, family and children's services to be analyzed by group workers in cooperation with other social workers. In local communities, through chapter work, group work must become a recognized part of the social work profession. This will involve working out more clearly than has yet been done the mutual interests and the distinguishing characteristics of group workers in relation to professional recreational workers and to educate toward both formal and informal. I believe that the development of a more generic approach to the practice of social work is important to emphasize in the coming decade. It is important that the concern be generic social work, not generic case work."

With strong accent on the word teamwork, another one of our contributors said, "It is my growing belief that in the coming years, the teamwork approach to social problems must become more workable in the total field of social service. Group work can no longer work as a separate entity, nor can case work or community organization. Techniques in all of these fields need to blend in common service to persons and areas of community life. This seems particularly true in the urban communities where there is much change and mobility. I believe that group workers must take the initiative in developing such ways of work because they understand the ramifications of group relationships, not only with clientele but with staff also. The same principles ought to hold good for developing the teamwork approach. I say that group work will have to develop much of this way of work because of our convictions generally and because we have the 'know how' of give and take. We have learned to see the person as a total personality and that I believe is the way of work which will meet the present needs and perhaps help the social welfare field make a more outstanding contribution to society today. To my way of thinking a teamwork approach will not be easy, not as easy as writing it here now. It means some drastic changes in philosophy in all of the areas of practice. It means continued effort in the educational field to blend generic training and at the same time not lose the techniques of the specializations. It will mean that the professional organization will need to give direction to agencies through worker-awareness and a quality of social pioneering must become part of the philosophical approach as well as 'know how' to do this type of service. This also means not only a knowledge and acceptance of other disciplines on the part of group workers but an understanding of the interlocking of the services to the benefit of the persons served."

Area 2. Group Work and Job Classification

Throughout our replies, it was evident that many group workers are increasingly concerned about the shortage of professionally prepared workers. These people felt that a major task for our profession is to study the job of the group worker. What kinds of groups need a professionally educated group worker? How can we make most effective use of our personnel when at the present time we do not have enough trained workers to go around? What kinds of jobs can we expect the untrained worker to perform? What is the role of the volunteer group leader?

In the words of one of our participants, "We have not yet faced up to the serious responsibility for determining the most effective utilization of our insufficient personnel. Until this supply of qualified workers begins to increase, it is imperative that we make better use of what we have. Critical reappraisal by all segments of the profession is needed at two levels. First, a review of staff positions to determine which must be filled by trained personnel and which can be filled by others and second, a review of how the time spent in these priority positions can best be expended."

Another writer said it this way, "The most important task for group workers to work on in relation to their own profession seems to me that of clear job classification. We should know which jobs can be carried by people who have no professional education, which jobs can be carried by those with bachelor's degrees, which must be carried by those with master's degrees. This kind of work has to be done in all of social work to make it finally possible for us to become a profession. We should not expect too much of people on all levels in the area in which we are working. In group work we will have to clarify which jobs in the so-called group work field must be carried by persons trained in social work and which jobs can be better carried by those trained in education or in recreation."

Still another observer remarked, "Another area in which leadership must be given at the national level is in the process of classifying group work tasks. Only as this is done will it be possible to identify the levels of group work practice and to specify the type of training needed by each level. This process of classification is essential to the accomplishment of another task, namely the more efficient use of the partially trained worker. It is clear that for the next decade at least, the field will use many such workers and it needs to be concerned with developing more effective ways of training and supervising these workers on the job."

Number one on the list of another respondent is this same problem of job study. "Further classification of the contribution of group work to informal education and recreation services is needed. By this I mean we should analyze more fully the types of positions in the field of practice which require professionally trained workers. This would give us some understanding of what we can expect from other staff contributions, volunteer leadership and the like. I think sometimes we are more clear about what a group worker does in a hospital or a children's institution than we are in a recreation agency. There is too much generality or an 'overallness' in our approach. Are we really aiming at having all workers trained group workers or do we need to do what has been done in the nursing field: that is, clarify the particular responsibility of the trained nurse and the practical nurse?"

From these remarks and many others that we received, it seems apparent that we must move quickly and vigorously into a national study aimed at job classification. Since this is needed throughout all of social work and will require substantial research funds it appropriately should be done on the national level with local cooperation.

Area 3. Need to Recruit More Group Workers.

It was not surprising that high on the priority list was the need to recruit more group workers. Again and again people said that we must work harder on the task of recruitment.

One of our respondents put it this way, "The most important task ahead for group workers in the next decade on both national and local levels is recruitment for the professions and for professional education to equip people to do more group work jobs. There is such a shortage of staff, that in many places people are being denied the services they need. Because there is such a shortage of staff, and since as yet staff workers are so far removed from giving direct service to clients, it seems to me there must be more use of professionally educated staff in direct leadership, with the focus on the professional use of the group process. The task of recruitment is a major one, in order to fill up the gap in the profession so that the actual group work services can be carried on by people who have a group work orientation."

Another respondent said it this way, "Recruitment of professional leadership is certainly a major task before us, not just in terms of declining school registration and shortage of workers for jobs, but the more basic questions and problems which result in these dwindling numbers. Some questions are: What is the place of social work in our society? What is the community attitude toward continuation or expansion of social work programs? What about the resultant uncertain status of the social worker and the profession? Study of such questions would help to clarify the role of social work as distinguished from sociology, psychology and psychiatry, and the contribution of group work as a specialization within generic social work."

A third observer said, "I would put at the top of my list the task of recruiting to the profession for the obvious reason that what we are able to accomplish in the next decade will depend upon the number of trained persons we have available to do the job. Recruitment in the final analysis must be done at the local level, but it requires strong support at the national level in the form of promotional material and the use of the mass media of communication. Recruitment to professional education suggests two other important jobs at the national level: the securing of scholarships on a large scale and the improvement of professional education."

The final reference to the problem of scholarships is of extreme importance. None of the branches of social work have a sufficient number of scholarships. Group work is particularly deficient in this area. Almost every week we come in contact with apparently qualified young people who would like to secure professional education and would like to become group workers but they are unable to afford the cost of graduate study. Furthermore, group work is in a competitive position with business and industry and in many cases the same young people who want to become social workers are helped to secure higher education by committing themselves to the business enterprise.

It seems that another point might well be made in this area of recruitment. Group workers come in contact with millions of young people who might be interested in the profession if it is properly interpreted to them. In camps, in clubs, in classes, in special interest groups, in all kinds of settings, the group worker every day of his work comes in contact with potential recruits for the field. It would seem only obvious that group workers should explore ways and means of recruiting through their program groups.

Area 4. Building Better Public Understanding of Group Work.

There was almost unanimous agreement that one of the important tasks which must be tackled is that of building better public understanding of group work. The need for continuous interpretation was voiced again and again. While it is certainly true that all of social work needs continuous interpretation, it seems that group work has a particular stake in this problem because of its relationships with recreation, health and physical education, adult education and community programs generally. The problem seems to be that of pinpointing the difference between what the trained group worker does and what the person in a related field does.

A broad-scale long-range program of interpretation would center upon the following points:

1. The objectives of group work, or what the group worker tries to help happen in the lives of people.
2. The philosophy of group work or why it is regarded as being of crucial importance in modern society.
3. The group work method or the ways that group workers go about doing their work.
4. The agency and its particular function.

The story of group work is a warm, human story which can best be told through the use of examples from actual group records. Little has been done in this area but much can be accomplished.

AREA 5.   GROUP WORK CONTRIBUTIONS TO RECREATION AND
EDUCATION.

A good many of our respondents stressed the importance of clarifying the contribution that group work makes to recreation and education programs.

As put by one of our respondents, "Group work must come to grips, and soon, with its relationship to recreation. As a method of working with groups, its application is universal. Linking group work so much with recreation limits its use, status and financial support. Once and for all, we must resolve the conflict in our own minds about group work and social work. Is group work a social work method primarily? If it is, there are broad implications for how it is practiced. Certainly its use should not be limited to the recreation agencies."

Another respondent pointed out that, "We need more experimentation in the use of the group work method in work with adults. I have special reference to the whole adult education area, considering the terrific amount that needs to be done to help all citizens understand more about our national and international situation and to live more effectively in the complex society of today. Adult educators as such have made many attempts and have had a certain degree of success. It would seem, however, that group work as a method has much to contribute in this whole area, and that the surface has not been scratched as yet. Some of our agencies have done considerable, but in certain others we have tended to work particularly with underprivileged people with many special problems. I would not mean that this should be discontinued, but rather that all kinds of agencies would experiment with working with more of a cross section of adults in their respective neighborhoods and communities in ways particularly geared to them in this day and age. Sometimes it seems we tend to infantilize, mother, or dominate adults with whom we are working, rather than to enable them to achieve much in their own right."

Another of our participants suggested that, "There should be further study and emphasis on group work relationships to public schools. Should the group worker be a consultant to teachers? How much direct work should group workers do in the public schools? Is there a place for a school group worker, working with the co-curricula program activities? Are group work specialists needed in the broad area of group life in the school?"

Similar questions were raised with reference to the field of camping, and with reference to the field of physical education and health education. Many respondents said that group workers should take the initiative in calling together recreation, physical education, health education, adult education and other leaders in their local communities to discuss mutual areas of concern and to map out ways in which it might be possible to work more closely with one another.

AREA 6. GROUP WORK IN RELATION TO THE SOCIAL SCIENCES.

A considerable number of participants in our study emphasized the importance of utilizing new knowledge which is coming to us from the social sciences. While group workers have always been interested in this area of knowledge, it now becomes apparent that a more systematic way must be found to put the social scientists and the group workers in continuous communication with each other.

As stated by one of our respondents, "I see clear evidence that group workers are beginning to develop a healthy respect for the social sciences. More and more we are trying to understand and apply in our work what the social sciences have to offer. This should be encouraged. But in order to make full use of social science material, the practitioner will need to work closely with the scientist toward the accomplishment of two objectives. First, the formulation of useful research programs, and second, the translation of research and theory into terms which the practitioner can use. The curricula of the schools of social work include a course or two in the growth and change of the individual. We need to develop comparable courses in the growth and change of the group or community. The reason why all of this is important is that it provides the means by which we may be able to build the theoretical base for practice which we have lacked so far. If we are really to be a profession, practice must stem from a scientific discipline."

In a somewhat broader vein another participant made these comments. "There needs to be more recognition of the sociocultural factors which play into the lives of people whom we serve. As we become more clear and more astute in our use of material out of the body of knowledge of the dynamics of individual and human behavior, we have sometimes lost track of the dynamics of group and societal behavior. We have been less aware and less clear about the various subcultural values existing in our society. We have been naive about the social stratification and the existent status systems, and we have known little about the leadership or power structure within our community. We have veered away frequently from anything which speaks of politics so that we have been surprised when certain issues which we believe in with all our hearts get by-passed on the local, state and federal governmental scene. We have frequently ignored the body of knowledge about population movement and community development and about the new developing set of institutions around community planning so that our agency services have not always been located where they could be of greatest value. There is available to us an ever-growing body of knowledge in all of these areas from the social sciences, so that there is less excuse for us to come out lacking, with good will but insufficient social science knowledge. These socio-cultural aspects of the practice of social group work must be a part of the equipment of every professional worker which means that such content must be taught in our professional schools and must be drawn upon from undergraduate social science background which is applied in practice. Since this knowledge is available to us, it behooves us to know more about it, to do more writing about it, and to do more discussing of it in our professional practice."

A similar thought is expressed in this remark. "I have been interested in recent social work conferences in the up-to-date information from sociology and anthropology as it has particular pertinence in our field. While this is not a trend in just the group work discipline, I think group workers can perhaps take advantage of this material more quickly and make use of it and possibly help the entire social work profession more than some of the other disciplines. I do not mean that we should not keep in touch with the field of psychiatry, but this has been an accepted part of our thinking for a long period, it seems. Also we need to continue to be in touch with some of the new research in the area of group dynamics and other scientific methods for examining inter-personal and inter-group relations."

Another participant in our study brought out this point. "Group work will need to clarify its relationships to the emerging field coming to be known as human relations. In the field of industrial relations, management studies of supervision and group relationships have been going ahead rapidly, apparently quite unaware of the concepts and experience of social group work. Much of it sounds like preliminary exploration in fields group workers have known for a long time. Some of these developments have the aspect of cults; at times they seem competitive to group work philosophy and practice. At the same time, new insights have been emerging of which many group workers seem quite unaware. Many of these fields could undoubtedly profit from the steadying hand and the guiding influence of some of our more able group workers. At the same time group workers must be ready to learn from them."

These four comments are but samples from the many we received. In the light of these remarks, it would seem particularly important for the new professional association to move quickly toward the establishment of sound lines of communications with various learned groups in the social science area. This is a continuing task which should prove to be rewarding for group workers and the social scientist and, more important, for the people whom we serve.

AREA 7. GROUP WORK IN SPECIALIZED THERAPEUTIC SETTINGS.

The rapid advancement of group work in therapeutic settings brought forth numerous interesting reactions from our participants. On the one hand there was considerable interest in exploring this whole matter further and in extending group work's efforts in the direction of the therapeutic setting, but a number of people injected a note of warning. Let us look at some of the comments we received.

One person said, "It seems to me that the use of group work in a variety of settings, particularly therapeutic settings, needs further study and emphasis. Where the group worker serves as a member of the total treatment team, he has a function in diagnosis, in helping patients respond to treatment, in providing ego-support for patients during treatment, and at spots being part of the treatment. All of this is an area which needs further understanding and emphasis. Such group work seems to be extending to hospitals, guidance centers, services for the handicapped such as the blind, hard of hearing, the crippled, in institutions for children, unmarried mothers, the aged, and the like. I am not speaking of group work as recreation which can be carried by the recreation therapist, but actually of group work treatment where it is part of the total treatment program of the patient and has equal status in the total program. This is an important advance in our profession, and I believe it should be carried forward."

Along this line of the use of group work in nontraditional settings, another one of our respondents said, "I am impressed with the tremendous growth of the so-called nontraditional settings. The recent study of graduates of group work schools indicated that at least one-third of the graduates of the past five years are now employed in nontraditional settings such as treatment homes, children's institutions, detention homes, mental hospitals and the like. I think this area of work has tremendous possibilities for future development. This increase in the nontraditional settings has unfortunately seemed to indicate a decrease of interest on the part of the trained group worker in the more traditional settings. I feel that we have definitely lost ground with many of our national agencies in the youth field. This either means that we are becoming too specialized in our relationship to social work or we have to think of ways of broadening our contribution to encourage its development in the more traditional settings."

Injecting a sharp note of anxiety, one of our respondents said, "Another trend concerns me. It is the trend toward glamorizing the practice of group work in specialized settings. I am concerned because the hard core of practice in the community centers and traditional agencies is acquiring a lower status. It seems to me that we need to stress the importance and the comparable sophistication of group work practiced well in the traditional settings."

With even more vigor, another respondent protests the move of group work into the treatment area in these words. "I think there is a danger at this point in our development that we may be moving in the direction of a psychiatric group work area of specialization. I know that there are a great many sincere protestations that group work is group work wherever it is practiced, and that the psychiatric setting does not in itself carry any special mark of honor or prestige. But I know, too, that case work went down the same road, protesting all the while and is actually still insisting that the family setting demands as much skill and sensitivity, while at the same time sponsoring the development of a privileged elite which sees itself as exclusively psychiatric. I would hate to see us fall into the same trap and I am not quite clear at the moment as to what we can do about it. I think perhaps the schools of social work may have a special role to play in the squelching of this illusion before it develops out of hand. Perhaps too, we should be extremely vigilant in our interpretation to the community with respect to the possible dangers in this situation and above all, we must ourselves be perfectly clear that the skill and understanding required of the neighborhood group worker is at least as great as that demanded of those working in agencies and institutions administered by the medical profession."

In the light of the above comments, it seems apparent that

group work must rethink its role in the therapeutic setting. A great deal of conscientious study must be made if we are to move with clarity and a sound sense of direction for the future.

AREA 8. GROUP WORK PERSONNEL PRACTICES.

Despite the progress that has been made in the past decade with reference to the development of adequate codes of personnel practices, a considerable number of our participants placed emphasis upon this area. They saw four things that we should work on during the period ahead.

1. We should continue to refine our personnel practices code and should endeavor to interpret it to employing agencies so that they will understand and make use of the experience we have had.
2. We should work upon the development of a code of ethics for group workers. This is a natural counterpart of the personnel practices code and should be undertaken at the earliest possible moment.
3. We should work upon the problems of staff evaluation. Increasingly throughout the country it was observed that group workers are not receiving the kind of careful evaluation of their work that is needed to insure their growth and their development. It was suggested by some of our participants in this inquiry that we have a national committee to seek out ways and means of improving evaluation procedures.
4. The fourth area which received a large number of votes is the area of certification and licensing. It was felt by many that we should participate in all efforts to bring about certification of the trained group worker by our professional association and licensing by the various state governments. It was felt that this would do more than

anything else to increase the level of professional competence and to protect the public from many people who do not have sufficient background and training to work with groups.

AREA 9. GROUP WORK PHILOSOPHY, OBJECTIVES AND METHODS.

Everyone who replied to our letter had pertinent comments to make regarding group work objectives, philosophy and method. This is to be expected because naturally we will be most concerned about such questions in the work of our professional association.

In the area of philosophy the following comment seemed to be pertinent. "I am concerned about the fact that far too many of our present day professionally educated group workers tend to see themselves as 'technicians' involved in doing a routine job without strong and clearly defined convictions about the profession of social work and more particularly about group work method. Our new national organization and its chapters might be of assistance to our schools of social work as well as to the employing agencies where group workers work and to present day workers by further evolving a philosophy for social group workers. This philosophy, it seems to me, needs to re-emphasize our basic convictions about the worth of the individual, the value of group experience, and democratic methods. It might also more clearly define the limits within which group work methods are effective and the role of the group worker in social action."

In the same area of philosophy, one of our respondents said, "Today we must deepen our understanding and working knowledge of the democratic process. We have, too long now, mouthed words about this process. The trends in the world about us toward totalitarianism are real dangers. Democratic concepts need to be taught from the cradle to the grave everywhere and to all people. What better group of professionals can help with this teaching than group workers? This means that we must see our function as group workers to extend far beyond the doors of the agency and we as people must live and act and struggle in the everyday world to do our part in carrying on with these principles. I guess what I am saying is that as professionals we must become active promoters of this philosophy, drawers of water and hewers of wood. What that says to me is that as professional social workers all of us must become vitalized doers, less objective theorists. We need to develop in our trained workers and in all persons in the field of social work, more feeling tone for this business of a democratic way of life. Perhaps our coming emphasis ought to be less objective and less sitting on the sidelines of life with intellectual approach and more spiritual commitments to the method of work we believe is the democratic way of life. In our zest to become professional, and rightfully so and naturally inevitable, we have gone over backwards and weighted our approach with objectivity and intellectualism. Now in the coming years we need to develop workers who are committed with real fervor and zeal to the teaching and developing of understanding and commitment to our way of work. This means that we can no longer think of our professional field as having techniques alone. We have to learn ways of spreading the knowledge and skill to many others. We must simplify and teach what we believe to be the way of work which can be meaningful to a total nation."

Another of our participants indicated that in his judgment we needed to work very hard on the problem of conceptualization. In his words, "We have failed to develop an adequate and consistent body of theory which underlies group work. We have not achieved an adequate definition of group work method and this, I believe, is an area in which we have stood virtually still for the past ten years. We have made tremendous progress over the same period in developing our understanding of the people with whom we work, of the communities in which we live, and of our relationship to the broad fields of social work and social welfare. We have, I feel, done fruitful work in hammering out conceptions of function of purpose and of overall goals and these developments have come home to us in the form of an increased respect for our services and a growing tendency to include group workers in the councils of community welfare and social planning but the major task of defining our specific methodological contribution to the total social welfare scene remains largely undone. This failure has also come home to us in many ways. First, in our inability to achieve public understanding of group work skill. Second, in the constant struggle to interpret the need for professional training at the practitioner level. Third, in the subservient position we play to other and more highly developed disciplines. And fourth, above all in our own inability to communicate with each other except in pat and stereotyped terms which have lost their meaning. While we once thought we had a common understanding of concepts like motivate, enable, relationship, limits and many others, these terms have ceased to be conceptual and now, vague and entrenched, mean many things to many different workers.

"We have worked ourselves into the unenviable position of having no theoretical issues in contention and this represents stagnation for the young profession. Workers who actually disagree profoundly on method find themselves in perfect agreement with the accepted and official statement put forward by AAGW, by the textbooks, and by the leading writers in the field. Our early insistence on a flexible terminology was, I believe, appropriate and conducive to growth. Now, I feel, we have reached the point where this reluctance to be pinned down represents a kind of resistance to broadening our areas of consciousness to include problems of practice we have been handling intuitively for the most part. In short, what I am calling for is a concentration of our creative energies on the theoretical problems involved in developing an understanding of the nature of the helping process. What do we mean by the notion of 'enabling'? What is it to 'use program as a tool'? When do 'limits' become shackles? How can the worker reconcile and synthesize the goal of 'member autonomy' and 'self direction' with that of 'socially desirable' values and actions? In order to clarify these problems for ourselves, we need to theorize and base this theorizing on our actual experiences with people. Our continuous pleading for empirical research has been fruitless, not because we have been unwilling to do research, but because we have not reached that stage in our development where sound theoretical speculation has produced the necessary testable hypotheses. We need to teach our students to theorize, to challenge text book conceptions, and to probe beyond the accepted statements and official terminology. In this manner to enable to limit, and all the rest will become questions for them rather than answers."

Strong as the above words may seem to be, they were echoed by numerous people who suggested that the time has come for group work to develop and state a conceptual framework similar to that which has been done for the method of social case work. This is a big job which will require a great amount of time, energy and effort. It must be done if we are to advance beyond our present level of practice.

AREA 10. GROUP WORK AND THE COMMUNITY AND AGENCY SETTING.

A number of our participants made comments about the need to rethink group work in its relation to the community and the agency. While there was some difference of opinion, on the whole the major points of question seemed to be in the areas of the use and function of the building and the use of sectarian groups.

One respondent raised this question about the building. "In the area of agency functioning, I think that the increasing and deepening trend toward street club and community work will produce a thorough-going re-evaluation of the function of the building in group work practice. We need to redefine our concepts of service so that we may go more realistically to the heart of community needs and community strengths. We have for a long time been 'building bound' and 'desk bound,' imposing conditions of agency behavior and agency loyalty that many people have been unwilling or unable to meet. I think that we are becoming increasingly less satisfied with merely declaring that these people are 'resistive to help' and instead we are beginning to view our agencies as part of an overall pattern of community service demanding no special loyalties and offering help not on our own special terms, but in relation to the people and situations that need help. In this respect I think that we are gradually learning the complex implications of our off-repeated phrase that people must be accepted where they are. I think, too, that we are beginning to understand that true acceptance of people cannot be based on a temporary tolerance which imposes the condition that they be willing to move to where we think they ought to be."

Another observer put it this way. "In recent years we have improved our effectiveness as group workers by borrowing from the psychiatric learnings. We have increased our understanding of individuals in our groups and have become more effective helpers on the basis of this understanding. On the other hand we have, it seems to me, lost some of our early awareness of community forces and have tended to operate too much separated from our communities and have not helped our groups as well as we might to see themselves as responsible parts of their community. I believe that our new national organization and its chapters can help us to correct present oversights and to benefit from new methods and insights developed by joint thinking and joint study."

In the area of the sectarian settings several of our participants raised questions. For example, one person asked these questions and made these remarks. 'What are the conditions prerequisite to the effective practice of group work in a sectarian setting? Is the context of a particular agency philosophy an inhibiting or an enabling factor? Those of us who contend that a religious philosophy and social work are compatible and mutually supportive, recognize that questions have been raised as to whether group work can help the individual achieve his fullest potential in anything but a truly non-sectarian setting. There are many implications to this question which would benefit from full study."

Another participant put it this way. "We ought to face the question of whether the sectarian sponsorship of group work services tends to limit contact between different religious groups and ways of bridging differences to promote constructive interaction."

AREA 11. GROUP WORK AND THE FAMILY.

A number of our respondents placed emphasis on the importance of rethinking group work and its relation to the family and to family life education.

As put by one of our writers, "There are many reasons why the family must assume a high priority in the consideration of group workers. For example, the centrality of the individual is a concept which has been well developed by sound group work. As in social case work, the individual cannot be aided effectively except as this is done in relation to his family situation. Many agencies which utilize the practice of group work serve or can serve all the members of the family. The meaning of this for effective practice needs to be explored more fully.

The family is the basic unit in our society. All services capable of strengthening the family should recognize this responsibility. Group Work is in the exceptionally fortunate position of being able to affect the wholesome development of family life and should give due concentration to this challenge."

Along the same line, another writer said, "Another emphasis which I see as a growing trend is the emphasis in many agencies on work with the whole family in an integrated way. I do not mean requiring the whole family to be members of the agency, but providing services for the whole family and collaboration of staff on service to various family members on a planned basis. This is particularly true of some settlements and community centers and ranges everywhere from play school programs, programs for young parents, programs for the aged, but always on an integrated family basis where information coming from one contact with a family member is used consistently throughout the whole agency in order to give a total social service function and treatment program to the family."

A great many workers commented on the important contribution that group work has to make to the growing program of family life education. In the words of one of our participants, "I feel that we should have a committee to study the potential contribution of group work to family life education. In our community, family life education discussion groups are growing in numbers. In many instances, it seems to me, they could profit from the constructive participation of the group workers who have an understanding of group process and have a skill in discussion method. In fact, I would go so far as to suggest that family life education is much more of a group work function than it is a case work function even though the programs are usually sponsored by the case work agencies."

While we might not agree with these observations, it seems readily apparent that we have an area for exploration which needs to be tackled by group workers on both the local and the national level.

AREA 12. GROUP WORK AND SOCIAL CHANGE.

In our analysis of the replies, we noted that numerous people commented upon the importance of developing a more realistic approach to the use of group work in helping to bring about social change. As one writer put it, "Back some 20 years ago there was a lot of talk about group work in relation to the kind of world we lived in and the kind of people that would be most effective in that world. I think we need a renaissance of that spirit but with somewhat more vigorous attention to the problems and the process. In what kind of a social climate will we live? What kind of behavior, insights, outlook and faith will be most helpful to men in that social climate?"

Another person said, "Increasingly we need to have a more active role in the area of legislation. For example, the present curtailment of public housing will probably cause increasing hardship in many of our communities. Group workers need to be aware of tensions arising from crowded housing conditions and be prepared to take some action on such matters. Although it is a little early to tell, it looks as if there may be some significant changes in our federal public assistance program. Group Workers have as much responsibility as case workers to be aware of changes in legislation and to be prepared to handle the problems which may arise from such changes."

Another person said, "I think we need further study of the basic minimum program of recreation which a community should provide through its tax-supported and voluntary services. Much thought is being given to this already on the part of community organization groups. I would hope that group workers could relate closely to community organization workers throughout the country in further developing such ideas in the next decade."

Another worker said, "I think that as a profession we have to revitalize our alertness to community trends and to their effect on people. Because of group work's firsthand experience with the impact of these developments, I believe that our profession has a triple function around them. First, there is continuous study or 'feeling the pulse' and doing this more scientifically than we have done in the past. Second, there is interpretation to the community and by this I mean interpretation of the human aspects which must complement the statistical facts presented by other institutions and professions. Third, using our method in part to ameliorate the effects of these trends and in part offer it to communities so that they can utilize it to counterbalance them."

From another point of vantage we received this expression from one of our respondents. "It is the opinion of some economists that we are moving from a so-called capitalistic economy to a consumer economy or at least the significance of capital is being balanced by the place of the consumer. This will probably call for more and more government participation in economic processes and the group worker of tomorrow must have some opinions about maintaining democratic participation while at the same time increasing structured areas of life through governmental rules and regulations."

Another worker said, "I see a great opportunity for us as group workers to reaffirm and revitalize the relationship between social work and social change. Here, too, some re-examination of our traditional assumptions would seem to be indicated. Our traditional approach, so largely identified with the settlement movement, needs to be examined and studied with recognition of the present body of knowledge in social work which in some ways goes beyond what was taken into account by the early settlement pioneers. Furthermore, we must study our relation to the public social welfare services and our role in relation to them. Case work has gone much farther than we have as group workers in relating to the steady growth of public programs. I feel this is an area where we have never honestly faced the issues and the implications."

In connection with group work and social change it was pointed out again and again that group work must state the values that it holds and must take a more active role in local, state and national legislative processes. Furthermore, it was indicated that group work must concentrate upon the improvement of community life and the building up of community strength. Furthermore, it was suggested that a critical examination of the process of social change would reveal to group workers the fact that there are many avenues of social change which have not yet been properly explored.

Area 13. Group Work Communication Through Publications.

A substantial number of our participants in this inquiry made note of the fact that group work needs a vastly expanded program of publications so that workers can be kept abreast of current developments and trends. Many indicated that the new association might well sponsor a comprehensive publication program through a monthly journal and through the release of various reports and documents. Our group work literature has increased in depth and richness during the last ten years; a considerable amount remains to be done in the actual writing up and analysis of current group work practice. A national committee on publications was suggested by several persons. They thought that such a committee might block out a long-range statement of the areas where literature is needed and might launch a systematic campaign of securing material that is felt to be desirable.

AREA 14. APPLICATION OF GROUP WORK PROCESS TO ADMINISTRATIVE GROUPS.

While some work has been done on the use of group work principles and methods with administrative groups, numerous persons remarked that we need to push forward in this realm. Accent was placed on the fact that there is a tremendous need for agency administrators today and there will be an even greater need in the future. It was pointed out that most schools of social work give little training in the area of administration and this would seem to be a leading priority for the future. Many people commented on the need to develop better understanding of citizen boards and how to use group work methods with them. In general it was thought that the group process in administration should be studied on the local level with special attention being given to the role of the executive.

AREA 15. PROFESSIONAL EDUCATION FOR GROUP WORK.

While this study was not particularly related to problems of professional education for group work, a sizable number of respondents thought that we should be given a great deal of attention to professional education during the period ahead. Specifically, it was felt that we should define the place and responsibility of the undergraduate program, particularly as it relates to graduate work. It was felt, too, that we should have a thorough evaluation of educational methods on the graduate level. Some persons felt that we should explore the need for advanced work beyond the master's degree. Some felt that we should make a special attempt to provide professional training for the many untrained workers who hold jobs in our agencies. Many people felt that we should make a concerted effort to interpret the need for professional education to the community so that additional scholarship support would be forthcoming.

AREA 16. EVALUATIVE RESEARCH, THE ESSENTIAL FRONTIER.

One of the most important jobs for group work in the next decade is to develop a program of evaluative research. Almost everyone who participated in our inquiry felt the same way about it. As one worker put it, "We must find ways to measure the effectiveness of our work. In order to interpret group work to the community, we must have some concrete proof of what the presence of a group worker means to the group."

Another worker said, "We can interpret our function from here to eternity, but until we can prove with competent research programs that we have a unique contribution, we cannot justify the cost of education for social group work practice or the cost of services we provide."

Another worker said, "I am sure we have strong desires for research findings in our field in areas which are actually not appropriate. I think we want research in areas X, Y and Z, when it still has to be done in areas A, B and C."

Another worker said, "I think that the field at the practice level must provide the setting and structure which will make research possible. Group workers cannot be proud of their record in the research area. Group work is not geared to research and the bulk of our experience is lost and the development of our skills correspondingly stinted because of these circumstances."

Despite these candid observations, a good many of our participants sketched out some interesting outlines and approaches to the research problem. We have selected a number of them for discussion purposes and it is our opinion that they will be helpful.

The first selection has to deal with the twofold frontier of theory development and experimentation. In the words of the writer, "Theory and research is in my mind the most extensive frontier for group work. We must do two things. We must try to conceptualize the social group work process around well-integrated theory. We must test and retest that theory in the laboratory and in the field. Let me elaborate a little. On theory development a few of the tasks that need to be undertaken are:

1. Identifying and defining in operational terms the dimensions along which groups move in the course of their development.
2. Identifying the various phases of the 'life cycle' of groups and attempt to specify what is normal for each of these phases.
3. Define operationally what is meant by such processes as group self-determination, acceptance, limiting and the like.
4. Attempt to define in operational terms the role of the social group worker.
5. Specify in observable and measurable terms the predicted effects of social group work experiences upon the participants.

"Then in regard to experimentation, we need to develop and refine a body of theory through systematic programs of research. Practitioners either through their professional organizations or in their agencies ought to be working in close cooperation with skilled researchers in the welfare councils or in the schools and universities. Good theory is built through the integration of two kinds of research: that which is done in the field in the reality situation, preceded or followed by that which is done in the controlled laboratory situation. Every community which has an AAGW chapter or a chapter of the new single professional association, as well as a school of social work with a research program, could and should become a center where this kind of needed research could be developed. Before this can happen however, we will have to do a better job than we have done of educating persons who have research competence as well as competence in the practice of their profession."

Another respondent submitted a list of possible research areas without attempting to define the material in terms of hypotheses. He suggested that we should be studying: "Size of group as an influence in group dynamics; Program content and relation to personality development; Stages of movement in the growth of groups; Limits and dimensions of professional worker's function in the group; Influence of the sex of the worker in relation to a given group of either sex; The relationship of family participation to the intensity of participation of individual members; The relationship of family participation to the intensity of individual participation according to sex and age; The development of program content according to developmental levels; Membership participation in the overall administration of the agency; Staff participation in the administration of the agency; Participation of the individual in groups according to variety of size, and intimacy of participants; What kind of groups is it desirable for individuals to hold membership in? What should be the intake policies on given agencies in terms of needs of the community? Under what conditions may group work processes be used with therapy goals? This brief remark refers to all types and conditions of therapy goals."

Another participant suggested that research effort should investigate the following problems:

1. Deepening and widening our conceptualizations.
2. The problem of groupings—this encompasses the following questions:
   a. What personality make-ups affect what others, in what ways, in what kinds of group situations?
   b. Provided we find some answers to the above questions, how should this influence the current policies of most

agencies with regard to voluntary grouping? What in fact will it do to our basic axiom of voluntary participation?

We need more research into the process of program development. For instance, how does program come about in different types of groups? In this particular area we have well-formulated principles and we have broad practical experience, but it seems to me that they need to be consolidated and scientifically substantiated.

The most important thing is to do research into the results of group work. How do experiences in social group work affect groups, and to what extent do they influence personal adjustment and growth; personal readjustment and rehabilitation? What attitude changes take place in individuals, and how consistent and lasting are such changes. To what extent do attitudinal changes of some individuals influence in turn the attitudes of others? To what extent do experiences in social group work groups influence the individual's social participation in other groups in the community?

Another practitioner suggested, "I should like to see group workers participating in some of the research that is being done under the 'group dynamics' title which provides much needed information on group process but is lacking in the impact on the process of a leader with certain knowledge and skills. I would also like to see group work develop research indicating the type of groups in group work which should be led by professionally trained workers, the type that can be led by supervised leaders, either volunteer or untrained. Such research, of course, would be tied in with increased clarification of the function of the group worker and may have to await the time when we are more clear as to the tangible knowledge and skills required for leadership. I should also like to see some research on group selection, group composition, group formation, group disbanding, that would tackle the difficult question always facing a group worker when a situation arises that indicates that membership in a group is occasionally disastrous for the individuals who are members. It was a real shock to me personally, I recall, to discover that not all groups are healthy. What are the elements that make the experience healthy and productive, would be the general question I suppose from which the research would stem."

Another participant outlined fine areas where he thought research was important. He said, "First, evaluation of results obtained through group work services, validating or modifying our principles and theories, is long overdue. Second, measures of need for group work services to be used in agency and community planning; development of adequate measures is not entirely dependent upon evaluative research. Third, increased application of knowledge borrowed from the allied sciences; we are already lagging in this respect and will have to catch up particularly with regard to the social sciences. Fourth, division of responsibility between the professional training school, the agencies, the professional associations and foundations for research effort; what has been everyone's responsibility has been no one's. Fifth, reaching the nonparticipants and the unreached; there is a wealth of data gained, both in and out of the profession, indicating that large portions of the population are not effectively related to organized community processes, agency or otherwise. These nonparticipants are people for whom we have a special responsibility although we seldom find them among agencies' constituencies. We consider participating citizenry essential in a democracy, yet we have been little concerned about those who cannot or do not participate in community associations. I do not presume that everyone ought to be in an agency program, but I do think we ought to be very much concerned about the forces which prevent many persons from participating in all kinds of organizations."

Another person placed emphasis on the need for evaluative research. "One of the obvious needs is for evaluative research, testing and validating our theory. We must develop instruments that can prove that group work accomplishes something and in detail, and under what conditions and what circumstances. This will establish levels for the use of volunteers and trained staff. It will take the guess out of our work. All factors must be evaluated in a scientific manner appropriate to our kinds of skills. Research into grouping, methods and co-related results, the friendship group and its structure barriers, status, the effect of the outer directed personality pattern and group work practice objectives, contagion, and so forth, are urgently needed."

Another person approached the research area with these words, "It seems to me that we have arrived at the point in our professional development where we must begin to do research on the group process in the kind of voluntary groups, interest or activity groups, or mass activity groups which are part of the program of the regular agency. We must take certain concepts about groups, such as group formation, decision making, group morale, group control and the like, and do actual research with live groups in the voluntary agencies to substantiate these concepts. Most research on group process has not been upon the kind of groups led by group workers and frequently has not been done with the same frame of reference which the social worker has. Therefore, the time has come, I believe, when in our profession we must make provisions for advanced research which would go very deeply into one specific concept and test it out in a variety of kinds of settings where group work as we know it is being practiced. This it seems to me is the greatest task ahead for group work in the next decade."

Another writer outlined the following areas where research is needed, "Further developments along the lines of measuring the quality of group work experience and its effectiveness, including individual growth and development along with group growth and achievement, the study of criteria for performance for group workers other than graduation from an accredited school of social work, and years of experience in certain kinds of agencies. It seems to me we need to measure what actually is instead of always placing our usual emphasis on what should be. While our assumptions need to continue to be tested, we also need to focus on our practice in the light of the assumptions and in the light of reality factors."

If we had the means of bringing together the people we have quoted in this section of our study, no doubt we could hammer out around the conference table a definitive long-term approach to research in group work. This, in fact, is one of the major steps which must be taken if we are to move beyond our present level of practice.

In the period which lies ahead group workers along with all other social workers have tremendous opportunities and equally huge obligations. Mighty forces are at work in the world. Civilization is being challenged as never before in all of history. As Franklin Delano Roosevelt wrote at the hour of his death, "Today we are faced with the pre-eminent fact that, if civilization is to survive, we must cultivate the science of human relationships—the ability of all peoples, of all kinds, to live together and work together in the same world, at peace. . . . The only limit to our realization of tomorrow will be our doubts of today. Let us move forward with strong and active faith."[1]

[1] *Franklin Delano Roosevelt—A Memorial.* Edited by Donald Porter Geddes, Pocket Books, Inc., New York 1945, pp. 246-47.